UNWILLING GERMANS?

UNWILLING GERMANS?

THE GOLDHAGEN DEBATE

EDITED BY
ROBERT R. SHANDLEY

WITH ESSAYS TRANSLATED BY
JEREMIAH RIEMER

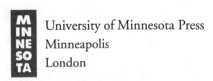

University of Minnesota Press
Minneapolis
London

For information on the original publications
of the essays in this book and
permission to reprint them, see p. 287.

Published by the University of Minnesota Press
111 Third Avenue South, Suite 290
Minneapolis, MN 55401-2520
http://www.upress.umn.edu

Library of Congress Cataloging-in-Publication Data

Unwilling Germans? : the Goldhagen debate / edited by Robert R.
Shandley ; with essays translated by Jeremiah Riemer.
p. cm.
Includes bibliographical references and index.
ISBN 0-8166-3100-X (hc : alk. paper). — ISBN (invalid)
0-8166-3101-8 (pbk. : alk. paper)
1. Goldhagen, Daniel Jonah. Hitler's willing executioners.
2. Holocaust, Jewish (1939-1945)—Causes. 3. Antisemitism—
Germany. 4. War criminals—Germany—Psychology.
5. National socialism—Germany—Moral and ethical aspects.
I. Shandley, Robert R.
D804.3.G3483U59 1998
940.53'18—dc21 97-49282

Printed in the United States of America
on acid-free paper

The University of Minnesota is an equal-
opportunity educator and employer.

10 09 08 07 06 05 04 03 02 01 00 99 98   10 9 8 7 6 5 4 3 2 1

CONTENTS

T his volume is the product of cooperation on the part of many people. I would like to thank all of the contributors. Each of them greeted this project enthusiastically, making it a pleasure to complete. They have all done a service to the understanding of this most horrible human event. The editors at Hoffmann and Campe assisted me tremendously in my initial contacts with many of the contributors. Toward the end, Arthur Heinrich and the editors of the *Blätter für deutsche und internationale Politik* were instrumental in completing the collection. Likewise the staff at the Siedler Verlag in Berlin were generous in their assistance. This volume and the debate as a whole is much richer due to the efforts of Andrei Markovits.

I received institutional support to pursue this project both from the Department of Modern and Classical Languages and the Interdisciplinary Group for Humanities Studies at Texas A&M University. Arnold Vedlitz and the Center for Public Leadership Studies at the George Bush School of Government and Public Service at Texas A&M University provided generous financial support.

Alexandra Kluge supported me at the outset of this project. It would not have happened without her editorial assistance. Wayne White and Tara Warren helped with valuable research assistance. David Pickus, Brent Peterson, Judith Stallmann, and David Myers were careful readers. Richard J. Golsan provided valuable advice in bringing the project to fruition. Micah Kleit and

Acknowledgments

Jennifer Moore at the University of Minnesota Press have been extremely cooperative and helpful. To these and many others, I owe great thanks.

I dedicate this volume to my mother, Mary Shandley, who more than anyone else has inspired me to understand history.

R. R. S.

Robert R. Shandley

On March 10, 1997, Daniel Jonah Goldhagen received the Democracy Prize from the *Blätter für deutsche und internationale Politik* (Journal for German and International Politics). The journal, a broadly based political magazine, had awarded the prize only once before, in 1990, to the leaders of the pro-democracy movement in East Germany, who had negotiated the end of one-party rule there. The award ceremony, at which Jürgen Habermas gave the laudatory remarks and the historian Jan Philipp Reemtsma gave a commentary, capped approximately one year of debate, controversy, and media attention to Goldhagen's book *Hitler's Willing Executioners: Ordinary Germans and the Holocaust.* Although much of the reception and coverage of the book was pure spectacle, it remains true that Goldhagen's book achieved a broader resonance in the German public than any other treatment of Germany's genocidal past. Goldhagen encountered strident criticism from most senior scholars of modern German history, from an ideological cross section of opinion writers and essayists, and from German politicians across the political spectrum.

Much of the criticism was territorial, that is, it reflected resentment that this book, rather than other supposedly more original, better written, and better researched works, received so much attention and debate. But as Habermas put it in his laudatory remarks: "The question is not who among contemporary historians deserves the attention of a wider public but, rather, how we are to understand the unusual degree of public attention that Daniel Goldhagen's book has in fact received" (Chapter 29 in this volume).

But Habermas's comments came at the end of a year-long discussion in Germany about *Hitler's Willing Executioners*. The book's reception, sometimes referred to as a debate, a controversy, even a syndrome, went through three phases. The first was a general rejection of the book, its theses, and its author, prior to the publication of its German translation. Upon publication of the book in German, the reception shifted to a tentative, albeit critical acceptance of the book by critics and a popular acceptance by the general public. Finally, Daniel Jonah Goldhagen and the book were celebrated for effecting an important change in how Germans regard their national past.

The broad reception started as a well-orchestrated debate. On April 12, 1996, Volker Ullrich, the political editor of the German opinion weekly *Die Zeit,* initiated a discussion of Goldhagen's book on the front page of the newspaper. He called the book the beginning of a new *Historikerstreit,* referring to the 1986 dispute among historians regarding the uniqueness of the Holocaust and the normalization of German history. Since only a few scattered reviews had appeared up to that moment, Ullrich's remarks are a call to debate rather than an actual report of events.[1] In the course of the following six months, *Die Zeit* actually staged such a debate, involving some of the most prominent Third Reich and Holocaust historians in Germany and the United States. Shortly after Ullrich's initiative, much of the rest of the German media, from television and radio talk shows to weekly youth magazines and party organs, chimed in, and a discussion ensued that went well beyond the entirely academic *Historikerstreit* of the previous decade.

In what follows, I will introduce and delineate many of the important arguments that appear in the present volume. Although it is not my purpose to provide my own reading of *Hitler's Willing Executioners* or a definitive critique of the entire debate, along the way I will interject my own critical remarks where I see them as helpful in furthering the general understanding of the reception of Goldhagen's book. This volume is intended not as a final word on the place of the debate surrounding Goldhagen's theses but, rather, as a starting point for us to begin to make sense of the historiography of the Holocaust in Germany as it now presents itself.

The fact that the first phase of the debate happened prior to the publication of the book's German translation tells much about the political culture and the cultural politics of postunification Germany: It reveals a continuing nervousness in German public spheres about how much their nation's past still reverberates in the rest of the world.

When Ullrich claims, as he did in the article that appears here as Chapter 1, that Goldhagen has provoked a new *Historikerstreit,* he is referring to the controversy that erupted in 1986 regarding the uniqueness of the Nazi extermination camps and the political use of German history. That dispute was argued in many of the same publications and by many of the same writers.[2] It became a debate about the relativization and normalization of Nazi history.

The residues of the previous struggle are visible in the initial reception of *Hitler's Willing Executioners.* The suggestion that certain historians had failed to treat the Holocaust with the necessary earnestness (another aspect of the *Historikerstreit*) placed conservative German historians on the defensive for years following. Therefore, should an occasion arise to reopen the issue of whether or not the Holocaust was being taken seriously, that discussion would necessarily contain unresolved repression, as the valence would testify not only to the matter at hand but to the memory by German historians of the earlier controversy, in which they had been tested. As is often the case with repression, the issue returned with that much more intensity.

THE EARLY RECEPTION OF *HITLER'S WILLING EXECUTIONERS*

The work that would be published by Alfred A. Knopf on March 29, 1996, as *Hitler's Willing Executioners* was already distinguished. In 1993 Goldhagen was awarded the Harvard doctoral award, known as the Sumner Dissertation Prize. In 1994 the American Political Science Association awarded him the Gabriel A. Almond Award for best dissertation in the field of comparative politics. Critics, especially in the book's early reception, often referred to these awards during the debates without naming them.

The book received a degree of publicity that is not unusual for a commercially listed book but that is quite rare for a first book based on a dissertation. Goldhagen supplemented the publication with a *New York Times* op-ed piece on March 17, 1996, and immediately set out on a book tour. Galley copies were sent both to the leading American scholars in the field and to scholars and publicists in Germany.

On April 8, 1996, the cable channel C-SPAN broadcast a discussion of the book held at the U.S. Holocaust Museum and Memorial in Washington, D.C. Knopf marketing personnel contacted the museum to arrange a symposium and discussion to which such dignitaries as Habermas and former German president Richard V. Weizsäcker were invited. These two prominent Germans declined the invitation. Instead Goldhagen shared the stage with American historian Christopher Browning, Israeli scholar Yehuda Bauer,

German historian Hans-Heinrich Wilhelm, and Konrad Kwiet, a German professor from Australia (see Chapter 6).

Meanwhile, in Germany the debate was gathering momentum. Ullrich's call for a new *Historikerstreit* worked. By mid-April every major national newspaper had published a review, and *Die Zeit* had initiated a series of articles on the book that would continue for a year. In May and again in August Germany's leading glossy news magazine, *Der Spiegel,* dedicated a cover story to Goldhagen's book (see Chapters 4 and 17).

It is important to note that in the debate as it played itself out in summer 1996, almost all reactions to *Hitler's Willing Executioners* were, if not entirely negative, highly critical. In fact, after the American historian of Germany Gordon Craig encountered an admonishing letter from Marion Countess Dönhoff for his relatively positive review in the *New York Review of Books,* he chose to publish a much more critical take on the book in *Die Zeit* on May 10, 1996. Among the leading historians of Germany on both sides of the Atlantic, there was little defense of Goldhagen's theses.

Die Zeit and *Der Spiegel* are no longer the dominant opinion makers in Germany in the weekly news market that they once were. The two do continue, however, to enjoy a critical hegemony in regards to public discussion of historical issues. The founder and publisher of *Der Spiegel,* Rudolf Augstein, immediately took an interest in the theses of *Hitler's Willing Executioners.* His first response to the book came in an article published on April 15, 1996, entitled "The Sociologist as Hanging Judge" (see Chapter 4). This topic apparently continued to bother him so much that he returned to it repeatedly. Rather than reviewing the book, Augstein's initial comments appear designed to convince the readers of Germany's largest-circulation news weekly to dismiss the book without reading it. The book was so unimportant that Germany's most influential journalist felt the need to urge his readers to ignore it.

Frank Schirrmacher, the conservative coeditor of the *Frankfurter Allgemeine Zeitung (FAZ),* made his displeasure with the book known in a diatribe published on the same day as Augstein's piece (see Chapter 3). Both contributions displayed indignation at the "widespread" acclaim the book enjoyed in the United States. Schirrmacher questioned the intellectual state of a society (the United States) that would regard Goldhagen's work as scholarly progress. Important for both pundits were the implications of this book for the German geopolitical situation. They saw Goldhagen's argument as a hindrance to Germany's ability to take on a world leadership role and as an affront to German national consciousness. These polemics, whether or not they were intellectually influential, at least provided cover for a cadre of historians who would soon join in the fray.

THE GUILD

In the months between the book's U.S. publication on March 28, 1996, and its German publication on August 6, 1996, a highly negative response to *Hitler's Willing Executioners* established itself in the German press, primarily from German historians. But to simply understand the responses to the book as negative would be to disregard much of what these critics had to say. And any such monochromic reading would also necessarily and erroneously presume that the initial detractors only intended or attempted a discussion of the book. What emerges from the body of criticism is a landscape of responses juxtaposed in varying relationships to Goldhagen's theses, Holocaust historiography, German political culture, and ethnic, ideological, and generational backgrounds.

Even the positive reactions are similarly mapped out. As Andrei Markovits points out, most of the favorable critiques in the press accounts came from German Jews. Julius Schoeps's *Die Zeit* article of April 26, 1996 (see Chapter 8), which spoke primarily of the merits of Goldhagen's book, serves as a fine example. Josef Joffe, in his generally negative critique, occasionally found room to praise redeeming qualities in the book in his first review, on April 13, 1996, in *Die Süddeutsche Zeitung*. The version of Joffe's article reprinted in Schoeps's collection of essays on the Goldhagen controversy, *Ein Volk von Mördern?*, later in 1996 was a much more balanced, indeed favorable, critique (see Chapter 26). This does not mean, however, that all German Jews reacted positively. Michael Wolffsohn, a Jewish emigrant to Germany from Israel and a visible member of Germany's conservative Christian Democratic Union (CDU), provides an unsparingly negative and personal critique of *Hitler's Willing Executioners* (see Chapter 7).

The passion of the early panning may be best understood as the aforementioned reaction to an earlier dispute. The *Historikerstreit*'s most forceful impact was on academic historians. Thus they seemed to be the ones with the most at stake in the public reception of Goldhagen's book. For them, the controversy was a zero-sum game. Either Goldhagen's work or their own was to be taken seriously. For Eberhard Jäckel the solution was simple. He dismissed *Hitler's Willing Executioners* as "simply a bad book" and recused himself from the discussion as it played out in the following months (see Chapter 10).

But other, often younger, historians were not as confident in where they would come out in the discussion. This uncertainty resulted in a much more dialectical critical stance, what I would call, paraphrasing Freud, a *Deckkritik*, that is, a screen of criticism put in place to hide a hint of praise. Ulrich Herbert provides the most accessible example (see Chapter 13). Herbert evidently found that in order to react positively to any part of the book, he had to preface that reaction with a dismissal of the book's overall value. Herbert's reading, although not necessarily recommending of the book, is much more balanced than his insistent dismissal indicates.

Sketching a few of the arguments in detail is important here to show how the "received wisdom" of the discussion gradually shifted. Perhaps the most detailed critique in the early debate came from the prominent modern German historian Hans-Ulrich Wehler (see Chapter 11). Having been a prominent contributor to the last two historical disputes, namely, the debate about Germany's special path to democracy (the *Sonderweg* debate) and the *Historikerstreit*, Wehler's comments may provide the most thorough indicator of how much of the Goldhagen discussion was initially a continuation of the *Historikerstreit*.

As did Herbert, Wehler declares the sincerity with which he is going to treat the book by providing six reasons why one should read Goldhagen's book and take it seriously. His positive comments are based on an assessment of the eleven chapters of case studies that the book contains, that is, the depictions of the police battalions, work camps, and death marches. After providing his own *Decklob* (screen of praise), he then neatly comes up with six reasons why Goldhagen's arguments are "untenable." Wehler becomes the most prominent of the historians to reject Goldhagen's cultural explanations because they supposedly espouse *collective guilt* as a mode of understanding. This reading is curious both because it has little to do with the arguments in the book and because, as Wolfgang Wippermann argued later (see Chapter 27), the accusation of subscribing to a collective guilt thesis was always a red herring. One would be hard-pressed to find a serious argument in favor of the notion of collective guilt either in or outside of Germany.

Wehler argued that despite having won a prize for best dissertation in comparative politics, the book, which is significantly similar to the dissertation, in no way resembles a comparative approach. If Goldhagen is right, according to Wehler, we are left at an explanatory dead end with regard to every other genocidal act of this century and the last. Wehler, who in the *Historikerstreit* rightly dismissed any understanding of the Holocaust that would lead to relativization and normalization of this history, suddenly sounded like an advocate of such thinking, but this time with a bizarre twist. Wehler questioned the right of a son of a Holocaust survivor to tell this history. He created a set of false oppositions between real historical research on a genocidal event and work being done by the progeny of a victim:

> Take, for example, the Turkish massacres of millions of Armenians: Instead of trying to provide an explanation in terms of a cluster of very varied causes and motives, should we simply give up and hand the job over to a young Armenian historian, so that he can then trace everything back to the centuries-old tradition of "Ottoman butchery"? . . . Take the even more appalling decades of millionfold murder under the dictatorship of Lenin and Stalin: . . . should we simply give up and hand the job over to a young Ukrainian historian, so that he can then trace everything back to the centuries-old tradition of "Russian barbarism"?

Wehler's diatribe was remarkable in that it clearly went beyond his reading of the book. It is also remarkable in that he did not adhere to the careful argumentative style that had made him so famous. The book clearly created in him a blind spot whereby he confused or identified the advocacy of monocausal explanations with genetic descent. For one of Germany's most eminent historians, *Hitler's Willing Executioners* is a personal affront, a sign of everything that is wrong with the academy, by which Wehler implicitly means the U.S. academy. This conclusion leads him to a harsh critique of Goldhagen's dissertation committee, wherein he proclaims: "The episode raises the whole question of quality control in the academic world . . . with Goldhagen, we have reached a new low." So the reception of the book had escalated from calling it "simply bad" to considering it a harbinger of Western intellectual decline.

Wehler ends his piece by discussing the political ramifications of this book. He decries the popular reception the book enjoyed in the United States: "For some sections of the American public, the book has been a quasi-scientific confirmation of deep-seated resentments and prejudices." He closes by expressing his own fear of what will become of the discussion in Germany. Realizing that the critical pendulum may have swung too far and fearing the appearance of censorship through neglect, Wehler paradoxically ends by demanding that Germans acknowledge the legitimacy of Goldhagen's right to his argument, before they go ahead and dismiss it.

The obvious defensiveness of many of the critics is surprising, given that they have dedicated their lives' work to serious study of the Holocaust. Kurt Pätzold noted later in the summer of 1996 that many of them were reacting as Germans and not as historians. Christopher Browning's response in *Die Zeit*, which was a version of the talk he gave at the U.S. Holocaust Museum and Memorial, was, for obvious reasons, much different. Browning is cited in almost every critique as the authority on the complicity of ordinary citizens in Holocaust atrocities.[3] After noting that there are some points on which he and Goldhagen agree, Browning, who is the subject of much criticism in the endnotes of Goldhagen's book, then goes on to discuss how one can study the same information and reach radically different conclusions. By entering the German debate, Browning serves, even if not intentionally, as a prime example of the tactic by which a critic can disregard *Hitler's Willing Executioners* while supporting the idea that Germans may of their own volition have committed the unspeakable acts it details. And while he does have the greatest territorial interests in the dispute, his contribution reflects little of the personal defensiveness so evident in the responses of his German colleagues.

Initially virtually all reviews of the book were devastatingly negative. By the end of May 1996 it looked as if the German reviewers had succeeded in dismissing *Hitler's Willing Executioners* as unworthy of the attention of the German public. The best of the reviews said nothing more than that the book, albeit weak and ill grounded, should be read. The dominant understanding of the book in the press was that it was so bad that it barely warranted translation. Up to that point, no one had declared firm support for Goldhagen's scholarly approach or theses about the willingness of Hitler's executioners.

This hegemonic attitude, especially among historians, encountered the earliest resistance from Wehler's own camp, namely from the Universität Bielefeld. The historian Ingrid Gilcher-Holtey engaged those who had up to then panned the book in her contribution to the *Die Zeit* debate (Chapter 12). She noted that their resistance to the book may well have been based on their having overlooked what Goldhagen was trying to do, namely apply a "sociology of knowledge approach" to the study of the Holocaust. She called the book "above all a methodological challenge to historical scholarship" in that in it Goldhagen transcended the tired polemics of the "intentionalists" versus the "structuralists." Below I will discuss these terms, both of which were (perjoratively) applied to Goldhagen at varying points in the debate. Although not engaging any of the claims about the historical veracity of Goldhagen's work, Gilcher-Holtey thus made a strong case that Goldhagen's approach as a whole be given proper consideration.

By June the relative one-sidedness of the German debate led the American political scientist Andrei Markovits to enter the fray (see Chapter 15). He found that many of the reviewers had stressed that much of the material Goldhagen discusses had already been included in Browning's *Ordinary Men*. Markovits asked why it should diminish the work of Goldhagen that after reading much of the same material, he reached a vastly different conclusion. Remarking on many critics' self-righteousness about the amount of important work by German historians that Goldhagen fails to mention in his book, Markovits points out that only two Americans, Browning and Goldhagen, had done any work on this unique set of files about German perpetration.

Perhaps most significant in Markovits's remarks are the anti-Semitic tendencies he notes in the German reception of Goldhagen and his book. He takes the German reviewers to task for their overemphasis of Goldhagen's parentage, as if being the son of a camp survivor rendered Goldhagen unfit for scholarly discussions of the Holocaust. Markovits asks whether being the son of a perpetrator would make a German historian unfit to discuss the topic. Likewise he indicts many of the critics, most notably Augstein, for slipping into the most common of anti-Semitic clichés.

Had the debate ended with Markovits's entry, it would have remained a hostile but forgettable journalistic discussion of a U.S. dissertation on the Holocaust. The debate would have been remarkable for the personal and angry tone of the arguments. It would, however, have affected neither the way in which the German public understood the Holocaust nor the way in which scholars study it. In fact, it would have remained exactly what some of Goldhagen's worst detractors dismissed it as, a media sensation. Indeed, having the debate stop here seems to have been the intent of a number of the critics. Despite the angry response and high visibility the book and its author had attracted, *Hitlers willige Vollstrecker,* the German translation, had yet to appear in Germany. The response was only beginning.

Although the reception of the book changed dramatically once it was available to a broader public, some facets of the controversy remained the same. Through the entire affair, the discussion stayed, for the most part, highly personalized. Daniel Goldhagen continued to refer to *Hitler's Willing Executioners* as "my book" and to see himself as being on a personal mission to change the ways in which the Holocaust was discussed. And many of his detractors continued to accuse him of self-promotion, if not even worse: as Jost Nolte put it, a "rage of Old Testament breath" (see Chapter 5). *Der Spiegel* devoted space to an interview with Erich Goldhagen, Daniel's father, himself a Holocaust scholar. The interviewer seemed more intent upon ascertaining the psychology and motivations of the younger Harvard scholar than on intending to understand the motivations of the German executioners. "Could it be," speculates Henryk Broder, "that Daniel at twelve or thirteen knew more about Adolf Eichmann and Heinrich Himmler than he did about Tom Sawyer or Huckleberry Finn? . . . Could it be that he had no other choice than to flee to the front of the pack and take over the heritage and mission of his father?"[4] But when this debate turned truly personal, Daniel Goldhagen won over many of his most ardent detractors.

Goldhagen was not always consistent in his reaction to the private attention he received. Yet, even if there is some contradiction to be found in Goldhagen's reaction, there is little doubt that there was more at stake for his critics than just discontent with a bad book. The reader can detect an anxious tone in the book's reception, especially in the early reviews of the book. Dozens of books appear yearly on the Third Reich, World War II, and the Holocaust, books that make much more egregious claims than those made by this Harvard political scientist. Indeed much of what is written about this topic warrants outrage. Some of the bile directed toward *Hitler's Willing Executioners* was probably due to the commercial gloss that accompanied Goldhagen's contribution to the debate. A lingering distrust of mass culture is detectable in much of the criticism. The early reception also frequently referred to Daniel Goldhagen's claims to have effected a shift in the paradigm of Holocaust scholarship as simply arrogant.

Can any of these factors account for the fireworks surrounding this debate? Not entirely. Much of what made this debate personal was generational and territorial. Hans-Ulrich Wehler, Eberhard Jäckel, and Hans Mommsen are at the end of careers devoted to careful consideration of the intricacies of modern German history. Younger historians such as Norbert Frei and Ulrich Herbert in Germany and Christopher Browning in the United States have established themselves through a slow and meticulous exposure of their work to the academic public. And finally, writers and publishers such as Marion Countess Dönhoff and Rudolf Augstein have enjoyed a place of honor as village sages, with almost unquestioned authority on matters of memory and German history. Goldhagen's highly visible tome dismisses much of the work they represent, and it comes from the ultimate in New World academic legitimacy, namely, Harvard. Given the obvious fact that this most sensitive of German historical topics was again being dominated by someone outside their sphere of influence, it is not surprising that initial reactions to *Hitler's Willing Executioners* ranged from incredulity to rage. Unfortunately, these early critics and their anxious attitude in this case add little to the cause of learning more about the Holocaust. Their comments are, however, quite revealing of the current state of the cultural battle around a unified Germany's "collective memory."

In their recent book, *The German Predicament,* Andrei Markovits and Simon Reich refer to collective memory as a "contemporary experiencing, a constant reinterpretation, of the historic past," one that "is in constant flux, subject to relatively sudden changes."[5] Collective memory, not unlike myth, "plays a key role in the symbolic discourse of politics, in the legitimation of political structures and action, and in the justification of collective behavior."[6] If we accept their postulation of the importance of collective memory, then we can see that the stakes for the political culture in Germany are considerable, particularly in the case of *Hitler's Willing Executioners,* a book that, because of the media attraction it drew, had the potential to influence the present life of the past in Germany immensely.

While the collective memory model, put forward by Markovits and Reich following the work of Maurice Halbwachs, explains much about the hegemonic struggle for the control over the telling of German history, it presents certain pitfalls that must be avoided. In 1986 Jürgen Habermas warned of the tendency of historians to legitimate the West German state through a normalizing view of German history; indeed, that is the project for which Michael Stürmer was taken to task in the *Historikerstreit.* Habermas was responding to Stürmer's comment that "in a country without history, he who fills memory, defines the concepts and interprets the past wins the future."[7] Stürmer's comment would seem to advocate "collective memory" as a interpretive model and justification for an event such as the Goldhagen debate. Habermas does not necessarily dismiss this theory of historical knowledge. He does, however, warn that one must be mindful "of the dependence of every historiography on its (historical) context." He goes on to insist that contemporary context does not mean that the historian can arbitrarily choose whatever images from history are appropriate at the time.[8] Thus if we advocate an understanding of current historiography as a struggle over control of "collective memory," we can only do so, according to Habermas, if we "expose our own identity-forming traditions in all of their ambivalence."[9]

But the use of the word "collective" remained in dispute throughout the controversy. The editor of *Die Zeit,* Robert Leicht, noted in an essay in the fall of 1996: "His equivocally alternating use of language ('the Germans,' 'these Germans'—all in all, his frequent resort to the collective designation 'Germans') . . . makes it evident that he is imputing a collective disposition" (see Chapter 24). Goldhagen, unwilling to buck common wisdom about the status of "guilt" in Germany, denies and decries any reference to "collective guilt." To whom, then, is he referring as "ordinary Germans," one might ask? To be sure, the case studies in *Hitler's Willing Executioners* provide bone-chilling examples of individuals making relatively uncoerced decisions. But much of Goldhagen's theoretical argument about the culture of "eliminationist anti-Semitism" relies on the possibility of a collective will. What is interesting about every mention of "collective guilt" in this discussion is how

Robert R. Shandley

much absolute denial that it is an explanatory model has become prescribed and how much of that denial is focused on the first word, namely, "collective." Whether or not "guilt" (in German, "*Schuld*") is a very useful word for addressing the responsibilities and culpabilities for the German crimes of the Nazi era was never called into question. Nor, in a controversy where many old taboos were shattered, did any of the commentators bother to question whether there may have been a productive, nonreactionary way to talk about "collectivity." Instead of criticizing the tendency to see collectivity in the actions of Germans, hardly an implausibility, the critics fixated on collective "guilt," a word that rarely appears in Goldhagen's otherwise damning prose.

The ways in which this debate would transform the German public sense of collective memory shifted throughout the debate. Clearly part of the early dismissal of *Hitler's Willing Executioners* was intended to mitigate any effect it might have on the politics of memory. To understand how it may have had an impact, it is first important to see how the reception of the book shifted once it was published in German.

FROM ARROGANCE TO CHARM: THE RECEPTION OF HITLERS WILLIGE VOLLSTRECKER

At the end of May 1996, after a steady barrage of German media attention, Daniel Goldhagen published a notice in *Die Zeit* declaring that he would avoid all public events until his book appeared in German three months later. While the debate raged on, Goldhagen remained out of view of most of the press. He reemerged again at the beginning of August just prior to the publication of *Hitlers willige Vollstrecker*. The first appearance was in the form of an extended response to his critics, a response published in *Die Zeit*.

In the rebuttal of his critics Daniel Goldhagen returns to the core of the argument he put forth in the book, essentially providing his own review of his work (see Chapter 16). He takes up many of the individual points brought up by his critics, in almost every case calling them misreadings of what actually appeared in his book. He is indignant that his critics, to that point, had gotten away with irresponsibility in their critique of his work: "Even if some were to conclude that I am not entirely correct about the extent and character of German anti-Semitism of that time, it does not follow that this invalidates my study and my conclusions about the material at the heart of my book."

Along with claiming that his critics misread what he wrote, Goldhagen continues by arguing that they invented arguments from his book that are not there. He refers to these and to the continuing psychologizing regarding his father, a Holocaust survivor, as defamatory, and he follows with a remark in kind: "Anyone who discusses my background, identity, or alleged character and motivations is clearly not engaged in scholarly inquiry and unwittingly betrays that his is not a reputable scholarly voice in the discussion."

Shortly after publication of that response and the publication of the German edition, Rudolf Augstein invited Goldhagen to an island resort in Germany for an extensive interview (see Chapter 17). This was a dramatic reversal of the attitude of the septuagenarian founding editor of *Der Spiegel* toward the young American. The interview became a section of the second issue of *Der Spiegel* dedicated to the debate. The intensity of generational and cultural conflict evident in their exchange was put to constructive use. Both defended their radically divergent epistemologies vigorously while at the same time easing the personal antagonism that had been Augstein's initial reaction to the book. *Der Spiegel* actually reported on the change in demeanor that took place in the course of their discussion. As the interview between the two came to an end, "the initial reservations were barely noticeable."[10]

And yet Augstein, the dominant journalist of the last fifty years in Germany, turns the discussion of personal background on its head by claiming that Goldhagen's life history does not allow him sufficient insight into the mind-sets of the perpetrators. He displays an irritation with the young Harvard scholar that manifests itself in an occasionally patronizing attitude: "A good week ago in the *Die Zeit* you published a long, egocentric article, which, to put it frankly, I regret because you presented your opponents with just the thing they hold against you." What Augstein saw as arrogant, Goldhagen perceived as a necessary defense of himself and his work.

A problem arises in their exchange that is inherent to contemporary historiography in general and to the study of the Holocaust in particular: It is the tension between older historians (or, in the case of Augstein, journalists) who also lived in the period under investigation and younger historians who do not risk being asked for an explanation of their own actions. Although the tone between the Augstein and Goldhagen was reported to be friendly and conciliatory, Augstein's sense of frustration that his historical experience is not valued was obvious: "As a young American who grew up in a democracy, you cannot imagine what conformist pressure—in its worst form, moral cowardice—could be like, certainly not during the Hitler dictatorship." There is a gap between their viewpoints that they will not overcome. But Goldhagen clearly seemed to convince Augstein that even if the former did not have the latter's personal experience, he clearly had a firm command of the historical research. The transformation of Augstein's view of the author and his book had begun.

During the early part of what became "the Goldhagen controversy" the author was so much under attack that it was difficult to imagine him on the offensive in any way. Yet Goldhagen was not above using foils. Throughout the year-long debate, individual critics either singled themselves out or were chosen to occupy the position of the natural enemy. It is no surprise that this seat was initially occupied by Christopher Browning, the one scholar whose work is closest to Goldhagen's. In fact Browning continued to play that role in the U.S. debates, with exchanges in conferences and in the pages of *The New Republic*. Browning's German counterpart was the eminent German historian, from a famous German historian family, Hans Mommsen, whose forefathers include, among others, the first recipient of a Nobel Prize for literature. Mommsen has spent a lifetime analyzing the underlying reasons for the Third Reich's atrocities and rule. More than any of the other critics of Daniel Goldhagen's work, Mommsen reacted vociferously and indignantly to the charge by the American scholar that Holocaust research had failed to take notice of the most important aspect of the crime, namely, the inhumane bureaucratic structure of the Third Reich. Mommsen was highly critical, indeed, as hostile as any of Goldhagen's most outspoken opponents. The structure of his own critique reveals the underlying antinomy of their approaches to the history of the Holocaust.

Although Mommsen led the charge in the debate with Goldhagen, his entry into the debate was radically different from that of Hans-Ulrich Wehler. Both in Mommsen's first response to *Hitler's Willing Executioners,* a lecture given in Munich and published on July 21–22 in the *Süddeutsche Zeitung,* and in his article in *Die Zeit,* Mommsen provided not so much a critique of the book as an alternative methodology to solving the enigma of the Third Reich.[11] In his first response to Goldhagen, there is little of the personal vilification or dismissal that characterized the first round of debates. He does not deign to review the book, and he makes very little reference to the author. Instead he decides to take up the challenge of giving an alternative answer to the question he sees Goldhagen posing: "Why, in an advanced and highly civilized country like ours, was the relapse into barbarism and the systematic liquidation of millions of people, primarily Jews, possible, without anyone having made an earnest attempt to stop it?"[12] What followed was a sophisticated account of a "structuralist" approach to the answer, dense in detail and differentiation. In writing this article, Mommsen shifted the terms of the debate, yet he still did not provide an answer to the challenge Goldhagen presented regarding the motivations of the perpetrators.

Up to this point, the terms "structuralist" and "intentionalist" had not been used much to characterize the debate. "Structuralist" (which in the course of this debate was not differentiated from the broader term "functionalist") approaches to the Holocaust tend to hold that the carrying out of the Final Solution was primarily a bureaucratic function, one that continued to succeed because of favorable work environments, competing claims on bureaucratic territories, and varying levels of professional opportunism. The "intentionalist" approach starts out with the premise that everything emanated from the Nazis' command structure and their desire to kill Jews. The two approaches are generally understood as mutually exclusive. In this debate Eberhard Jäckel is the most prominent proponent of the latter way of reading the Holocaust, whereas Mommsen best represents the former.

Mommsen's critique of Goldhagen is programmatic. Because the latter's work is not structuralist, it is, in Mommsen's viewpoint, not rigorous. In practical terms, this means that some of Goldhagen's basic premises would not hold up under the only type of analysis that Mommsen finds legitimate. "In the differentiated viewpoint of recent Holocaust research, anti-Semitism appears as a necessary but by no means sufficient condition for the implementation of the 'Final Solution.'" Mommsen continues with a sentence cast in the perfect grammar of the structuralist study of the Holocaust: "The structure of the regime, aligned around permanent competition among self-dissolving institutions, together with processes that discouraged the safeguarding of political interests, fueled a process of cumulative radicalization whose inevitable endpoint was the liquidation of the Jews" (see Chapter 21).

With this statement it is not hard to see why, in the debates that followed, Goldhagen and Mommsen clashed so vehemently. Goldhagen's methodology is laid out quite early in his book: "The first task in restoring the perpetrators to the center of our understanding of the Holocaust is to restore them to their identities, grammatically by using not the passive but the active voice in order to ensure that they, the actors are not absent from their own deeds."[13] According to Mommsen, Jews were killed through the cumulative radicalization of structures and institutions. Goldhagen argues that individuals who understood themselves to be, above all, Germans killed Jews because they believed it was right. If Goldhagen eventually succeeded in having his work at least read by a general public, he never bridged the gap between himself and Mommsen. Nor would he wish to do so.

Not unlike Christopher Browning, Götz Aly was one of the figures to whom critics referred when they sought a model of a scholar who has provided authoritative research on the atrocities of the Third Reich. Unlike Browning, however, Aly did not necessarily play the role of the noble opponent that was set up for him. His essay began with a qualified praise: "Everything Daniel Jonah Goldhagen tells us is true—and yet it is only the tip of the iceberg." A renowned structuralist, Aly differentiated himself from

Goldhagen by referring to the latter as a superintentionalist. But instead of treating these varying approaches as moral categories, Aly claimed to have assumed his position as a student of structures not out of moral conviction but out of emotional self-protection.

Aly commends Goldhagen for being able to do the kind of work and personal writing that he himself apparently found too painful. As an example that both affirms Goldhagen's theses and marks the difference between structuralist and intentionalist approaches, he recounts a story that he had removed from a book he published almost ten years earlier. It is the story of a family torn apart by their own inhumanity, a story that supports much of what Goldhagen argues about how deep the sentiments against Jews went. With an example as good as any Goldhagen offers, Aly shows that those acts that led to the coining of the phrase "crimes against humanity" were actually viewed in the Third Reich as legitimate personal choices.

Aly dismisses out of hand Goldhagen's claim of having proposed *the* theory that explains the Holocaust. But he does so while affirming much of what Goldhagen does present. He agrees that the controversial theoretical findings are not only something of which one needs to be reminded (as did the early reviewers) but also material that is valid and useful to the entire scholarly pursuit of understanding. In order to provide a slight corrective to Goldhagen's argument, Aly mentions the other writer often cited in the debate to either confirm or dispute Goldhagen's findings. He quotes the late Victor Klemperer, a professor of literature from Berlin and Dresden and the author of the famous *Lingua Tertii Imperii (LTI: The Language of the Third Reich)*, whose published memoirs and journals shared the bookstores' bestseller shelves with Goldhagen's book. Klemperer kept meticulous diaries during his years of persecution as a Jew in Nazi Germany. Aly quotes Klemperer's observation: "I become more and more convinced that Hitler really is the spokesman for almost all Germans" (see Chapter 19).

In what became a series in the *Süddeutsche Zeitung,* Jan Philipp Reemtsma did an extensive comparative reading of Klemperer and Goldhagen, beginning with the same quote provided by Aly.[14] Overlooking what he refers to as "breathtaking arrogance," Reemtsma finds Goldhagen's premise accurate. Indeed, he complains over and over again that despite having some intelligent and worthwhile arguments to make, Goldhagen was sloppy and made it too easy for his critics to dismiss the book.

Reemtsma directly takes on the comparison that others (apart from Christopher Browning himself) only mentioned. In a very close reading of Browning's *Ordinary Men* and *Hitler's Willing Executioners,* Reemtsma shows that the two are not necessarily so far apart. If, as Browning attempts to show, the actions of Reserve Police Battalion 101 are taken to show the potential of "ordinary men" to easily convert themselves into mass murderers, this does not exclude the possibility that in the specific case of the police battalion, their initial readiness to do so was not necessarily related to their ideas about the worthiness of Jewish lives: "Every historical explanation must go back and forth between the historical specificities and that which is predictable in general human behavior."[15]

Reemtsma's entry into the debate is also important because of two other events associated with him in 1996. In the spring of that year, at about the time this debate was beginning, Reemtsma, who is director of the Hamburg Institute for Social Research and heir to a family fortune, was kidnapped and held for millions of marks ransom. This placed him in the national press in a way usually reserved for pop stars and, in fall 1996, for Daniel Goldhagen. Reemtsma then remained in the headlines for reasons related to his professional position: In 1995 his institute organized an exhibit on the role of the *Wehrmacht* (German army) in the Nazi atrocities. Not unlike Goldhagen's theses, the *Wehrmacht* exhibit broke with many of the narratives told earlier about the Third Reich's army and the Holocaust, showing quite clearly the complicity of a large number of conscripted soldiers in genocide. In this case the reception was the reverse of that afforded the Goldhagen book. Although both the *Wehrmachtausstellung* and *Hitler's Willing Executioners* enjoyed popular success, the German exhibit received far better critical reception than did the American's book.

During much of his book's early reception, Goldhagen was accused of harboring distinct anti-German sentiments; that is, he was said to hold present-day Germans responsible for the crimes of the past. In the English edition, albeit in a footnote at the very end of the book, Goldhagen had already commented on cultural changes that occurred after the war that affected the way Germans related to Jews. If those remarks were insufficient, much of the foreword to the German edition is dedicated to the task of distinguishing present-day Germans from their Nazi counterparts: "The political culture of the Germans has obviously changed in the fifty years since the end of the Second World War."[16]

Whereas the provocative nature of Goldhagen's theses carries much of the responsibility for the uproar caused among the academic class in Germany, the foreword to the German edition is a great part of the answer to the question of why the book and its author eventually enjoyed such overwhelming popularity. Goldhagen differentiated pre-1945 Germany from the Federal Republic, noting that after 1945 "German society underwent a gradual change." He argues that young people are brought up to believe in the equality of all human beings and that racial theories no longer inform what is taught in schools. He continues: "Since people's fundamental views are, to a great extent, imparted to them by their society and their culture, the creation of a new public political culture in Germany and generational replacement has produced what one would have expected: a decline and a fundamental change in the character of anti-Semitism."[17] For many observers of postwar German culture, despite the occasional neo-Nazi flare-up, this is a plausible reading. It is important that it comes from someone whom no one can accuse of trying to relativize German history.

Numerous critics have complained that Goldhagen contradicts his positive assessment of a shift in German opinion forty-five pages later in the body of the text when he states that no matter how much anti-Semitism seems to have disappeared, "it is always there waiting to be aroused and uncovered."[18] But it should be noted that nowhere does Goldhagen make the claim he is accused of making, that is, that postwar Germans have freed themselves completely of anti-Semitism. He is more reserved than that. He simply says that anti-Semitism in Germany has changed. The old form, which he calls "eliminationist," no longer enjoys any legitimacy. This differentiation puts postwar Germans in a more positive light than is often the case in discussions about the Holocaust and its bearing on the present.

Although the commercial success of *Hitler's Willing Executioners* in Germany may have been, after a certain point, predictable, one could not have foreseen the popular reaction to the book. Daniel Goldhagen went to Germany to defend his book and, through his *Der Spiegel* interview and rebuttal in *Die Zeit,* to ask the public to give it a chance. When he returned a month later, it was to respond to widespread demand for an encounter with a bestselling author whose book had begun to resonate broadly throughout popular culture. In addition to countless interviews and signings, the tour was highlighted by five large fora. These events were the aspect of this debate that differentiated it from any other historiographical discussion in memory.

All sides seemed to agree that Goldhagen's most vociferous critics should be invited to participate in the five public discussions and in one televised debate. Indeed, many did choose to attend. In "A Triumphal Procession" (see Chapter 22), Volker Ullrich recounts in detail the specifics of the tour, in which Goldhagen managed to convince his detractors that he was a serious scholar. In the process, the German public found a figure whom they appeared to trust to tell them their history. In the course of the tour, the popular press, even the tabloid press, paid close attention, treating the American scholar as a celebrity.

This is not the first time that discussions about the Holocaust and its representation have become big news in Germany. The premiere of the television miniseries *Holocaust* in 1979 and the 1994 release of *Schindler's List* both created public stirs. But it is unique in the German public reception of the history of the Holocaust that a debate among scholars filtered into the general populace to this extent. Moreover, Goldhagen and *Hitlers willige Vollstrecker* met with overwhelming public sympathy despite making a damning argument regarding Germans and the darkest parts of their cultural heritage.

This is the first major historical debate of the postwar era in which none of the primary participants (apart from Augstein, who served in the war) have their personal histories to defend. Thus the memory of the events being discussed is only an acquired "collective memory." It reflects how Germans have come to terms with a history that they did not live. In the process of understanding the motivations of the murderers of millions of Jews, Goldhagen created an emotionally vivid and personal picture of perpetration that, despite the horrific story he told, explained the Holocaust in terms much more understandable to average, intelligent readers. Among the many reasons this book was received so well in Germany, the vivid and individualized presentation was most often cited as primary.

IN THE WAKE OF THE TOUR

Immediately after the tour the debate turned into a kind of spin-doctoring contest, that is, competing attempts to analyze the media in a way that would serve whatever argument was being presented. Ullrich's "A Triumphal Procession" justified his earlier claim about the book's provocation of a new *Historikerstreit*. In his afterword to the U.S. paperback edition of his book, Goldhagen provided his own reading of his reception in Germany: "Fifty years after the end of the war, many Germans want to have an honest reckoning with the past. They are not satisfied with the myths and misleading perspectives that have dominated public discussion of the Holocaust." The author then claimed that Germans rose up against the deceptive coverage his book had received and that this rebellion was "yet another indication of how radically transformed democratic Germany has become in the latter half of the twentieth century."[19]

The debate did not end upon Goldhagen's departure from Germany, but the trip changed everything. Shortly after his departure a dispute broke out at the forty-first annual convention of German historians, *Deutscher Historikertag*. Normally a report about the *Historikertag* would not be one that editors would readily pick up off the wires. But the 1996 meeting came on the heels of one of the most visible debates in memory on German history. The press was primed to continue the discussion.

Hitler's Willing Executioners was not an official topic of discussion at the meeting. This left the chairman of the Association of German Historians, Lothar Gall, to defend both the conference's failure to include a discussion of Goldhagen's book and the almost complete lack of discussion of the Nazi era (to which only one of the forty sessions was dedicated). Gall claimed that the Nazi era had been so thoroughly researched that "there is not much left to take there." Rolf Ballof, the chairman of the Association of History Teachers, a sister organization for high school teachers, noted the difference between the opinion represented by the association and a more widely held viewpoint: "We are running away from exactly that which is currently being discussed in the Federal Republic."[20]

Throughout the conference a question often posed was why Goldhagen's book had such broad resonance whereas the many high-quality German works on Nazi history did not. Again the answer came back to the indigestible scholarly language. Gall conceded that the accusation in Germany of being a popularizer would ruin the career of a young historian. This contradicted the motto of the meeting, which was "History as Argument." The historians were forced to admit that if they wished to remain socially relevant they would have to learn to speak to a wider audience. This seems to be a lesson that German historians have taken away from the Goldhagen controversy.[21]

Daniel Goldhagen overstates the case a bit when he suggests that his positive reception in Germany is a function of the public's being fed up with misleading narratives of the past. To be sure, plenty of those have been proffered. Goldhagen makes a strong case that some of that research has missed important aspects of that past. But German historians have also contributed significant and important elements to our understanding of the Holocaust. Reaching synthesis on these points would have constituted a historians' debate, one that may well have taken place at the *Historikertag* in Munich but one that would hardly have found popular reception. Even if in the course of academic debate the factual presentations in *Hitler's Willing Executioners* had been found to be inadequate or if Eberhard Jäckel's assessment of the book had been held to be accurate, it would still be an important work. Goldhagen's specific contribution to Germans' understanding of their own history came in the passion of his inquiry. He asked why humans, who most definitely understood themselves as Germans, were motivated to kill other humans, whom they only saw as "Jews." And he did so in a language that demanded answers.

If Goldhagen's success was related to his compelling argument and clear voice, there are others who contributed equally clear commentary but who remained ancillary to the debate. On September 20, 1996, Dorion Weickmann wrote a letter to the editor at *Die Zeit* protesting the gender mix of the public fora. Weickmann noted that the results of the debate prove one thing for sure: "For the present, history is something to be made by men, written by men, and discussed by men." She then goes on to name possible female replacements for all of the participants in the debate. Likewise, she notes that the problem starts with Goldhagen's theses themselves, remarking that he bases his conclusion on the widespread nature of anti-Semitism on the claim that Reserve Police Battalion 101 was composed of representatives of all sectors of society. "This cannot be true," she argues, "unless one understands women as *quantité négligeable.*" Thus, playing upon the title of a Heinrich Böll novel, she calls the entire media event "a group portrait without lady."[22]

Furthermore, historiographically, the Goldhagen debate was firmly situated as a West German debate. In fact there was no sign of the East, either in his description of received history or in the dramatis personae of the participants in the discussion. The Berlin historian Kurt Pätzold provided a review for *Neues Deutschland* (the party organ of the reformed, formerly East German Communist Party) shortly after the book appeared in German (see Chapter 18). And indeed, there was a reaction from many of the weeklies and youth magazines of the former East Germany. But in the hegemonic debate, that is, in the fora where prominent historians were invited to discuss the book, no East Germans were represented. Moreover, in the debate, the cultural heritage that was discussed, that is, the historical ties to the Nazi era, was discussed directly through West German culture. And Goldhagen made perfectly clear that the "new Germany" that had changed so radically was Germany west of the Elbe. When he spoke of a changed political culture, he was talking of the one emanating from Bonn.

The theses about the willingness of ordinary Germans to commit extraordinary acts of violence against Jews took another step toward being an accepted basis of historical inquiry in that it coincided with the aforementioned exhibit on the *Wehrmacht*. The exhibit, which opened in Hamburg in March 1995, attracted added attention as it began to be compared to Goldhagen's work. The combination of the two radically expanded the perception of the number of Germans who were complicit in the atrocities of World War II. What was left of the false image that World War II and the Holocaust were events engaged in by strangers in faraway places was finally shattered in the public imagination.

The collective memory of that period, gradually becoming the only type of memory left to call upon, had been altered irrevocably. This does not mean that normalization tendencies will not again arise in Germany;

they most certainly will. It does, however, mean that they have increasingly greater obstacles to overcome.

Nobody understood this more than Peter Gauweiler, Munich chairman of the Christian Social Union (CSU), the Bavarian conservative party. On October 12, 1996, well after the tidal wave of media coverage had passed, the most visible member of the right wing of the party offered his opinion of the Goldhagen controversy in the CSU party organ, the *Bayernkurier*.[23] Gauweiler called Goldhagen's theses reverse racism. He referred to Goldhagen's rhetoric as *Volksverhetzung*, racial hate speech. As might be expected from a CSU leader, Gauweiler justified his relativizing tirade on the text of a speech given by his late party leader, Franz Josef Strauß. Based on unknown sources, Strauß claimed that the sum of all of those who had participated in atrocities never exceeded 50,000. "Of course, this 50,000 is too many, but in a people of 65 million they hardly constitute a substantial minority." Calling upon the German historian and son of the Nobel laureate, Gauweiler quotes Golo Mann as saying: "The realization of Hitler's Jew hatred was never popular in Germany." Not even the most conservative of German historians would now state the case in such an extreme way.

It is clear that Gauweiler is the self-appointed mouthpiece for the radical right in Bavaria, a German state where radical right parties have always enjoyed more success than elsewhere in Germany. That he would voice his reactionary notions of German history so vehemently suggests that he expects to find support for such ideas in his wing of the party and beyond. His entry into the foray also suggests that those conservative forces, most of which favor the push to normalize German history, were threatened by the public discussions unleashed by the book and the *Wehrmacht* exhibit.

The opposition parties in the *Bundestag* (the federal parliament) began to openly denounce the Bavarian politician. Joschka Fischer, the leader of the Green Party who was already sympathetic to Goldhagen's book, called for a debate of Gauweiler's statements in the *Bundestag*. His request was refused by the ruling Christian Democratic coalition, of which Gauweiler's party is a member.

Although the book and its reception had a geopolitical aspect from the start, that aspect had been effaced by a discussion of competing histories and identities. With the Gauweiler polemic the Goldhagen controversy took on the geopolitical tone of its *Historikerstreit* predecessor. The theses were again in the papers, and this time the polemics were such that anyone who was not a supporter of Goldhagen ran the risk of being seen as in the camp of the normalizers or even the deniers, at least of those denying that ordinary Germans participated. Careful reading of Goldhagen's text and careful rhetoric addressing it may well have still provided space for critique of *Hitler's Willing Executioners,* but to this point in the debate there had been very little precedent for that. Andrei Markovits, Christopher Browning, and numerous other non-Germans had contributed much toward the debate in factual terms. But this was an identity question; that is, it was effected by those who identified themselves as German and therefore carried the historical and cultural burdens of Germany's past.

By November 1996 the debate had gone well beyond a discussion of *Hitler's Willing Executioners* to a discussion of the discussion. A series of meta-commentaries on the book's reception began to appear on both sides of the Atlantic. Josef Joffe broached the topic in a long article in the *New York Review of Books* (Chapter 26). He claimed that in the reception of the book one could trace the differing reactions of three generations. "The grandparents came back from the war and hid behind self-imposed silence. The parents, teenagers at the end of the war, made an unconscious reckoning for themselves along these lines, perhaps: 'We were too young to be culpable, but we certainly paid the bill in the coinage of destruction and stigmatization; the accounts and squared and closed.'" The third generational reaction Joffe mentions is that of those presently younger than forty: "In reading Goldhagen's book, many felt, they could at least discover for themselves the evil their elders inflicted upon the world. They could unearth the knowledge that is necessary to step toward liberation and even redemption."[24] He is most certainly correct in his reading of those born in the generation referred to by Helmut Kohl as those, himself included, who enjoyed "the good grace of having been born later." In his differentiation of age groups, however, Joffe leaves out an important generation, namely, those born after the war. Gauweiler perjoratively named them the "Rudi-Dutschke Generation," referring to the slain student-movement leader of the late 1960s.

The role played in the debate by those born during the mid-1940s to mid-1950s (represented in this volume by, among others, Klaus Theweleit, Wolfgang Wippermann, Götz Aly, Volker Ullrich, and Jan Philipp Reemtsma) was critical. Although they did not represent a uniform opinion, their contribution is remarkable in that for the most part they did not resort to the same identity politics as had the preceding generation. This is the first major postwar historical dispute in which this generation was in a position to influence the outcome of the discussion. That is to say, inverting what Kurt Pätzold has noted apropos many of the early respondents, the "68ers" have reacted more as historians and less as Germans. Perhaps the most thorough and productive response of this type came from Wolfgang Wippermann (see Chapter 27).

After taking Goldhagen to task for having underestimated the severity of the Nazi racial ideology, Wippermann then becomes his most articulate defender. He weaves a critique of many of the chapters in this volume, which have been drawn primarily from the dominant press sources in Germany, as well as of less mainstream contributions to the discussion. And more than any observer up to that point, Wippermann makes a compelling case for the value of Goldhagen's contributions to current political culture in Germany:

> On the whole, the Goldhagen controversy—which began exactly ten years after the outbreak of the *Historikerstreit* and, quite obviously, has by no means reached an end—shows that the struggle for cultural hegemony in the present by mastery of the past continues, even if at the beginning of 1996 it still appeared as though the equalizers, relativizers, and deniers had already won. Goldhagen has written an important book at the right time.

THE PUBLIC PERFORMANCE OF HISTORY

When, in late December 1996, the *Blätter für deutsche und internationale Politik* announced that it would award its Democracy Prize to Daniel Jonah Goldhagen and that Jürgen Habermas would make the laudatory remarks, the debate was about to come full circle. Jürgen Habermas, the social philosopher who threw down the gauntlet in the *Historikerstreit*, the moral voice who made a compelling argument for an honest assessment of the horrors of the recent German past, was going to make his thoughts known on this matter as well. And given the role he agreed to take, it seemed unlikely that he would provide anything but a positive response.

Goldhagen's detractors were right when they referred to the book's publication and reception as a media event. By definition, any such widely marketed and reviewed book would be. They are wrong that such a designation is necessarily pejorative. Because of or perhaps even despite the blatant commercialism that surrounded the publication of the book, important issues were brought to the fore. These issues were especially critical for countering the destructive normalizing historiographical forces in Germany. When the book came out in March 1996, no one could have anticipated the quantity or quality of the roles that would be ascribed to the book and its author. By March 1997 Daniel Goldhagen, whom world-renowned and worthy scholars and pundits alike had attempted to relegate to the trash heap of historiographic oblivion by referring to him as "anti-German," would be celebrated as a friend of the Republic. By the "urgency, the forcefulness, and the moral strength of his presentation," Daniel Goldhagen has "provided a powerful stimulus to the public conscience of the Federal Republic"; he has sharpened "our sensibility for what constitutes the background and the limit of a German 'normalization.'" Jürgen Habermas's rendition of the declaration made by the Board of Trustees of the *Blätter* in awarding the prize to Goldhagen shows into what form the debate about *Hitler's Willing Executioners* finally grew. The reception of the book had mutated from a discussion about the motivations of individuals who chose to carry out the acts of genocide against European Jews into a discussion of the status of political culture in postunification Germany.

Habermas's entry into the discussion was the sine qua non for the book to acquire moral force. The social philosopher has never been deposed from the position of moral authority he acquired in the *Historikerstreit*. This time, however, the stakes were different; the debate never did run along the lines of its predecessor. In the Goldhagen case, the sides could legitimately oppose each other without fear of being regarded as outside of democratic political norms. The difference between Habermas's remarks in the Goldhagen controversy and in the *Historikerstreit* were visible in the fact that Habermas did not polemicize against those who disagreed with him. On the contrary, he names many of them and commends their work on the complex history of the Holocaust done "with the devotion of an entire professional career" (see Chapter 29). Thus he made it clear that he does not read this dispute as being morally divisive, as were the debates about the uniqueness of the Holocaust of ten years earlier.

Although the controversy remained highly polemical, no one could be branded a neofascist just for agreeing or disagreeing with Goldhagen's theses. (The case of Gauweiler is different in that he uses *Hitler's Willing Executioners* and its author only as an excuse for a Rush Limbaugh–like tirade.) Thus, insofar as it expanded the terms with which we discuss and understand the history of the Holocaust, the Goldhagen debate has arguably been much more productive than the *Historikerstreit*. This is counter to Reemtsma's assertion that as a "historians' debate" discussion of Goldhagen's book would necessarily fail (see Chapter 28). Reemtsma claims this is so because those who were dismissive of *Hitler's Willing Executioners* had, in effect, no argument to make contrary to Goldhagen's. The results of the public fora of September suggest this is true. Goldhagen and his critics were simply talking past one another. Nevertheless, this certainly does not detract from the fact that the occasion brought forth a forceful shift in public understanding of an important aspect of the Holocaust.

Without having been named as such, "History and Community" was the theme of the four speeches on the occasion of the presentation of the Democracy Prize. Discussions of the past, such as the Goldhagen debate, Habermas said, "concern how we as citizens of the Federal Republic can have mutual respect for one another." This statement is hard to dispute, but Habermas then jumps straight into the most controversial issue in the entire debate, namely, collective guilt: "This singular crime—a crime that first generated the notion of a 'crime against humanity'—has issued from the very midst of our collective life." In this way, Habermas provides a clear reading of the relationship of Goldhagen's theses to collective understandings of the responsibility for the Holocaust. He continues by asking, why, insofar as individuals can be held responsible for mass criminality, they did what they did: "And insofar as normative justifications were of decisive importance for the actors, were these rooted in the culture and in particular ways of thinking?" This, according to Habermas, is the greatest burden for the members of later generations in coming to terms with their own understanding of themselves and their communities (see Chapter 29).

On this occasion, the last of the large concert hall gatherings that Goldhagen was to encounter with this book, the primarily younger audience as well as the long list of elites invited to attend were to witness the final transformation of the discourse from a book reception into a debate on national identity. Reemtsma's role in the evening was to respond to Habermas's laudatory remarks. Instead of doing so, he continued in the vein of Habermas's discussion of the resonance of Goldhagen's book in Germany. Again Reemtsma contextualized the book's reception within the reception of his institute's *Wehrmacht* exhibit and the unexpected commercial success of Victor Klemperer's diaries. In all three cases, the history of the Third Reich and the German persecution of Jews moved from an abstract and distant set of events to an integral part of the everyday life of many Germans. Reemtsma praises his fellow Germans for their willingness to take the risk of recognizing their own forebears in the histories they read. That risk taking, he claims, deserves much of the credit for this turn in historical understanding.

The event ended, in a way, where the *Historikerstreit* of 1986 began, namely, with a discussion of the formation of what Habermas then called "postconventional identities." Daniel Goldhagen took the occasion of this award ceremony to speak about what he termed the "internationalization of German history."

In the *Historikerstreit* one of the key notions was *Sinnstiftung*, the "provision of meaning." It became the bad example against which Habermas posited historiography and scholarship as proper pursuits of coming to terms with the past. Although the constellation of arguments, of players, and of generations—indeed, the country itself—had changed since 1986, it is not difficult to see how it is that the German philosopher ended up allied with the Harvard scholar. The latter set out on a pursuit that addresses a historiographical question, without any expressed plan of engaging in current German politics. Although Goldhagen certainly seeks to change our understanding of German history, it is not a restorative project that could in any way normalize the horrors of German history and thereby release contemporary German politics from the burdens of the past.

Goldhagen's questioning of the motives behind what he views as personal decisions to kill Jews could well be read as what Habermas referred to as "the filter of universalistic value orientations" through which "national pride and collective self-esteem" in Germany would necessarily have been forced in order to achieve "signs of the development of a postconventional identity."[25] In Goldhagen's speech, it becomes clear that he believes that the reception of his book is a sign of the success of this filtering.

The other sign of development for Goldhagen is what he refers to as the "internationalization of German historical composition" (see Chapter 30). In 1986 Habermas called on Germans to see to it that "we have not completely wasted the opportunity afforded by the moral catastrophe."[26] He continued: "The unreserved opening of the Federal Republic to the political culture of the West is the great intellectual achievement of the postwar period."[27]

Goldhagen claims that as a part of that achievement, Germans have done something no other Western country has managed to accomplish, namely, open up the writing of their national history to foreigners. To be sure, he notes, at first they had no real choice. But what cannot be said for France, Britain, or the United States can be said for Germany, namely, that many of the most acclaimed experts in German history come from outside its borders: "However some in Germany might have wished or even tried to write a sanitized German history, it has simply not been possible because it would have necessitated altering the dominant framework of understanding, which has not been entirely under national control." The results of this lack of internal control are, Goldhagen argues, that "it is not a coincidence that the country that has succeeded best at dealing honestly with the least savory part of its past, Germany, is the country that has had the least control over the construction of its national history." He does not claim that they have always done it perfectly, but that they have been more successful than other nations in producing an accurate national history: "They have succeeded best at counteracting the prettifying, mythologizing, and self-deluding tendencies of national history writing."

This is Goldhagen's account of a "postconventional identity" that has already been accomplished. The Germans' (which, as the title of the speech indicated, necessarily referred only to West Germans) would, according to this argument, not have at their disposal control over national narratives that would provide for the "unified picture of history"[28] that Habermas attributed to the conservative historians. As such, Germans would be forced to accept the horrors as constituting a critical portion of their identity structure, thereby permanently preventing a conventional, normalized national identity.

Awarding the Democracy Prize to Goldhagen was justifiable. But the *Blätter* may have focused its award too narrowly. To be sure, it was legitimate to acknowledge an author and a book that in this postunification period, when the German Question had been answered but when many questions about Germany nevertheless remained, did much to mark a sensible path for a republic trying to find its way. But as even Goldhagen acknowledged, that prize could equally be shared by Habermas, Reemtsma, and the late Victor Klemperer. Indeed, in this case, it could be shared by some of Goldhagen's worst detractors. For even in their diatribes, they brought issues to the fore that have become part of a valuable debate.

Historical disputes have marked how Germans, mostly West Germans, have gradually over the last fifty years come to terms with their past. The results have not always been flattering. Much has been read about Germans and their treatment of their past vis-à-vis the Federal Republic's response to terrorism in the 1970s, the *Sonderweg* debate, President Ronald Reagan's visit to the Bitburg cemetery in 1985, the *Historikerstreit*, the fall of the Berlin Wall in 1989 and reunification in 1990, and the reception of *Schindler's List* in 1994. Volker Ullrich started this debate by again setting up the reception of Goldhagen's book as a bellwether: "How we receive his disturbing, disconcerting book—by this reading, much can be registered about the historical consciousness of this republic" (see Chapter 1).

One may not have anticipated it in May 1996, but from the viewpoint of May 1997, an openness toward an honest examination of the past exists in Germany to a greater extent than it has in the past fifty years. Alongside the continuing success of the *Wehrmacht* exhibit and of the powerfully moving personal writings of Victor Klemperer, the reception of *Hitler's Willing Executioners* may well be seen as that which many have demanded from Germany for fifty years, that is, an honest reckoning with their past.

The form that *Vergangenheitsbewältigung* [coming to terms with the past] has now taken in Germany can be seen as a watershed. For fifty years it has been all too easy (and often justified) for Western critics to point fingers at Germans for denying their past. Likewise it has been all too tempting for German historians and politicians to try to draw discussion of the Holocaust to a conclusion. To be sure, the construction of collective memory will always remain an issue for the present, and no one can predict how it will be pursued in the future. That is to say, mastery of the past is always a way of mastering the present. *Hitler's Willing Executioners* is a vigorous attempt to understand neglected aspects of Germany's past. What is critical, however, is the fact that its reception has been a way of making sense of that past for generations born thereafter. As such it may have done much to prepare Germany for the roles it will be required to play in the future. One of the disturbing trends of the entire Goldhagen debate was the way in which this most important debate became personalized. The issues at stake were much more important than any of the egos that were involved. Fortunately, the readers of Goldhagen and Klemperer and the visitors to the *Wehrmachtausstellung* seemed to recognize this. The German public's willingness to sustain a critical look at their own history shows that they, perhaps more than anyone else, are deserving of a prize in democracy.

NOTES

1. The first review to appear was a translation of a piece written by the American political scientist Jacob Heilbrunn in the Berlin daily *Der Tagesspiegel,* March 31, 1996.

2. See "Vergangenheit, die nicht vergehen will: Eine Rede, die geschrieben, aber nicht gehalten werden konnte," in *Historikerstreit: Die Dokumentation der Kontroverse um die Einzigartigkeit der national-sozialistischen Judenvernichtung,* ed. E. R. Piper (Munich: Piper Verlag, 1987). For Jürgen Habermas's contributions, see the original "Eine Art Schadenabwicklung: Die apologetischen Tendenzen in der deutschen Zeitgeschichtsschreibung," in ibid., 62–76. See also Jürgen Habermas, "A Kind of Settlement of Damages," trans. Jeremy Leaman, in *New German Critique,* no. 44 (Spring/Summer 1988): 25–39.

3. See Chapter 6. Critics refer to his book *Ordinary Men: Reserve Police Battalion 101 and the Final Solution in Poland* (New York: HarperCollins, 1992).

4. *Der Spiegel,* no. 21, May 20, 1996 (my translation).

5. Andrei Markovits and Simon Reich, *The German Predicament: Memory and Power in the New Europe* (Ithaca, N.Y.: Cornell University Press, 1997), 14.

6. Ibid., 15.

7. Quoted in Habermas, "A Kind of Settlement of Damages," 28.

8. Ibid., 38.

9. Ibid., 39.

10. *Der Spiegel*, no. 33 (1996).

11. See Hans Mommsen, "Schuld der Gleichgultigen: Die Deutschen und der Holocaust. Eine Antwort auf Daniel Goldhagens Buch *Hitlers willige Vollstrecker*," *Süddeutsche Zeitung*, July 21–22, 1996, and Chapter 21 in this volume.

12. Mommsen, "Schuld der Gleichgultigen."

13. Daniel Jonah Goldhagen, *Hitler's Willing Executioners: Ordinary Germans and the Holocaust* (New York: Knopf, 1996), 6.

14. "Die Mörder waren unter uns: Daniel Jonah Goldhagens *Hitlers willige Vollstrecker*. Eine notwendige Provocation," *Süddeutsche Zeitung*, August 24–25, 1996.

15. Ibid.

16. Daniel Jonah Goldhagen, *Hitlers willige Vollstrecker* (Berlin: Siedler Verlag, 1996), 12.

17. See the paperback edition of *Hitler's Willing Executioners: Ordinary Germans and the Holocaust* (New York: Viking Press, 1997), 482–83.

18. Goldhagen, *Hitler's Willing Executioners* (paperback), 45.

19. Goldhagen, *Hitler's Willing Executioners* (paperback), 465–66.

20. *Stuttgarter Nachrichten,* September 19, 1996.

21. Matthias Hoenig, "Goldhagen-Debatte offenbart Probleme deutscher Geschichtsschreibung," *Cannstatter Zeitung,* September 21, 1996.

22. Dorion Weickmann, "Gruppenbild ohne Dame: Die Goldhagen-Debatte. Ein Zwischenruf," *Die Zeit,* September 20, 1996.

23. Peter Gauweiler, "Ein deutsches Phänomen," *Bayernkurier,* October 12, 1996.

24. Josef Joffe, "Goldhagen in Germany," *The New York Review of Books,* November 28, 1996.

25. Habermas, "A Kind of Settlement of Damages," 38.

26. Ibid., 39.

27. Ibid.

28. Ibid., 38.

ONE

A PROVOCATION TO A NEW
HISTORIKERSTREIT

Volker Ullrich

T he great historical debates always begin with a provocation. So it was at the beginning of the 1960s when the Hamburg historian Fritz Fischer challenged the conservative guild with his book *Griff nach der Weltmacht* (Germany's aims in World War I). So it was in the mid-1980s when Jürgen Habermas gave the impetus to the *Historikerstreit,* the debate about the uniqueness and comparability of National Socialist crimes, with his response, in this paper [*Die Zeit*—Ed.], to Ernst Nolte and other historians.

Ten years later the prelude has been set for a second—and even sharper— *Historikerstreit.* The newly published work of the young Harvard professor Daniel Jonah Goldhagen, *Hitler's Willing Executioners,* is one of those provocations that lead to great debates. In August, Siedler Verlag will bring the book out in German translation. In the United States the book has already stirred up controversy, which is hardly surprising, for Goldhagen claims to definitively answer the two questions that continue to intrigue us a half century after the end of the Third Reich: How could the Holocaust, this most despicable of all human crimes, occur? And why in Germany in particular?

After 1945 historians quickly inclined toward blaming everything on Hitler's delusional ideas and on the small clique of fanatical SS men who put those ideas into action. Later, in the 1970s, this "intentionalist" interpretation was challenged by a "functionalist" one that sought the key in the internal systemic conditions of National Socialist rule, in the uncontrolled dynamic of a regime that spawned genocide in a process of "cumulative radicalization" (Hans Mommsen). Recently an attempt has been made to connect the Final Solution with the ethnic "consolidations" that the Nazis planned and practiced in the greater eastern European space they dominated.

In Goldhagen's view all these interpretations fall short: The Holocaust—so runs his thesis—can only be explained by relating it systematically to the society of the Third Reich and to anti-Semitism as its integral component.

At the heart of the book lie not the victims but the perpetrators, and not even the "desk perpetrators" but those people who—as members of *Einsatzgruppen* [task forces] and police battalions, as guard personnel in the camps and ghettoes, and as members of *Wehrmacht* units—participated *directly* in killing and exterminating actions. Their number was much greater than generally assumed; the author estimates it at several hundred thousand. These were not fanatical SS people but, rather, friendly fathers of families, ordinary Germans, a representative cross section of society. And they murdered, according to Goldhagen, not because they were forced to, not out of blind obedience or fear of punishment, but freely, eagerly, and without any moral scruples.

This finding is not all that new. Several years ago, Goldhagen's American colleague Christopher Browning, using the example of Hamburg Reserve Police Battalion 101, showed how "ordinary men" (the title of his book) became murderers. And the same picture came to light in the much-frequented and much-discussed exhibit on the *Wehrmacht*'s war of extermination at the Hamburg Institute for Social Research. Still, Goldhagen's case studies on the perpetrators and their motives are more broadly substantiated and more thoroughly considered than any previous investigation. This alone is a significant research achievement.

The author's ambitions, however, reach further. The analysis of the "ordinary" perpetrators serves for him as a window of recognition into why it was in Germany—and only in Germany—that this monstrous crime was possible. His central thesis reads: Nowhere else at the end of the nineteenth century had racially motivated anti-Semitism eaten its way so deeply into political culture and into all of society's pores; nowhere else did it gel into an *eliminationist mind-set,* a mentality of exclusion and elimination. Accordingly the ground was prepared for the program of extermination long before Hitler came to power. Seen this way, there reigned between the Nazi leadership and the great majority of the German people a silent agreement that Germany and later Europe had to be made *judenrein* [free of Jews]. Goldhagen speaks of a common "national project." For him, this explains why there were no major protests in spite of very wide knowledge of the mass crime. And ultimately it is to this that he attributes the police battalions' practicing their murderous craft without any awareness of injustice.

There is no doubt that strong objections will be raised against this thesis (to a certain extent, they have already been raised in the United States). Thus, for example, one has to ask whether anti-Semitism in the *Kaiserreich* really differed so significantly from that of other countries. And when (for purposes of comparison) one calls on the recently published diaries of Victor Klemperer—that most exact of all observers of everyday National Socialist life—one must have doubts about the picture of a society infected through and through with anti-Semitism. One must remain skeptical of all collective accusations. To be sure, collective guilt is not Goldhagen's subject, but his treatment comes substantially very close to making this charge.

Like many scholars who believe in their ability to overturn conventional wisdom, Goldhagen, too, inclines toward plain simplification. He argues more like a district attorney than a historian. In his dismal painting there is hardly room for opposing voices or opposing forces, for acts of contradiction and resistance. Thus his account creates the impression that the terrible events were executed with almost compelling logic. However, as important as anti-Semitism in the *Kaiserreich* was as a societal precondition for the Holocaust, there was no straight path from there to Auschwitz.

In spite of all objections, we are dealing with a very important book worthy of discussion. The radicality with which Goldhagen develops his theses compels us to rethink previous perspectives. The fierce commotion that the book's appearance has unleashed in the United States shows that it has struck a nerve. Perhaps what is being expressed are misgivings on the part of many Americans about a reunited Germany.

And here at home? Some have been lulled into believing, after the com-memorations marking the fiftieth anniversary of the war's end, that they were finally rid of the tiresome theme and could now without further concern de-vote themselves to the new "normality." And now along comes a brilliant Harvard lecturer who instructs us that we are a long way from being finished with the most frightful chapter of our past. How we receive his disturbing, disconcerting book—by this reading, much can be registered about the his-torical consciousness of this republic.

Originally published in *Die Zeit* on April 12, 1996

A PEOPLE OF "FINAL SOLUTIONISTS"? DANIEL GOLDHAGEN DRESSES AN OLD THESIS IN NEW ROBES

Norbert Frei

W hoever wants to find an audience in the tough, competitive media market of the 1990s needs a thesis with a bang. Long ago this unholy message reached the historians, too, but seldom has it been followed so consistently as in the case of a book just published in the United States. In his dissertation *Hitler's Willing Executioners,* Daniel Jonah Goldhagen, a young researcher from Harvard, takes the view that the National Socialists set into motion the murder of the European Jews during World War II with the knowledge and approval of nearly all the Germans living at that time. According to Goldhagen, not only hundreds of thousands but perhaps millions participated in the Holocaust; practically the whole of German society wanted the genocide.

The author and his publisher (Alfred A. Knopf) are aware of how spectacular this thesis is: "A work of the utmost originality and importance—as authoritative as it is explosive—that radically transforms our understanding of the Holocaust and of Germany during the Nazi period," it says on the dust jacket. In the book one constantly encounters formulations highlighting the claim. No doubt about it: Goldhagen is seeking to provoke. It so happens that Holocaust research in Germany—though indeed neglected in the first few postwar decades—had by the 1980s at the latest achieved such density and complexity that it is no longer so easy for individual scholars to stand out in the crowd. The central facts have been researched; the sequence of monstrous events is known. Formerly vehement debates about the question of how the Final Solution began and whether it even required a general "order" from Hitler (long sought in vain)—in other words, the oft-cited dispute between "intentionalists" and "functionalists"—these have faded into the background in the face of differentiated research into details. And it becomes ever clearer that those who (without themselves participating) knew about the mass shootings and extermination camps number in the tens of thousands, in spite of strict efforts at secrecy and camouflage, and that presumably millions had the opportunity to obtain this knowledge.

Favored by the discovery of new sources since the opening of the archives in eastern Europe, Holocaust historiography in the 1990s is meticulously reconstructing a number of killing actions and population resettlements that made up the genocide committed on the Jews "in the east." The latest research concentrates no less on the victims than on the perpetrators and the institutions that directly or indirectly participated in these deeds. These investigations will in turn significantly sharpen and enrich our picture of what happened.

Unfortunately the same can hardly be claimed for Daniel Goldhagen's book. The thesis, a dissertation that was awarded the American Political Science Association's dissertation prize in comparative politics, has but a tiny historical-empirical yield. Goldhagen's account of recent German anti-Semitism rests chiefly on secondary literature; much the same is true of his rather coarse portrayal of the stages of the National Socialists' Jewish policy, which in no respect broadens our knowledge on the subject. But even his four chapters on the police battalions that participated in mass executions behind the Eastern Front hold little new for those already familiar with the 1992 study on this topic by the American historian Christopher S. Browning (*Ordinary Men: Reserve Battalion 101 and the Final Solution in Poland*). For these sections of his work, Goldhagen spent a lot time in the relevant archives, but he has arrived too late to measure up to the high standard of innovation he has claimed.

In light of the positive reception given Browning's book, it may at first appear incomprehensible that Goldhagen should concentrate on the same police unit. The especially favorable source material—a dedicated prosecuting attorney's office in Hamburg had conducted a preliminary investigation from 1962 to 1972 against members of the battalion and had produced an abundance of unusually revealing depositions—must have influenced Goldhagen's decision. Presumably, something else was more important: His work was nothing less than a frontal assault on the "established" Holocaust research.

Goldhagen's comprehensive account is, at bottom, driven by a single thought, which he pursues with great acumen but occasionally also with an almost frighteningly argumentative hermetic: All research on the National Socialists' Jewish policy is noted for underestimating the power of the anti-Semitic worldview. The results are fundamental and numerous defects in interpretation as well as fateful historiographic dead ends.

If one pursues his version of the *Sonderweg* thesis pushed to its extreme, then anti-Semitism in Germany—unlike, say, in France or England—was already headed in an eliminationist direction at the end of the eighteenth century and took an exterminatory turn long before Hitler. When, after decades of unbridled anti-Jewish propaganda and after years of the most perfidious anti-Jewish policy, the opportunity finally arrived with the war against the Soviet Union, the Germans immediately succumbed to their deeply rooted destructive wish.

In view of this "radical break with everything known in human history," the notion that the Germans of the nineteenth and twentieth centuries were "more or less like us" proves to be incorrect, says Goldhagen. Whoever wants to understand the Germany of the Holocaust will therefore have to approach it with the methods of the anthropologist. Of course, this makes the Germans—at least those of the Hitler period—seem to be a unique species.

It requires no special imagination to suspect that such formulations and insinuations, which are accompanied by an overbearing style of argumentation, will not exactly lighten the task of substantive debate on Goldhagen's work. Nevertheless, cheap polemic is prohibited because the author has not made it easy on himself. This is especially true for those chapters in which he has us confront the dreadful details of the killing actions just before the war's end with an urgency and clarity only rarely to be found in the previous scholarly literature.

But this is also just the place that reveals the weakness of a book rigorously designed to portray these "ordinary men"—whose massive "readiness for action" was undoubtedly what made the Holocaust possible in the first place—exclusively as ideological perpetrators acting from conviction. This interpretation is of essential importance for Goldhagen's main argument. But as Browning shows on the basis of the same sources, it is an interpretation resting on shaky ground empirically. Browning plausibly works out the process-like and situational dimensions: highly pronounced notions of obedience, group pressure, emotional coarsening, alcohol abuse, reality loss, and diversion of aggression. He points out an entire bundle of factors that ultimately motivated upright fathers of families to massacre Jewish women and children. Against this, Goldhagen asserts the monocausality of an "exterminationist anti-Semitism"—with destructive orgies carried out freely and with complete conviction. To safeguard his basic thesis Goldhagen is naturally compelled to see no one but devout anti-Semites at work along the execution ditches. In the preliminary phase, too, when the Jews of the *Altreich* (Old Reich) were being segregated and deprived of legal rights, he discerns almost nothing beyond a massive, ideologically based approval by the Germans. He thereby misses a reality whose meticulous—and because of its very precision, deeply depressing—description we owe to a survivor like Victor Klemperer.

One example is the introduction of the Star of David in September 1941, which Goldhagen comments upon simply by remarking that this further aggravated the isolation and demoralization of the Jews while making it easier for the Germans to avoid people now marked as "socially dead." But in Klemperer's diary we read something different: The initially deep anxiety affecting him and those around him about venturing onto the street with the "yellow patch" proved to be only partially well founded. To be sure, Klemperer does record that youths hounded and mobbed him. More frequently, however—and totally surprising to him initially—he encountered gestures of friendliness and even shame. Not a few Dresdeners gave him to understand that they were not in agreement with the way that he and his kind were being treated. Of course, they also signaled their fear of being denounced at the smallest hint of human solidarity.

This epidemic readiness to denounce must be at least partly linked with that "eliminationist mind-set" that Goldhagen rightly sees as widespread in Germany—more widespread than portrayed by a historiography that for a long time sought, if anything, to repress the fact of the high degree of identification with Hitler and the National Socialist regime. But it is also correct that not all Germans embraced this mentality and that there was a minority who aided Jews and saw to it that ten thousand of them could survive in the underground. The lasting shame is not only for the many who turned out to be Hitler's zealous executioners but also for the millions who looked away when there was still time to look. In their moral indifference, the Germans of that time almost all became guilty—which does not mean, as Goldhagen believes, that the Holocaust was a "national project."

It may at least be doubted whether, in light of this sensation-seeking thesis, a new "and even sharper *Historikerstreit*" is forthcoming, as Volker Ullrich has now prophesied in *Die Zeit.* Ultimately there is too little that is really new in Goldhagen's book, and it will probably be unanimously criticized in the profession as soon as his extremely deterministic account gets a careful reading. Perhaps it is no accident that there were no experts among those who bestowed quotable advance praise on this work for the sake of its effective media debut.

Originally published in *Süddeutsche Zeitung* on April 13–14, 1996

THREE

HITLER'S CODE: HOLOCAUST FROM FAUSTIAN ASPIRATIONS?

Frank Schirrmacher

P irouettes are already being spun, new battles are already being proclaimed, and it has already started to matter who engages whom in conversation, and how. Elie Wiesel speaks of "irrefutable proof,"[1] and one German newspaper fancies a new *Historikerstreit* in the making. But so far the book that this is all about is only available in English, and the impact of its German translation three months hence remains to be seen. The young American historian Daniel John [*sic*] Goldhagen has written a dissertation with the title *Hitler's Willing Executioners* that has led to adulation and fierce controversies in the United States and that is now stirring debate and zealous manifestos in Germany. This is due not so much to the book's complexity as to the radical simplicity with which the author presents his theses.

Goldhagen believes that there is a specifically German form of anti-Semitism, deeply rooted in history, that differs from all other types of European anti-Semitism in its preconditions and aims. He comprehensively discusses the anti-Semitic currents, programs, and circles of the nineteenth century in order to demonstrate that "Nazi anti-Semitism had already taken shape in the nineteenth century . . . , was widespread in all social classes and deeply embedded in the cultural and political life of the country."[2] As early as the nineteenth century, large segments of German society wanted to exterminate the Jews, and this initially theoretical destructive fantasy was a distinctive characteristic of German Jew hatred from the start. This thesis—rendered as simply as it appears in the book—has far-reaching consequences. National Socialism is nothing but the wish fulfillment of an ambivalent national self. For in Goldhagen's view, the Germans have desired the liquidation of Jewry, or at least regarded it as necessary, for at least 150 years.

Goldhagen always speaks, intentionally, of "the Germans." That gives his book an almost pamphlet-like intensity. He avoids characterizing or even identifying social groups within society. In this way anti-Semitic remarks become, for him, the expression of a collective and, as it were, national will. By all appearances, he makes a break with the insights of modern research on anti-Semitism, research that traces every kind of Jew hatred back to its specific social, economic, or intellectual milieu. What perches on the horizon of this discussion is a kind of appended historical metaphysics whereby the Germans' wish to destroy the Jews gradually turns into an obsession.

JEW HATRED EVEN WITHOUT JEWS

It was surely the immediate political implications of this thesis that made the book well known far beyond the academic world. At one point Goldhagen explicitly says that it is fundamentally irrelevant for an anti-Semitic society whether anti-Semitism stays silent for fifty or a hundred years. He makes this comment in reference to the eighteenth century, but it gives rise to unsettling questions about the present. Whoever believes Goldhagen's argumentation must accept that German society, as it were, pursued a historically necessary anti-Semitism, a Jew hatred even without Jews.

In the central portion of this work the author attempts to corroborate his historically derived thesis. He does not analyze the SS or the *Einsatzgruppen,* not the desk perpetrators or the concentration camp guards, arguing, thoroughly reasonably, that such an analysis, as it were, delegates the Holocaust to institutions and thereby makes it morally tolerable. At the core of his researches are the police battalions, especially the thoroughly researched Reserve Police Battalion 101; the civilians, industrialists, and civil servants in the vicinity of the concentration camps; and the guardians of the death marches in which the murder of the Jews was literally continued until war's end. In all cases the outcome reads: It was in no way only, or even overwhelmingly, National Socialists who operated the machinery of destruction and who were capable of unimaginable acts of cruelty. Hitler's willing executioners were average Germans from all social strata, with a thoroughly bourgeois repertoire of moral and ethical notions. All National Socialism did was furnish them with juridical inviolability. The orgy of destruction, however, had been culturally programmed in them far earlier.

What counts for Goldhagen as one of the most telling examples in support of his thesis about the Germans' inherent homicidal drive is the murder of the Jews during the death marches, after Himmler had prohibited them on tactical grounds. Viewing the empirical findings through his cultural theory, the historian finally comes to the conclusion that more than a million Germans actively took part in the destruction of the Jews or that they at least regarded it as necessary. All in all, it is the collective guilt thesis that forms the core of this book, and the only remarkable thing is how Goldhagen radicalizes and sociologizes that thesis. He supplements it with the thesis of an eminently anti-Semitic and annihilation-prone German national character.

None of this is new; it could all have been taken straight out of the arsenal of instructional and self-accusatory literature of the early 1950s. The once common theses that drew a direct pathway from Luther to Hitler to Auschwitz and that conjured up the "Hitler inside us" belong here, just as does the writer Günter Grass's fear that Auschwitz is again possible in a nationalistic German state. The chutzpah with which Goldhagen ignores an extensive scholarly literature (on methodological grounds alone) is astounding. In a favorable review, Gordon Craig and Simon Schama have praised Goldhagen's "scholarly achievement," presumably in reference to the research he conducted in the *Zentralstelle der Landesjustizverwaltungen* in Ludwigsburg.

Goldhagen's thesis about the Germans' anti-Semitic feelings are based not at all on the sources but instead almost exclusively on a few recognized standard works and anthologies, from which he borrows the quotations for his arguments. But even the career records and biographies he was able to inspect in Ludwigsburg cannot justify the high praise from Craig and Simon. Ultimately what remains are impressive portraits of a few perpetrators that Goldhagen has independently researched and that portray animal-loving, anti-Semitic sadists. These vignettes must carry the burden of the thesis that all Germans were perpetrators.

Every voice that gives later generations a hint of the victims' suffering must be documented and heard. For this reason Goldhagen's scanty basic research is useful even though all it does is bring the ghostly poems of the perpetrators to light. His portrayal of the death marches is shattering and probably the most impressive chapter of the entire book. On occasion he succeeds in tearing away the veil and making the horror palpable across the distance of half a century.

But does this suffice to justify the claim made here: that it has been proved, by scholarly methods, that for centuries the Germans had the desire and the goal of destroying the Jews? Does it suffice to convince us that the Germans were conditioned to be culturally anti-Semitic and prepared—

above and beyond the call of National Socialism (for only in this way can the discussion of Himmler's rescinding of orders be understood)—to destroy Jews? It might just be possible to understand how, in a book on anti-Semitic deep culture, the names Mendelssohn and Heine do not appear. But one has to be taken aback by a prehistory of the Third Reich in which neither Lueger, Schönerer, Bismarck, nor Rathenau are mentioned.

The author hardly even tries his hand at the debate on the emancipation of the Jews, whose advocates do not appear. World War I does not take place, a sociology of the NSDAP [Nazi Party—Ed.] is not even touched upon, and the author is of the opinion that the Germans elected Hitler by parliamentary means. Even other theses of his about the history of National Socialism are, to say the least, questionable. For example, he believes that Hitler waited to exterminate the Jews until 1941 because he did not want to endanger the German-Soviet pact. That is, at the very least, a headstrong interpretation of established historical fact. There are almost no sources from the everyday life of the Third Reich that could testify to anything about the purported anti-Semitic zeal of the population. The significance of party membership appears to have escaped the author totally because he seems to know nothing about the frequent interruptions in the application procedures for joining the NSDAP. It fits the picture that one document was apparently falsely interpreted in the initial disposition of the thesis. It is hardly more of a surprise to see the consistent misspelling of the name of one of the most important German historians of the SS state.

AT THE START OF A NEW *SONDERWEG*

Especially irritating is the mechanistic psychology to which Goldhagen is devoted. In the nineteenth century sources he sees not only documents of racist delirium but also instructions for a collectively expressed will. One often has the impression that the author is not a historian but an information scientist who reads historical processes and documents like the components of a gigantic piece of software, which issues mathematically precise commands that the actors cannot evade. In a curious schematization of "the dominant beliefs of the Germans about Jews, the mentally ill, and Slavs" appended to the book, Goldhagen provides the basic data for this program. The data shape not only Hitler's code but also, in Goldhagen's view, that of the Germans.

So caution is advised in speaking of Goldhagen's scholarly achievement. His book proves nothing. Like a computer program, it merely executes a series of typesettings and instructions that produce a logically unobjectionable but factually questionable result. What remains is amazement that in 1996 historical writing can again be presented as anthropology while four decades of hard research are roundly ignored. In the 1950s, whose air this book breathes, *Hitler's Willing Executioners* would certainly have evoked less sensation and far more embarrassed silence. Today the eminently political aspect of the incident cannot be overlooked. In many respects Goldhagen is pursuing a remythologizing of the Holocaust. It leads him back into the Faustian depths of German consciousness and thereby distances him from a rational grasp of the subject. If one believes this book's theses, the Germans' pathway into the twenty-first century can only be regarded with skepticism and fear.

These theses are all, to state it clearly, merely opinions. Goldhagen's book has little to do with scholarship and with demonstrability. It is a curious countermanifesto against the civilizing efforts to which the Germans have subjected themselves since 1945, and in its attitude and language it recalls the many psychological reports that the Allies had drawn up all over the country from March 1945 until the summer of 1947. It gives rise to that kind of inconsequential self-accusation that is really nothing other than a comprehensive form of self-appeasement. Instead of explaining something, it escapes into a general realm in which all relationships turn gray and become expressions of a mythical self.

It is questionable whether Goldhagen was actually interested in real scholarly achievement. He has surely written his book, first and foremost, with a view to the U.S. public. There is no other way to explain the abbreviations, definitions, and schemata. If what is going on here is correctly understood, then it has to do with again pinning the Germans to a *Sonderweg* for the next century. The U.S. reader who knows little about recent German history will find here the ethnology of a people who never quite left the Middle Ages, for whom anti-Semitism was a personal, perverse form of the "pursuit of happiness." These are the sort of theses that, as Karl Kraus once said, cannot be contradicted without dumbing oneself down. Goldhagen's book leaves questions open, including questions about the intellectual condition of a society that regards such theses as intellectual progress.

Originally published in *Frankfurter Allgemeine Zeitung* on April 15, 1996

NOTES

This article's original title was "Hitler's Code: Holocaust from Faustian Aspirations? Daniel John [*sic*] Goldhagen's Remythologizing of the Germans." Corrections were made to Goldhagen's name as well as that of American Gordon Craig

Frank Schirrmacher

when the article was reprinted in Julius Schoeps, ed., *Ein Volk von Mördern?* (Hamburg: Hoffman and Campe, 1996), 99–105.

1. [In his March 31, 1996, review in the British paper *The Observer,* Wiesel wrote that Goldhagen "offers a wealth of proof . . . with the overwhelming support of documents and facts."—Trans.]

2. [This appears to be a translation of a quotation from page 77 of *Hitler's Willing Executioners,* where Goldhagen writes: "The cognitive model of Nazi antisemitism had taken shape well before the Nazis came to power, and . . . this model, throughout the nineteenth and early twentieth centuries, was also extremely widespread in all social classes and sectors of German society, for it was deeply embedded in German cultural and political life and conversation, as well as integrated into the moral structure of society."—Trans.]

FOUR

THE SOCIOLOGIST AS HANGING JUDGE

Rudolf Augstein

A picture goes round the world. In the foreground a muscular, stout SS man is one link in the chain of SS men, behind whom festively costumed young peasant women seek to storm their Führer at the harvest thanksgiving on Bükkelberg near Hamlin. The picture's caption says: That's how they looked, the Jew killers of tomorrow.

The picture sets the mood for the new book by Daniel Jonah Goldhagen, thirty-five, junior professor of sociology at Harvard University. Its German title might be translated *Hitler's willige Vollstrecker*. So far the author and his publisher can be content, girding themselves as they are for a new *Historikerstreit*.

Something will surely come of their efforts. The nonhistorian Goldhagen blocks out whatever does not suit him from past Holocaust research. He wants to denounce the Holocaust-era Germans as a group as the worst, and as unique, anti-Semites—"a provocation with an eye on outrage," as the *Frankfurter Rundschau* quite mercilessly maintains.

One need not judge so polemically. But one should be allowed to ask what new information we are supposed to derive from this book. The results are thin; one can go so far as to say: close to zero.

That is what the relevant Israeli historian in this field, Raul Hilberg, believes, as does the British historian Paul Johnson. Hilberg laments the "unhistorical" excursion of this charming perpetrator of conviction, whose "sociobabble" Johnson cannot warm up to.

But it would be mistaken to ascribe the U.S. debate solely to the mostly Jewish columnists (to nonhistorians, in other words). Even the grand old Gordon A. Craig praises the "fresh look at the nature of German anti-Semitism." Craig is a profound authority on Germany and a highly regarded historian. However, one cannot call him an expert on the Holocaust.

Johannes Heil, a scholar at the Zentrum für Antisemitismusforschung [the Center for Research on Anti-Semitism] at the Technical University of Berlin, cannot make much of Goldhagen's "one-track explanation" and regards it as "not worth debating." But that—unproductive debate—is what this polite pamphlet is aiming at.

I know at what cost the *Wehrmacht* was retrospectively included among those held to account for the crimes of the Nazi dictatorship. That has been achieved. It was a step forward.

But what kind of breakthrough is Goldhagen supposed to be aiming at here? Reports about the murderous and criminal deeds of the Nazis are always ghastly to read. That there were police battalions involved—at least 15,000 persons—is knowledge that *Der Spiegel* made public in a two-part series three years ago (based on the standard work of the American historian Christopher R. Browning). This is the most important part of the Goldhagen book; nothing new here.

With respect to the systematic annihilation of the European Jews, this sociologist who teaches at Harvard regards it as beyond question that "the mode of self-understanding of Germans in no way led them to carry out the mad plans of a criminally insane man. Rather they were in agreement with the necessity of such radical action in order to secure the existence of the people. The persecution of Jews appeared to them to be a national project."

It is clear that these lowly police battalions embodied not the elite of the nation, not the elite of the party, the state, or the *Wehrmacht,* that they were honest, ideologically uninterested beer drinkers and skat players, not important activists. Anyone brave and clever enough could also dodge the murdering.

But those assembled here were not the bravest and cleverest but, rather, pardon the phrase, the dregs of people with families who could still be trapped into these battalions. If they murdered "voluntarily," they had one thing in mind: What should I do if I don't do this here?

We did not learn all this just since Goldhagen started his research. We knew it before he even existed as an academic celebrity.

His invention is the thesis that the banality of evil at that time was restricted to the Germans. Such a "plainly absurd" notion (expert Walter Pehle), such a "naive construct" (historian Johannes Heil), can, to be sure, make the intended debate inevitable.

The result, however, is already apparent. "Much ado about nothing." In the end, all one may say of Goldhagen is that he writes well but thinks ahistorically. The debate about the singularity of Auschwitz, now that it has been settled, cannot be rolled out anew every year.

We need not learn from people who really know nothing about this. "Pre-war Germany was a country sui generis, the product of a unique history of anti-Semitism" (*Newsweek*). All our federal presidents, with the exception of the current one (because of when he was born) and all our federal chancellors—again, with the exception of the current one—must accordingly have grown up in this swamp of potential Jew killers.

"The Germans were anti-Semitic, and therefore they murdered the Jews." If that is how it was, says Konrad Kwiet, "there is no need to teach history any more." Kwiet is a professor at Australia's Macquarie University, where he teaches "Comparative Genocide Research." Indeed, his chair would be superfluous if Kwiet had to confine himself to Hitler's Germany.

Goldhagen's assertion that the Germans "really hated the Jews with a passion that they worked up into a national psychosis" is, naturally, pure nonsense.

The handicapped historian should have played a mouse during the night of the 1572 Saint Bartholomew Massacre in Paris. Then he would have learned how "orders" can turn independently into cruelty. Sadism is not a purely German invention. Nonetheless, Richard Bernstein in the *New York Times* says that Goldhagen's book deserves the designation "pathbreaking."

We do not dispute the cruelties; we have never disputed them for as long as we have known about them. But we do dispute that in Germany prior to Hitler ("pre-Hitler Germany") the anti-Semitism that was no doubt present was so "intent on elimination." Not only do we dispute it, we find the assertion at best ignorant, if not downright mean-spirited. It is understandable that Nobel Prize winner Elie Wiesel declares the book to be a "gigantic contribution toward understanding the Holocaust." Wiesel does research on nothing else.

Another Nobel Prize winner, Henry Kissinger, would not be able to share Wiesel's opinion; indeed, he would find it dangerous. According to Kissinger, "The Germans were no more anti-Semitic than others." He is not just saying this now; he has been saying this for over thirty years.

Lord Acton is supposed to have remarked last century that a historian should view himself as a "hanging judge" who is called upon to condemn the sins of the past. "Hanging judge" is the caption under Goldhagen's picture in *Time*. The historian, however, should have his craftsman's tools together: It does not suffice, as *Time* writes, "to have a pen in one hand, a noose in the other."

Originally published in *Der Spiegel* on April 15, 1996

FIVE

SISYPHUS IS A GERMAN

Jost Nolte

t is said that Sisyphus seemed to achieve what was denied all mortals. For a time, at least, he outsmarted Thanatos, the ruler of death's realm. In order to punish the sinner for this and other acts of impudence, the gods finally condemned him in the afterlife to push a gigantic rock up a hill with his bare hands. He was supposed to lose his grip on the burden each time he came just short of his goal, so that his torment would last forever. For this the man remains in human memory even today.

The twentieth century has invented other, tougher tortures, but it has nonetheless never forgotten this one. In the Neuengamme concentration camp, there was a steep ramp over which the inmates, under the blows of the *Kapos,* had to transport iron wagons full of clay into a factory making cinder blocks. Inside the manufacture of the bricks proceeded apace using modern technology; outside the most primitive and harshest labor served the purpose of killing the prisoners. Work did not free the people; it annihilated them. The SS had taken the measure of Sisyphus's suffering.

Still, any myth worthy of the name should have room for more than one truth. It is also true that a certain type of past keeps looming in front of the Germans—the past in which its people followed Hitler. Put another way, we find a kind of cycling of the arguments here. There was no lack of them, and in time the early accusation of collective guilt for the crimes of the Nazi years would evolve into the absurd claim that Hitler alone was culpable for everything. At some point it came to be assumed that the calamity of the National Socialist period had emerged from an almost anarchic system of diverse levels of command, so that ultimately everything came down to "structures" into which any such notion as responsibility hardly fit. Afterward it could not fail to happen, sooner or later, that somebody would again shift responsibility for their misdeeds back onto every last German.

The most recent interpreter of German guilt to appear is the American sociologist Daniel Jonah Goldhagen—with a book whose title speaks of *Hitler's Willing Executioners* or, more accurately, of his obedient hangmen. In the United States Goldhagen has reaped, quickly, passionate approval along with vigorous protest. When his pamphlet comes out in German this August, it may lead us to a new *Historikerstreit.* Thereby is given unto the author not so much an understandable rage of Old Testament breath as the success that guarantees controversy for him and for his technique of simplification and generalization.

For example, he follows his countryman Christopher Browning, who investigated the way the Hamburg Reserve Police Battalion 101 committed murder against thousands of Jews after Hitler's victorious march eastward. Browning saw in these policemen "ordinary Germans [*sic*]" for whom the anti-Semitism of their milieu lightened the bloody business. Now Goldhagen quotes one of them making hideous utterances and without much fuss ascribes these—as evidence for a general mental constitution—to all Germans who marched eastward at Hitler's command. Apparently all of them at this time not only knew everything that was happening in the conquered territories; they approved of it, too. On top of that Goldhagen is convinced that they passed it on without encountering protest anywhere. In this direct fashion genocide again becomes collective guilt and unexpectedly, above and beyond that, original sin. For as Goldhagen wants to see it, long before 1933—in the nineteenth century at the latest and probably even earlier—the Germans generated a hatred of Jews that was distinguished from every other kind of anti-Semitism by its bloodthirstiness. Accordingly Auschwitz could never have matured in Polish or French heads, only in German ones.

It is true that those are the heads in which it matured. But it is also true that death camps were unimaginable in Germany before 1933 and that they have been unthinkable here since 1945. This shows that Goldhagen's speculations about the murderous German soul are themselves racist. We need not agree with Rudolf Augstein, who in a recent issue of *Der Spiegel* ascribed the implementation of German crimes in World War II to the "dregs" of "beer drinkers and skat players." Those responsible for these misdeeds certainly included more Germans of that generation—including *Wehrmacht* commanders and their subordinates from staff level down to the commandos ordered to "shoot in the neck." But proof of an inherited criminal character among the Germans can in no way be derived from this.

To put the point as soberly as possible: The pamphleteer Daniel Goldhagen unloads a problem on the Germans that, God only knows, has human dimensions. As stupid as it is to exonerate Hitler's Auschwitz by balancing it against Stalin's Workuta, it is just as blind to overlook what made either one of them possible. There is a mechanism for justifying torture that exists worldwide: Its banal company secret consists of withdrawing from every disturbing entreaty of one's conscience by convincing yourself that one is among the winners and that the victims are the losers delivered to you by fate.

More than half a century after Hitler's death and after the *Wende* of 1989–1990, which rattled at the outcome of World War II, it finally looked as though the Germans would be released from Sisyphus's fate. Goldhagen has tried his best to push them back into damnation.

Originally published in *Die Welt* on April 16, 1996

SIX

ORDINARY MEN OR ORDINARY GERMANS

Christopher R. Browning

n the spring of 1990 a conference was held on the campus of UCLA that was devoted to the issue of "probing the limits of representation" in writing Holocaust history. At that time I noted in my discussion of the problematic sources used in writing a history of Reserve Police Battalion 101 that "different historians reading the same set of interrogations would not produce or agree upon an identical set of 'facts'—beyond an elementary minimum—out of which a narrative of events . . . could be created." I also identified the particular questions that shaped the construction of my narrative and concluded: "If other kinds of questions had been asked, other aspects of the testimony would have seemed more important and been selected instead; a different story would have been told."[1] I must confess that at the time I wrote these words, I did not imagine that a confirming example of an alternative history would be forthcoming either so quickly or so starkly as it has in the form of Daniel Goldhagen's *Hitler's Willing Executioners: Ordinary Germans and the Holocaust.*

On two issues we do not in fact disagree, namely, the extensive participation of numerous ordinary Germans in the mass murder of Jews and the high degree of voluntarism they exhibited. These conclusions are not original with Daniel Goldhagen, the inflated claims of much recent promotional literature to the contrary notwithstanding. We do disagree, however, in our explanations of the motivation behind the participation and voluntarism of these Germans. What is at the crux of this divergence?

In acknowledging how little we know as yet about the motivations of non-German collaborators, especially the eastern European *Schutzmänner*, Daniel Goldhagen calls for a study of the "combination of cognitive and situational factors" that brought such perpetrators to contribute to the Holocaust.[2] This is a suggestion I would support. But Goldhagen does not employ such a combined approach for studying German perpetrators of the Holocaust. He writes emphatically: "With regard to the motivational cause of the Holocaust, for the vast majority of the perpetrators, a monocausal explanation does suffice."[3] The "one explanation" that is "adequate" is "a demonological antisemitism" that "was the common structure of the perpetrators' cognition and of German society in general."[4] Because Hitler and the Germans were "of one mind"[5] about the Jews, he had merely to "unshackle" or "unleash" their "pre-existing, pent-up"[6] anti-Semitism to perpetrate the Holocaust.

According to Daniel Goldhagen, therefore, one question historians like myself should not pose and need not answer is how ordinary Germans overcame reluctance and inhibition to become professional killers. There was no reluctance, aside from sheer squeamishnesss at the sight of too much blood and gore, because ordinary Germans "wanted to be genocidal executioners."[7] Given the chance, the vast majority killed with "gusto";[8] they had "fun";[9] they enjoyed themselves; they "killed for pleasure."[10] They did so "equipped with little more than the cultural notions current in Germany."[11]

I have taken the wrong track and posed the wrong question, Goldhagen writes, because of at least two factors: (1) I have not been sufficiently rigorous in excluding mendacious, self-serving, and exculpatory postwar perpetrator testimony,[12] and (2) I have naively studied these events through my own non-German cognitive lens rather than—like the anthropologist—discovering the very different cognitive world of the Germans that was so saturated with anti-Semitism as to make it part of the "common sense" of the day.[13]

One way to test our differing views is to look at the rare testimony of Jewish survivors who worked among German reserve policemen over an extended period of time. Three comments can be made about such witnesses: (1) They were in a position to know the ambience and dynamics of such units; (2) they had no motive similar to that of the German police to distort and falsify their testimony; and (3) they should have been quite sensitive rather than blind to the pervasiveness and intensity of the policemen's anti-Semitism.

Allow me to share a letter I received following the publication of *Ordinary Men:*

> Your book deeply affected me, because I personally experienced the German *"Schutzpolizei,"* the good and the bad. As a fifteen-year-old Jewish boy, I was sent by the *Judenrat* as a punishment to my father to do maintenance work in the headquarters of the German police. The town then called Auschwitz had no running water. I carried the water and polished their boots until March 1941, when the whole Jewish population had to leave. The whole police company came from the town of Waldenburg in Silesia. I came across men who in my opinion could not hurt a fly. Walter Stark, Max Maestig, Walter Kraus, Joseph Grund, *Polizeimeister* Sebranke, his deputy Orlet, and so on. Two of them were willing to make out false papers and send me as a Pole to work in Germany, apparently knowing what was coming . . . As I mentioned before, this whole company came from the town of Waldenburg. As fate would have it, in October 1944, I was taken to the KZ Waldenburg. In January 1945 we were taken to dig so-called *Panzergraben* [antitank ditches] on the outskirts of town in the direction of Breslau. One evening going back to the camp a child was playing on the sidewalk. I recognized him as Horst Maetzig, who[m] I met with his parents in Auschwitz. His father Max Maetzig was one of the policemen. Of course, you know we were guarded by SS. I could not help it; as we lined up with the boy, I exclaimed, "Horst." He took a look and ran away. The next day he was standing there with his mother Elisabeth, and [she] just nodded with her head. I appreciated that now very much. For the next two months, she and her boy stood there, it was a tremendous boost for my morale. I will never forget it. I wonder what happened to this police company, if they wound up to do what you describe in your book. Maybe you can find out for me, I would be grateful.[14]

I do not in fact know what this company of middle-aged policemen from Silesia did subsequently. If they were called upon to kill Jews, my guess is that, just as in other such units, most of the policemen would have done so, and some probably would have behaved with gratuitous and unspeakable cruelty. But I doubt that most would have killed willingly and enthusiastically, motivated by the lethal and demonological anti-Semitism uniformly attributed to such ordinary Germans by Goldhagen.

We do know, however, what a group of middle-aged reserve police stationed in the Belorussian town of Mir did when called upon to kill Jews. In the winter of 1941–1942, shortly after their arrival, these German police led Belorussian *Schutzmänner* into the surrounding countryside to murder scattered Jewish communities—"clearing the flatlands" as the German documents put it. In August 1942 they helped liquidate the Jewish ghetto in Mir. And through the following autumn they engaged in the infamous "Jew hunts," tracking down and killing Jews who had escaped the earlier massacres. What distinguishes this police station, then, is neither its personnel (randomly conscripted middle-aged reservists) nor its actions (systematically killing Jews) but the fact that a Jewish survivor, Oswald Rufeisen, passing as a Pole, worked inside the station as an interpreter for eight months. How has he described the ambience and dynamics of the *Gendarmerie* outpost in Mir? Nechama Tec, in her book *In the Lion's Den,* reports that according to Rufeisen there was

> a visible difference in the Germans' participation in anti-Jewish and anti-partisan moves. A selected few Germans, three out of thirteen, consistently abstained from becoming a part of all anti-Jewish expeditions . . . No one seemed to bother them. No one talked about their absences. It was as if they had a right to abstain.

Among these middle-aged gendarmes too old to be of interest to the army, Rufeisen noted the presence of enthusiastic and sadistic killers, including the second in command, Bruno Schultz, who was described as "a beast in the form of a man." "Not all the gendarmes, however, were as enthusiastic about murdering Jews as Schultz," Tec notes. Concerning the policemen's attitude toward killing Jews, she quotes Rufeisen directly:

> It was clear that there were differences in their outlooks. I think that the whole business of anti-Jewish moves, the business of Jewish extermination, they considered unclean. The operations against the partisans were not in the same category. For them a confrontation with partisans was a battle, a military move. But a move against the Jews was something they might have experienced as "dirty." I have the impression that they felt that it would be better not to discuss this matter.[15]

In short, Rufeisen's testimony about the Mir *Gendarmerie* outpost—neither tainted by a credulous acceptance of postwar German mendacity nor blind to the cognitive world of pre-1945 Germans—does not confirm the image of men uniformly possessed of a "lethal, hallucinatory view of the Jews" who viewed their killing of Jews as "a redemptive act."[16]

To maintain his image of uniformity and totality, Goldhagen is particularly keen to discredit the estimate I hazarded in *Ordinary Men* that some 10 to 20 percent of the reserve policemen refused or evaded and became "nonshooters." It is an estimate, he says, that has no evidentiary base.[17] I would note in this regard that even in his own account of the Helmbrechts death march, he refers to a minority among the older guards who according to a Jewish witness "were for the most part good-natured and did not beat or otherwise torment us."[18] And according to Rufeisen, three of thirteen German reserve police in Mir, that is, 23 percent, did not take part in the killing of Jews. This would suggest that my estimate is not so wildly improbable after all.

The number of nonshooters may not have been large, but the issue is important. The existence of a small minority of nonshooters suggests the existence of an even larger group of accommodators drawn from the indifferent majority of German society, a group who did not share the regime's ideological priorities but who, despite initial reluctance and lack of enthusiasm, became killers. This approach is in line with the interpretations advanced by such diverse historians of German public opinion as Ian Kershaw, Otto Dov Kulka, and David Bankier. To quote Bankier, who in no way downplays the breadth of anti-Semitism in the German population: "Ordinary Germans knew how to distinguish between acceptable discrimination . . . and the unacceptable horror of genocide . . . the more the news of the mass murder filtered through, the less the public wanted to be involved in the Final Solution of the Jewish question."[19] If such a group of "indifferent" Germans not only gave the regime the autonomy to implement genocidal policies but also provided many of the killers, then the focus of explanation would shift from Goldhagen's single cognitive model producing a uniform group of willing killers to the combination of ideological and situational factors that allowed a popular, ideologically driven dictatorial regime and its hardcore followers to mobilize and harness the rest of society to its purposes. In such an approach, anti-Semitism would certainly not be absent, but it would also not be sufficient.

Allow me to turn to a second issue, namely, the comparative treatment of Jewish and non-Jewish victims. Goldhagen repeatedly—and for the most part I think correctly—makes the point that Jews were systematically treated worse than other terribly abused victims of the Nazis. He attributes this difference not so much to Hitler's priorities and the regime's policies but, rather, once again to the pervasive lethal anti-Semitism of ordinary Germans. They could not, he implies, have acted similarly toward other victims.

As one example, Goldhagen notes that when Reserve Police Battalion 101 carried out its first reprisal shooting against Poles in the village of Talcyn in September 1942, Major Trapp wept. At the same time, he notes, the policemen were ruthlessly deporting or killing on the spot the entire Jewish population in the region. Reluctant to kill Poles, they simultaneously "slaked their Jewish blood lust."[20] But Goldhagen is comparing apples and oranges. Trapp wept before and while he carried out the initial massacre of Jews at

Jozefow as well. More telling, however, is the behavior of the middle-aged re-serve police in a subsequent reprisal action against Poles, which Goldhagen does not mention. In January 1943 a group of reserve police were about to visit the cinema when they received word that a German policeman had been shot by Polish assailants. The men hurried to the village of Niezdow to carry out a reprisal, only to discover that in anticipation of the German reaction all but the most elderly inhabitants had fled. Even though word came in the middle of the action that the German policeman had only been wounded and not killed, the Germans shot all twelve to fifteen elderly Poles—mostly women—and burned down the village before returning to the cinema.[21]

Can one be as confident as Goldhagen that these men would not have systematically killed Polish men, women, and children if that had been the policy of the regime? Goldhagen does not ignore the fact that millions of Russian POWs perished in German camps, that Slavic populations were rou-tinely subjected to selective massacres, and that Gypsies and the German men-tally and physically handicapped were systematically murdered. Each of these mass killings, he notes, had its own ideological basis.[22] Yet the *Wehrmacht* mas-sacres of Italian POWs (just days earlier German allies) in 1943 and of villagers in central Italy in the summer of 1944[23] as well as the killing of Greek men, women, and children in the village of Komeno[24] would indicate that neither a singular brand of German anti-Semitism nor even long-held German views about Slavic inferiority or "eugenics" were an essential motivation for Ger-mans to carry out wartime massacres if such were legitimized by the regime.

A third issue concerns non-German perpetrators and the importance of situational factors. Goldhagen argues: "Because each of the conventional ex-planations explicitly or implicitly posits universal human traits, the conven-tional explanations should hold true for any people who might find them-selves in the perpetrators' shoes. But this is obviously and demonstrably false."[25] The notion that ordinary Danes or Italians could have acted as Ger-mans, he says, "strains credulity beyond the breaking point."[26]

Allow me to examine one example of cross-cultural comparison that suggests otherwise. In addition to the middle-aged reservists from north Germany, Reserve Police Battalion 101 included a contingent of young men from Luxembourg, which had been annexed to the Third Reich in 1940. The presence of the Luxembourgers in Reserve Police Battalion 101 offers the his-torian the unusual opportunity for a "controlled experiment" to measure the impact of the same situational factors upon men of differing cultural and national backgrounds.

The problem is the scarcity of testimony. Only one German witness de-scribed in any detail the participation of the Luxembourgers in the battalion's activities.[27] According to this witness, the Luxembourgers belonged to Lt. Buchmann's platoon in First Company. On the night before the initial massacre at Jozefow, Lt. Buchmann was the sole officer who said he could not order his men to shoot unarmed women and children and asked for a different assignment. He was put in charge of taking the work Jews to Lublin, and according to the witness the Luxembourgers under his command provided the guard. Hence they did not participate in the massacre.

Thereafter Lt. Buchmann continued to refuse participation in any Jewish action. However, those in his platoon, including the Luxembourgers, were not exempted. According to the witness, the company captain took considerable care in the selection of personnel for assignments. "In general the older men remained behind," he noted. In contrast, *"the Luxembourgers were in fact present at every action"* (emphasis mine). "With these people it was a matter of career police officials from the state of Luxembourg, who were all young men in their twenties." According to this testimony, it would appear that the Luxembourgers became the shock troops of First Company simply because of their younger age and greater police experience and training, the absence of singular German anti-Semitism notwithstanding.

None of the Luxembourgers of Reserve Police Battalion 101 was interrogated by the German investigators. However, two of them, Jean Heinen and Roger Wietor, wrote brief accounts of their wartime service with the German police that were published in Luxembourg in 1986.[28] According to this testimony the Luxembourgers in question were not career police but prewar volunteers in Luxembourg's army—the so-called Luxembourg Voluntary Company. Fifteen of these Luxembourgers, all between the ages of twenty and twenty-four, were sent to Hamburg in early June 1942. One fell ill there, but fourteen departed with Reserve Police Battalion 101 on June 21 for the Lublin district.

Two aspects of the accounts of Heinen and Wietor stand out. First, they portrayed themselves as victims of both German conscription and the horrors of war. Second, both men portrayed the actions of the Luxembourgers as consistently nonsupportive of the German cause. The local population in Poland could easily distinguish the Luxembourgers from the Germans because the "latter, exclusively reservists, were twice our age."[29] Thus the Luxembourgers were contacted by the Polish resistance, and Wietor claims to have provided them both information about impending searches and arrests as well as captured guns and ammunition, at great risk to himself.[30] Heinen claimed that on several occasions Luxembourgers assigned to machine-gun duty did not shoot in action and feigned jams, since machine-gun crews would immediately draw concentrated enemy fire and suffer excessive casualties.[31] Beginning in June 1944 five Luxembourgers successfully deserted and two others were killed trying to go over to the Russians.[32]

Most notable, given what we now know about the battalion's mission in Poland, is that neither account mentions even the presence of Jews, much less the battalion's participation in their mass murder. At most, there is a slight hint behind several of Heinen's comments. He notes that though the battalion was engaged in numerous actions, the Luxembourgers did not suffer their first casualty until mid-1943.[33] Thus the early actions could not have involved serious antipartisan combat. A tacit consensus for silence among themselves emerged in the postwar period, he concludes: "When we meet one another by accident now, we no longer speak of our tour of duty in Poland, or at most of the great amount of vodka that helped us through many difficult times."[34]

In my opinion, one can make a very strong argument from the silence of the German and Luxembourger testimony. The Luxembourgers detailed every aspect of dissident behavior that they could. If they had been among the nonshooters in anti-Jewish actions, would they not have claimed this to their credit in postwar accounts? Many German witnesses could still remember the nonshooters in the battalion twenty years later, yet the Luxembourgers attracted no comment whatsoever in this regard. Did the Luxembourgers stir no memories and cause no comment by German witnesses in the 1960s precisely because they were behaving like most of their German comrades in 1942?

To my mind the basic question still remains: How and why could ordinary men like the *Schutzpolizei* in Auschwitz (men who "could not hurt a fly") and the *Gendarmes* in Mir (who considered Jewish actions "dirty") and the Luxembourgers in Reserve Police Battalion 101 become Holocaust killers? I do not think the answer is that they "wanted to be genocidal executioners" because they were "of one mind" with Adolf Hitler about Jews. Demonological German anti-Semitism is in fact not a sufficient explanation.

I would now like to turn from particular issues and examples to a broader approach, examining how Goldhagen has gone about constructing his history of Germans and the Holocaust. His background chapters on pre-Holocaust German anti-Semitism are an example of what I would call "keyhole" history; he views events through a single narrow vantage point that blocks out context and perspective. Goldhagen's imperial Germany is one in which conservatives and *völkisch* nationalists form the vast majority, a tiny liberal elite is fighting a *Kulturkampf* against Jews rather than Catholics, and Socialists are invisible. Rather than a society beleaguered by social and ideological divisions, it is unified in its anti-Semitic consensus, albeit temporarily distracted by the "false consciousness" of a growing concern for foreign policy issues on the eve of World War I.[35] The keyhole approach inexorably leads Goldhagen to the conclusion that anti-Semitism "more or less governed the ideational life of civil society" in pre-Nazi Germany.[36] Blocked from the pogroms for which they yearned by the restraints imposed by the Imperial and Weimar governments, the Germans "elected"[37] Hitler to power, for the "centrality of anti-Semitism in the Party's worldview, program, and rhetoric . . . mirrored the sentiments of German culture."[38] The Holocaust represented the congruence of Hitler and ordinary Germans; ultimately, the camp system, the cutting edge of the Nazi revolution, exposed "not just Nazism's but also Germany's true face."[39]

Let me make clear what is not at issue here. Many historians would agree that in nineteenth-century Germany Jewish emancipation was more strongly opposed and anti-Semitism more widely visible in German culture and politics than in that of the rest of Western Europe. Many historians would agree that this was an element of the illiberal political culture that was in turn a constituent part of a German *Sonderweg*. And many historians would agree that German anti-Semitism helped shape the political climate in which National Socialism came to power. But Goldhagen is arguing for a viewpoint far beyond this. He is arguing that virulent, lethal anti-Semitism is the veritable leitmotiv not only of Hitler's ideology but of 150 years of German history.

Goldhagen's keyhole view of German history is not, of course, incidental to what follows. Only a history of modern Germany constructed in this manner makes plausible his subsequent interpretation. But if Goldhagen has viewed modern German history through the keyhole, one should wonder, I think, whether he might not also have viewed the voluminous postwar testimony that he consulted in the same manner. In fact, he leaves the reader in no doubt.

In the appendix on methodology at the end of the book, Goldhagen frankly admits that he rigorously excluded any uncorroborated perpetrator testimony that he deemed self-exculpatory. Goldhagen argues that to do otherwise would be the equivalent of writing "a history of criminality in America by relying on the statements of criminals as given to police, prosecutors, and before courts."[40] This is but one of many instances in the book in which Goldhagen argues from the basis of a false dichotomy, painting any position but his own as an opposite and obviously untenable extreme.[41] In doing so, Goldhagen effectively ignores the possibility that a historian might judiciously accept some self-exonerating testimony that is uncorroborated in the particular instance but corroborated by other testimony as having occurred on occasion. Goldhagen's approach likewise prohibits the historian from selective use of unusually detailed and vivid testimony that has a "feel" of plausibility about it, especially in comparison to the formulaic and transparently dishonest testimony so often encountered.

Allow me a dramatic example. One reserve policeman, interrogated in November 1964, claimed to remember only several minor deportation actions: "It may sound unbelievable but it is true," he insisted in a typical example of perpetrator denial.[42] Two days later the same man reappeared uninvited and recalled in painful detail his experience in the forest outside Jozefow:

> The shooting of the men was so repugnant to me that I missed the fourth man. It was simply no longer possible for me to aim accurately. I suddenly felt nauseous and ran away from the shooting site. I have expressed myself incorrectly just now. It was not that I could no longer aim accurately, rather that the fourth time I intentionally missed. I then ran into the woods, vomited, and sat down against a tree. To make sure that no one was nearby, I called loudly into the woods, because I wanted to be alone. Today I can say that my nerves were totally finished. I think that I remained alone in the woods for some two or three hours.

He then went on to explain his unusual return to the office of the investigators. "I showed up here again today, to be rid of what I just said . . . The reason for my return was to unburden my conscience."[43]

This is a kind of testimony that Goldhagen's methodology excludes, and the result is a kind of "methodological determinism." Screening out much that could give some texture and differentiation to a portrayal of the German killers, he is left almost solely with those admissions that confirm both the hypothesis with which he began his research[44] and his unremitting portrayal of German uniformity. Given his methodology, he could scarcely have come to any other conclusion.[45]

Indeed, it is this uniform portrayal of Germans—undifferentiated, unchanging, possessed by a single, monolithic cognitive outlook—that is at the heart of Goldhagen's interpretation. When combined with his intentionally vivid descriptions of horrific events of murder and torture,[46] the cumulative emotional effect is overpowering. Not once as I read the 600 pages did it ever occur to me to ask about the perpetrators: "What would I have done in their place?" It is, of course, exactly their place or situation that Goldhagen considers irrelevant; it is only their alleged beliefs on the one hand and their terrible actions on the other that matter, and both are totally alien. Goldhagen's "ordinary Germans"—uniform and alien—are in effect dehumanized, his own disclaimer that "Germans should not be caricatured" notwithstanding.[47]

In addition to dehumanizing the perpetrators, Goldhagen repeatedly defines the historical situations he analyzes one-dimensionally, that is, as test cases solely of the perpetrators' anti-Semitic convictions torn from any situational and comparative context. For example, Mark Mazower has studied the *Wehrmacht* massacre of Greek men, women, and children in the village of Komeno.[48] Like Goldhagen, he concluded that for most of the perpetrators, killing women and children was much more difficult than killing men. But Goldhagen immediately moves past the age and gender issues to focus on ethnicity and forces the conclusion that because the perpetrators mentioned women and children specifically, they had no problem with killing Jews in general.[49] This in turn is invoked to support his general thesis of wide approval of the extermination. Taking a testimony about a policeman's difficulty in shooting Jewish women and children and turning it into a scholastic argument for broad German approval of the Final Solution is symptomatic of the single-issue, agenda-driven approach of the book.

The impact of Goldhagen's one-dimensional analysis is especially crucial in his dismissive attitude toward the issue of conformity and peer pressure. If the men fear being seen as cowards but not as "Jew-lovers," Goldhagen argues, this "can only mean" that there is "an essentially unquestioned consensus on the justice of the extermination" within the unit. "If indeed Germans had disapproved of the mass slaughter, then peer pressure would not have induced people to kill against their will."[50] But that presupposes that what is Goldhagen's sole interest, namely, a test case of anti-Semitism based on the Jewish identity of the victims, was also central to the policemen of Reserve Police Battalion 101. Were the perpetrators primarily concerned about the fate, much less the identity, of their victims, or about the looming test of their individual abilities to carry out the first difficult task assigned to the battalion in occupied territory during war? When a policeman whom Goldhagen cites as particularly honest was asked why he did not take up Trapp's offer, he answered: "I was of the opinion that I could master the situation, and that without me the Jews were not going to escape their situation anyway."[51] It was himself, not the victims, that was the center of his concern. Goldhagen is right that the ethnic identity of the victims should not be ignored, but this does not justify ignoring all factors but the victims' identity.[52]

One of the obvious situational factors that Goldhagen ignores consistently is the dictatorship itself. He pronounces the regime both dictatorial and consensual but analyzes German behavior as if there was no dictatorship and all expression was spontaneous and free. One of the hallmarks of modern dictatorship is the epidemic of hypocrisy in virtually all public discourse and the corruption of sincerity in public behavior that it engenders. In a dictatorship that strived to produce and orchestrate visible popular acclamation, silence did not mean support. The manipulative ritual, pageantry, and propaganda—such as "Jews not wanted here" signs at the edge of town—that aimed at creating the image of uniform German attitudes should not, I think, be taken as evidence for the spontaneous expression of a pervasive anti-Semitism.[53] The ubiquitous bickering about prices and shortages and other minor dissatisfactions, even the successful protest against the removal of crucifixes from classrooms, ought not be taken as evidence that anything could be freely said, as Goldhagen implies.[54] Repression was real. Bishop Galen, by virtue of his visibility and status, barely avoided his sentence of euthanasia. But students of the White Rose, who passed out leaflets condemning the mass murders of the regime, were arrested, tortured, and beheaded. Members of the killing units could individually abstain from shooting, but those who encouraged others not to shoot were court-martialed for defeatism and subversion of morale.[55] The Third Reich was not a benign dictatorship, and there were lines that could not be crossed.

Goldhagen emphasizes the horrendous and pervasive cruelty of the German perpetrators, arguing that "the quantity and quality of personalized brutality and cruelty that the Germans perpetrated upon Jews was also distinctive" and "unprecedented"; indeed, it "stood out" in the "long annals of human barbarism."[56] This singular German cruelty is again seen by Goldhagen as evidence of a singular, malevolent German anti-Semitism. I am not particularly comfortable in engaging in a competitive discussion of comparative cruelty, but since the issue has been put on the table, I would note that few historians familiar with the crimes of non-German collaborators, such as those that the Croatian Ustasha committed against both Jews and Serbs, would find German cruelty distinctive and unprecedented. Indeed, what state-sanctioned mass murder has not unleashed unimaginable cruelties, including those committed under the Khmer Rouge by Cambodians and during the Cultural Revolution by Chinese against their neighbors and countrymen? But these did not require a cognitive model of a singular, centuries-old demonological mind-set. Goldhagen's constant invocation of cruelty does not, I think, strengthen his case for an exclusive motivation of singular German anti-Semitism. The ubiquitous cruelty that accompanies mass murder points instead to the need for adding a wider perspective. Indeed, if ordinary Serbs, Croats, Hutus, Turks, Cambodians, and Chinese can be the perpetrators of mass murder and genocide, implemented with terrible cruelty, then we do indeed need to look at those universal aspects of human nature that transcend the cognition and culture of ordinary Germans.

Such an approach, no doubt, does lead to the "disjointed" and "strained patchwork" explanations that Daniel Goldhagen finds so wanting in comparison to his "single explanatory tract."[57] Like a latter-day Copernicus, he sees himself sweeping away the outmoded equants and epicycles of a superseded Ptolemaic system and replacing it with an explanation that is seductively attractive because of its simplicity. But history is not a natural science. In this regard I would note the words of a man far more eloquent than I:

> We also tend to simplify history; but the pattern within which events are ordered is not always identifiable in a single, unequivocal fashion, and therefore different historians may understand and construe history in ways that are incompatible with one another. Nevertheless, perhaps for reasons that go back to our origins as social animals, the need to divide the field into "we" and "they" is so strong that this pattern, this bipartition—friend/enemy—prevails over all others. Popular history . . . is influenced by this Manichean tendency, which shuns half-tints and complexities; it is prone to reduce the river of human occurrences to conflicts, and conflicts to duals—we and they . . . The desire for simplification is justified, but the same does not always apply to simplification itself, which is a working hypothesis, useful as long as it is recognized as such and not mistaken for reality. The greater part of historical and natural phenomena are not simple, nor simple in the way we would like.[58]

These are, of course, the words of Primo Levi, taken from his essay "The Gray Zone." It is precisely the "gray zone"—that murky world of mixed motives, conflicting emotions and priorities, reluctant choices, and self-serving opportunism and accommodation wedded to self-deception and denial—a world that is all too human and all too universal—that is absent from Daniel Goldhagen's Manichean tale.[59]

> This article was presented to the U.S. Holocaust Museum and Memorial on April 8, 1996 and was first published in *Die Zeit* on April 19, 1996. An English version also appeared in *History and Memory* (Tel Aviv: Yad Vashem Memorial, 1996).

NOTES

1. Christopher R. Browning, "German Memory, Judicial Interrogation, and Historical Reconstruction: Writing Perpetrator History from Postwar Testimony," in *Probing the Limits of Representation: Nazism and the "Final Solution,"* ed. Saul Friedländer (Cambridge, Mass.: Harvard University Press, 1992), 30–31.

2. Daniel Jonah Goldhagen, *Hitler's Willing Executioners: Ordinary Germans and the Holocaust* (New York: Knopf, 1996), 409.

3. Ibid., 416.

4. Ibid., 392.

5. Ibid., 399.

6. Ibid., 443.

7. Ibid., 279.

8. Ibid., 241.

9. Ibid., 231.

10. Ibid., 451.

11. Ibid., 185.

12. Daniel Jonah Goldhagen, "The Evil of Banality," *The New Republic,* July 13, 20, 1992, pp. 49–52.

13. Goldhagen, *Hitler's Willing Executioners,* 27, 32–33. According to Goldhagen historians must rid themselves of the notion that Germans in the Third Reich were "more or less like us" (27), that "their sensibilities had remotely approximated our own" (269). Instead scholars should approach them as they would the Aztecs, who believed human sacrifice was necessary to cause the sun to rise (28).

14. Personal letter of J. H. to the author, November 21, 1995.

15. Nechama Tec, *In the Lion's Den* (Oxford: Oxford University Press, 1992), 102–4.

16. Goldhagen, "The Evil of Banality."

17. Goldhagen, *Hitler's Willing Executioners,* 551, note 54.

18. Ibid., 360.

19. David Bankier, *The Germans and the Final Solution: Public Opinion under Nazism* (Oxford: Oxford University Press, 1992), 151–52. I find Goldhagen's attempt to dismiss the notion of "indifference" (439–41) quite unpersuasive. For instance, in discussing a report that described German reactions to a deportation as "*teilnahmlos,*" he objects to Kershaw's translation as "indifferent" and proposes "unsympathetic" instead (592, note 46). None of this discussion of the

subtleties of translation prevents him from concluding something far more sweeping, namely: "The deportations . . . were, with some exceptions, greatly popular among the populace" (104–5).

20. Goldhagen, *Hitler's Willing Executioners,* 240–41.

21. Testimony of Bruno P. Staatsanwaltschaft Hamburg, 141 Js 1957/62 (hereafter cited as HW), 1925–1926. This is a witness that Goldhagen in other matters considers trustworthy.

22. Goldhagen, *Hitler's Willing Executioners,* 410.

23. Michael Geyer, "Es muss daher mit schnellen und drakonischen Massnahmen durchgegriffen werden," in ibid., 208–38.

24. Mark Mazower, "Military Violence and National Socialist Values: The Wehrmacht in Greece 1941–1944," *Past and Present,* no. 134 (February 1992): 129–58.

25. Goldhagen, *Hitler's Willing Executioners,* 389.

26. Ibid., 408.

27. Testimony of Heinrich E., HW, 2167, 2169, 2172, 3351.

28. L. Jacoby and R. Trauffler, eds., *Freiwillegekompanie 1940–1945,* vol. 2 (Luxembourg: Imprimerie St. Paul SA, 1986), 207–21. I am very grateful to Dr. Paul Dostert, Luxembourg's representative on the International Committee for the History of the Second World War, for providing me with this material.

29. Ibid., 209 (Heinen testimony).

30. Ibid., 221 (Wietor testimony).

31. Ibid., 212 (Heinen testimony).

32. Ibid., 212–17 (Heinen testimony).

33. Ibid., 209 (Heinen testimony).

34. Ibid., 219 (Heinen testimony).

35. In regard to the issue of ideological division versus consensus, I would also note Robert Melson's conclusion that modern genocide is a product of war (often civil war) and revolution. Genocidal regimes are also revolutionary regimes trying to remake the national identity and impose a new ideological consensus. Such a situation is anything but indicative of a preexisting ideological consen-

sus. Robert Melson, *Revolution and Genocide: On the Origins of the Armenian Genocide and the Holocaust* (Chicago: University of Chicago Press, 1992).

36. Goldhagen, *Hitler's Willing Executioners,* 106.

37. Ibid., 419.

38. Ibid., 82.

39. Ibid., 460.

40. Ibid., 463.

41. Sometimes Goldhagen's false dichotomies are relatively harmless, such as when he argues for the constancy of Hitler's eliminationist anti-Semitism by posing the absurd opposite: "He never seriously considered or proposed that Germans could live together in harmonious peace with Jews" (134). Elsewhere the implications of the false dichotomy argument are more serious. The reserve policemen must have approved of the mass murder, he argues, because they were not motivated by "solidarity with the Jews" (549, note 41). They must have had genocidal beliefs because "the Nazi leadership, like other genocidal elites, never applied . . . the vast amount of coercion that it would have needed to move tens of thousands of non-antisemitic Germans to kill millions of Jews" (418–19).

42. Testimony of Franz K., HW, 2474–80.

43. Ibid., HW, 2482–87.

44. Goldhagen, *Hitler's Willing Executioners,* 463.

45. Goldhagen is selective in his treatment of the evidence in other ways as well. Testimony about incidents that do not fit his thesis of uniform voluntarism and eagerness are deemed "murky" and "sketchy." Ibid., 204; 535, note 4; and 541, note 74.

46. Ibid., 22.

47. Ibid., 382. I find unpersuasive Goldhagen's claim that it is not his but others' interpretations that deny the humanity of the perpetrators (392). Goldhagen's dehumanization of the Germans is crucial for understanding how he constructs the history of killing units like Reserve Police Battalion 101. In other instances Goldhagen is not insensitive to the importance of situational pressures. About German Jews, he writes: "The pressure on Jews of substantial cultural attainments to renounce their Judaism, a pressure that came from the wider German milieu, was so great that, during the middle part of the nineteenth century, two-thirds of culturally prominent Jews are estimated to have converted to

Christianity" (61). This was not a matter of forced conversion under dire threat. Yet clearly, bending to such pressures in no way implies that these Germans Jews "wanted" to convert, that they did so "willingly" and "enthusiastically," much less that their actions could only be interpreted as reflecting a strong embrace of Christian convictions. In this case Goldhagen is perfectly capable of understanding that framing the decision of mid-nineteenth-century Jews to convert solely in terms of religious belief would be absurd. Here Goldhagen has no difficulty understanding that people do not get to choose the choices they are offered, that choice does not always reflect willingness and approval, that belief and action are not always commensurate. Here he is capable of empathy with the subjects, of placing himself in their situation, of feeling their frustrations and aspirations.

48. Mazower, "Military Violence and National Socialist Values."

49. Goldhagen, *Hitler's Willing Executioners*, 541, note 69. Another example of Goldhagen's imposing a one-issue, noncomparative analysis on events is his treatment of Trapp's speech at Jozefow. Trapp—the weeping major—becomes a latter-day Goebbels calculatingly activating the men's ingrained anti-Semitic notion of threatening world Jewry by referring to the Allied bombing of German women and children (404–5). Yet the same incitement of German troops by referring to the Allied bombing of German women and children is made in *Wehrmacht* exhortations for drastic reprisals against Italian civilians. Michael Geyer, "Es muss daher mit schnellen und drakonischen Massnahmen durchgegriffen werden," in *Vernichtungskrieg: Verbrechen der Wehrmacht 1941–1944*, ed. Heer and Naumann, 231. A comparative perspective makes clear that the Allied bombing of civilians in Germany was used to justify German slaughter of unarmed civilians, regardless of the identity of the victim.

50. Goldhagen, *Hitler's Willing Executioners*, 251, 383–84.

51. Testimony of Erwin G., HW, 1640.

52. Goldhagen writes that "crimes of obedience . . . depend upon the existence of a propitious social and political context, in which the actors deem the authority to issue commands legitimate and the commands themselves not to be a gross transgression of sacred values and the overarching moral order" (*Hitler's Willing Executioners*, 383). But his one-dimensional analysis, focused solely on anti-Semitism, prevents him from seeing the legitimacy of the Nazi regime stemming from other than an anti-Semitic consensus and from seeing the common values of the men deriving from commonly accepted obligations of loyalty to one's unit and country in wartime.

53. Ibid., 92–93.

54. Ibid., 116, 430.

55. Testimony of Willy Schmidt, LG Hanover 2 Ks/65 (Strafverfahren gegen Pradel und Wentritt).

56. Goldhagen, *Hitler's Willing Executioners,* 386, 414.

57. Ibid., 391; 582, note 42.

58. Primo Levi, "The Gray Zone," *The Drowned and the Saved* (New York: Vintage International Edition, 1989), 36–37.

59. I delivered the preceding paper at a symposium at the U.S. Holocaust Museum and Memorial on April 8, 1996, where I was part of a panel that had been asked to discuss Daniel Jonah Goldhagen's interpretation of the "perpetrators." I do not wish to alter the text of the remarks I made at the time, but I would like to comment briefly on several aspects of Goldhagen's book that were not within the purview of my panel assignment.

The first aspect is Goldhagen's "straight road to Auschwitz" account of the development of Nazi Jewish policy. He emphatically insists upon the "constancy" of Hitler's maximalist approach and ignores evidence to the contrary, particularly for the 1939–1940 period. Here I have taken the view that if one wants to know what Hitler was thinking, one should look carefully at what Himmler (who sensed and anticipated his master's desires better than any of his rivals) was doing. Himmler was engaged in various manic schemes of "ethnic cleansing" to engineer a demographic and racial reorganization of German-occupied territories in eastern Europe, of which first the Lublin Reservation and then the Madagascar Plan were one part. Brushing aside the evidence, Goldhagen instead "reads" Hitler's mind. Goldhagen confidently states that Hitler did not immediately proceed with the extermination of Polish Jewry in 1939–1940 because, believing that the Soviet Union was controlled by the Jews, he must have feared the intervention of Stalin. In Goldhagen's methodology, clairvoyance supersedes evidence.

The second aspect is Goldhagen's concept of "eliminationist anti-Semitism." Concepts are constructs of the mind that are useful and indeed necessary to the extent that they permit us to speak of the common features of diverse and individual phenomena. There is merit, I think, in Goldhagen's view that one of the distinguishing features of the various strands of German anti-Semitism was the notion that the Jews were quite alien and un-German and that the role of the Jews in German society should be "eliminated" one way or another. But as the book progresses, "eliminationist anti-Semitism" becomes increasingly concrete, a thing in itself, until Goldhagen embraces the metaphor of a cancerous disease. "Eliminationist anti-Semitism"—almost inevitably—"metastasizes" into a society-wide embrace of the Final Solution.

With its keyhole approach to German history, its stereotypical generalizations about the perpetrators, and, finally, the employment of the metaphor of disease to illuminate our understanding of a singular and uniform German anti-Semitism, Goldhagen's approach becomes an eerie mirror image of how anti-Semites write about Jews. I do not think such an approach explains the Holocaust.

SEVEN

A PEOPLE OF WILLING JEW MURDERERS?

Michael Wolffsohn

W ere "the Germans" of "the Third Reich" a nation of dedicated Jew-killers? Yes, says Harvard professor Daniel J. Goldhagen. They were (thus the title of his book) *Hitler's Willing Executioners*.

The number of these "willing executioners" was high, much higher than is asserted either generally or by scholars, adds Goldhagen. With respect to perpetrators and accomplices, the number reaches "into the millions." The Jew-killing will and mania of "the Germans" has deep roots reaching far back into the past, deeper than for other peoples. Since the Middle Ages and especially from the nineteenth century through to the modern period, German culture was shadowed by a murderous anti-Semitism.

"Nothing new under the sun" is what the preacher Solomon would have said about this. Déjà vu, déjà lu. Already seen, already read, and in the interim long since packed in mothballs in the closet of historical research.

Goldhagen: "Most other anti-Semites only wanted to drive the Jews out of their country; for the Germans, Jews were metaphysical enemies." Long before the Nazi era, Germany was "pregnant with lethal thoughts (against Jews)." In brief: For Goldhagen, the millionfold murder of the Jews is, so to speak, part of the German national character. So much for part one of his message.

Part two, which he has been pronouncing more in interviews than in the book, sounds more conciliatory, even if not exactly convincing (owing to part one) coming from Goldhagen's mouth, and hence has been less noticed by the German public.

This second message is really not that far wrong; just as little is it wholly new: "Germany is a thoroughly changed country" after World War II. Modern Germany is "the success story of the postwar era. Germans have transformed themselves into liberal democrats."

Goldhagen must know. In the first place, he researched for several months in the Germany of today. Second, the Federal Republic counts as one of the donors funding the Center for European Studies. Stubborn, supposedly eternal anti-Semites surely would not do this.

Was it all for naught, those fifty years of research on contemporary history, of social science education about how collective statements about "the Jews" or "the Germans" are wrong, misleading, and dangerous? Even the research on prejudice over the last fifty years seems to have fizzled out without any impact on Goldhagen.

Germans and Germany, not Eskimos or Martians, bear the responsibility for the millionfold murder of Jews ("the Holocaust") and answer for it. Should that (to exaggerate the point polemically) be the message? Who, aside from dangerous and aggressive marginal groups, seriously disputes this here at home? The doors that are supposed to be flung open are already opened wide. They were by no means closed after the "commemorative year" 1995. The overwhelming majority of "the Germans," "the Jews," and the world have seen to that. "Death is a master from Germany." Paul Celan phrased that for all time in his "Death Fugue." The best-seller and TV documentation by Lea Rosh and Eberhard Jäckel familiarized a public of millions here at home, well beyond readers of poetry, with thesis, title, and facts. They were not the first, and they will not be the last. Legion are the books, essays, and films showing this at home and abroad to a scholarly and a broader public.

Here and there Goldhagen adds to our knowledge. In metaphoric terms, the wheel has been invented, and America has also been discovered. Not the course of history but the development of research on contemporary history seems to have turned like a wheel—if Goldhagen's book should point the way, as Gordon A. Craig recommends.

Seeming to be dressed up like the naked emperor with his supposed new clothes, Goldhagen struts in with his book. Unlike in Andersen's fairy tale "The Emperor's New Clothes," there quickly emerged more than one boy who not only saw the emperor's nakedness but also spoke to the emperor and spoke out. Craig's or Elie Wiesel's praise changes this state of affairs not a whit.

At the last meeting of the German Studies Association, Goldhagen was virtually derided by renowned experts and colleagues in Chicago. Major Holocaust researchers like the Israeli Yehuda Bauer or world citizen Walter Lacqueur dismissed Goldhagen's book. Substantively and methodologically, they found it unsatisfactory.

This applies both to Goldhagen's prehistory and history of the Holocaust. How nice it would have been for my Jewish ancestors if murderous anti-Semitism had been restricted "just" to Germany. Millions might have survived persecution.

Goldhagen's Germanocentric perspective is profoundly ahistorical, and un-Jewish to boot. In the Passover story (the Haggadah), the Jewish book of memory par excellence, it literally says: "Not just once [namely, in Pharaoh's Egypt] did they want to destroy us [Jews], but in every generation there are those who want to destroy us. But the Eternal One, blessed be He, rescues us from them." This latter was seldom the case, but this is more a theological than a historical problem.

Nor was racial anti-Semitism restricted either to Germany or to the nineteenth and twentieth centuries. The Spanish Inquisition demanded "purity of blood" as early as the sixteenth century. For the Jews, Germany in the nineteenth and early twentieth centuries was also anything but a paradise.

But precisely because they were, in spite of all, more tolerant than other states, the Jews of eastern Europe at the turn of the century fled murderous anti-Semitism by the millions to the United States and by many thousands to Germany. This is part of basic historical knowledge. As a professor, at Harvard no less, Goldhagen should know this. "I always read the sports section [of the paper] first," Goldhagen confessed in an interview. It shows.

During the Holocaust, countless peoples in eastern and western Europe were willing helpers and apprentices to the German masters of murder. That cannot excuse a single German perpetrator or lessen German liability, but it is part of the historical truth and of the problem that Goldhagen proposes to solve: Why were people prepared to commit murder? How could one become a perpetrator?

Even in the Netherlands this has been an agonizing question for some years, even though that is where Anne Frank and her family were hidden by a courageous minority. The majority were fellow travelers, and many pitched in. In 1995 Queen Beatrix proclaimed this painful truth to her countrymen in no uncertain terms. Many did not want to hear it, but even more dealt with it, not least by reading *The Assassination* by Harry Mulisch.

In recent years, a heap of novels and nonfiction works have shown us how and why so terribly many people in Europe virtually conspired with the

German master killers in murdering the Jews. Just a few of what I consider the most outstanding names may be mentioned here: In the nonfiction category, Jörg Friedrich (*The Law of War*); for novels, Louis Begley (*Lies in a Time of War*), Robert Bober (*What's New from the Front*), Alexander Tisma (*The Blame Book*), and Janos Niyri (*The Jewish School*).

Unlike the situation during the Cold War, there is no longer any need for Goldhagen to spare Germany and "the Germans" for reasons of alliance politics. But that does not release him from the duty to work carefully as a scholar.

What is inexplicable is the position of the directors of the U.S. Holocaust Museum and Memorial in Washington, D.C. It was recommended that they sponsor a three-day symposium on Goldhagen's book. Richard von Weizsäcker, Jürgen Habermas, and Günter Grass were also invited to be present. It could hardly be assumed that they would relativize German guilt or lecture about the collective guilt thesis. In any event, they declined the invitation.

Daniel Goldhagen is the son of Erich Goldhagen, who until recently taught sociology of religion at the Harvard Divinity School. *Hitler's Willing Executioners* was dedicated by Daniel Goldhagen to his father, his "constant discussion partner." That also shows.

Three years ago I met Erich Goldhagen at Harvard, where I was presenting my new book *The Germany Files*.

"I don't believe this." That was Erich Goldhagen's comment on the plethora of facts I presented on "U.S. Jews and the GDR." One should perhaps remind father and son that history has less to do with questions of belief, with prejudices or collective judgments, and with legends than with facts.

Originally published in *Berliner Morgenpost* on April 24, 1996 and
Rheinischer Merkur on April 26, 1996

EIGHT

FROM CHARACTER ASSASSINATION
TO MASS MURDER

Julius H. Schoeps

T he excitement is not completely hard to understand. Ultimately, much of what Daniel Goldhagen formulates in his book *Hitler's Willing Executioners* has long been familiar to the experts. For years, Alex Bein, Helmut Berding, Werner Jochmann, Wolfgang Benz, Leon Poliakov, and many other well-known researchers on anti-Semitism have submitted books and treatises on the conditions and the course of the Holocaust as well as on the motives of the perpetrators, and they have pointed out the connection between traditional anti-Semitic prejudice and the National Socialist murder of the Jews. This did not trigger major debates.

Things are different with Goldhagen's book. His theses are designed to excite protest. Are all Germans, we are surely supposed to ask ourselves after reading this book, really born anti-Semites? And are the Germans to be held collectively responsible for the organized murder of the Jews?

It is absurd to blame "the Germans" in their totality for Nazi crimes. The accusation of collective guilt, which was leveled immediately after the war and stirred up violent passions then, is no more insightful just for being taken up again in 1996.

On the other hand, there were, as we now know, many more people participating in the deportations and killing actions in the east than was at first assumed. The frightening thing about this realization is not so much the fact itself. What is frightening is the realization that it was not only SS men and Nazi bureaucrats who participated, actively or passively, in the murders, the realization that, rather, completely normal citizens took part, people from all strata of society, of whom we would not normally expect this.

Before 1945, hardly any notice was taken of the information gradually seeping through about the crimes and killings committed in the National Socialist state. Initially the organized mass murder was something only whispered about behind cupped hands. Then, after 1945, when it was possible to talk openly about it, one discussed whether one had even known anything. And as one finally broke through to the admission that one could perhaps have known something, the extent to which this knowledge was widespread was then discussed.

Now, as then, the Germans have had considerable difficulty in relation to the Nazi past. Thus it is hard for them to ask about the degree of participation. Who was involved in the killing actions, and who not? In the meantime much has become known, and much else remains uncertain. Until today it has been impossible to comprehend how honest family fathers mutated into beasts and how normal housewives had no problem looking on as their husbands, police battalion officers ordered to the east, did their murderous handiwork.

In some of his observations, admittedly, Goldhagen operates close to the border of the tolerable. To be sure, in his book he does not claim that the Germans were all murderers (several newspaper reports falsely create the impression that this is what Goldhagen has done), but he does say that the machinery of murder could not have been set in motion if the "executioners" had not sensed strong backing from the population. This is something one can certainly discuss.

Goldhagen supports the thesis of tacit approval with, among other things, statements taken from the letters of members of Reserve Police Battalion 101 and with photos that capture the murder of Jewish men, women, and children. In these pictures one sees laughing SS officers, but one also sees friendly *Wehrmacht* soldiers looking on, soldiers who are obviously proud of being present at the killings. No consciousness of injustice speaks from their faces, but instead the certainty of having assigned themselves a task, and in the name of *"Führer* and *Volk."*

The major reason that Goldhagen is facing objections is that his book goes way beyond all the interpretations previously submitted by historians. The questions he poses are posed more radically than usual. For Goldhagen the issue is not just a question of whether there was an order to murder the Jews. The preoccupation with this question is, above all, a specialty of German historians. What matters for Goldhagen are the reasons, the motives, that moved many Germans to become "Hitler's willing executioners"—and, ultimately, the demonstration that a generally widespread climate of conscious belief was what initially made the Nazi murder of the Jews possible.

Goldhagen proceeds from the assumption that eliminationist anti-Semitism was no invention of the Nazis but, rather, had its roots within the deepest layers of German political culture. This thesis is not new, but the form in which it is brought to a head makes it highly irritating. The critics take exception, above all, to the fact that Goldhagen makes no allowances in his argumentation. This must also be the reason why they disqualify him with designations like "hotspur," "up-and-coming scholar," or "junior professor." They smugly refer to the fact that he does not stick to any of the current interpretations but, on the contrary, seems downright mad about picking a fight with everyone who has previously had a scholarly engagement with the Nazi murder of the Jews.

This latter point is, without a doubt, the book's weakness, but as paradoxical as this may sound, it is simultaneously also its strength: It forces the reader to come to terms with Goldhagen's reflections. In any event, he is correct when he points out that eliminationist anti-Semitism has a long tradition in Christian Europe. The image of the Jews shaped by the church was undoubtedly highly responsible for attitudes and policies regarding Jews. The enemies of the Jews, the people who called for their exclusion, were for the most part good Christians and churchgoers. It never occurred to them that something was amiss with their attitude toward the Jews. More to the point, they believed that they were acting justly in attacking the Jews.

The anti-Semite Hartwig von Hundt-Radowsky, for example, was not plagued by any scruples—and presumably felt in tune with the spirit of the times—when he agitated in his 1819 Würzburg publication *Judenspiegel* (Jewish mirror) on behalf of putting Jewish women in bordellos and castrating Jewish men, or permitting them to work only in mines underground, or for selling them to the English so they could be marketed as slaves in England's overseas colonies.

Hundt-Radowsky's demand to exterminate the Jews, or at least to drive them out of Germany, marks a new stage of hostility toward Jews at the beginning of the nineteenth century, which may be counted as an early form of modern anti-Semitism. Not a few Germans sympathized with slogans of this kind and made an effort to buttress them with detached images like that of the "parasite." It was suggested that Jews lived at other people's expense, that they conned their way into advantage with flattery and obsequiousness without performing truly productive work. When Hitler's henchmen put up cynical inscriptions like "Work Makes Free" on the gates of some concentration and extermination camps, this presumably corresponded to—as Gold-hagen correctly observes—many Germans' internalized image of the Jew.

The success that Hitler and his paladins enjoyed with the Germans can be explained, above all, by the fact that the *völkisch* ideology propagated by the Nazis had a religious Christian core. Anti-Semitism, and this is also *expressis verbis* Goldhagen's stated conviction, played not a peripheral but *the* central role here. As evidence Hitler's well-known formulation, written in his confessional book *Mein Kampf* and cited over and over again, may be adduced: "Thus do I believe myself to be acting according to the meaning of the almighty Creator: In defending myself against the Jew, I struggle for the work of the Lord."

Anti-Jewish stereotypes strongly shaped the consciousness of Germans both before 1933 and, especially, thereafter. Hitler and the Nazis knew about the impact of these stereotypes and employed them in a calculated fashion to stir up more hostility toward Jews in the population. The publications in which the Nazis incited these prejudices were countless. The *Picture Book for Big and Small* by Elvira Bauer (Nuremberg: Stürmer Verlag, 1936) is a good example. The book, which was a concoction of the worst sort, which carried the subtitle *Trau keinem Fuchs auf grüner Heid und keinem Jud bei seinem Eid* (Trust no fox on the green heath and no Jew at his oath), and which had a wide circulation, was designed to incite the population and prepare them mentally for what was to come. It remains to be examined whether this lit-erature did not contribute to breaking down the last inhibitions for many Germans. A great deal speaks for this.

Originally published in *Die Zeit* on April 26, 1996

NINE

THE MURDER OF JEWS AS A SOCIETAL PROJECT

Walter Manoschek

"Muss i denn, muss i denn zum Städtele hinaus" sang the members of the former Police Battalion Vienna-Kagran as they departed eastward from Vienna in June 1941. A few weeks later their battalion writer noted:

8-10-41: 7:00 liquidation of the Jews held in the prisoner collection camp Bialowiza. Seventy-seven Jews of the male sex aged sixteen to forty-five years were shot.
8-12-41: Morning drill formation. Afternoon repair of weapons and bicycles.
8-14-41: 5:00 implementation of the Jewish measure in Barewka-Mala. Two hundred eighty-five Jews were shot.
9-1-41: 5:30 implementation of the execution of the Jews arrested the previous day about ten km eastward Minsk. Three execution commandos were set up. The commando of the Ninth Company shot a total of 330 Jews (of which forty were Jewesses).

On the margins of the diary are pasted photos of smirking policemen and of Jews on their way to execution. A diary of everyday police life in the eastern deployment—for veterans' reunions, for the generations after the victorious war . . .

Kolomea, a city in Galicia. In the autumn of 1941, 60,000 Jews lived in

Kolomea. A Jewish ghetto was set up and placed under a division of thirty-five Viennese police constables. Just fewer than 200 Jews saw the police constables withdraw in February 1943. In the intervening sixteen months the Viennese policemen shot around 15,000 Jewish men, women, and children. In the killing actions they were actively supported by the other institutions of occupation: "The SS, the police constabulary, *Gendarmerie, Wehrmacht,* criminal police, and Ukrainian militia participated in actions like this." Whoever was spared the shootings landed in the gas chamber at Belzec: "The surviving Jews were loaded by us into wagons that departed for the gassing," a Viennese police constable laconically recorded after the war. Kolomea, Boryslaw, Sanislau, Lemberg, Drohobycz, Minsk, Riga, Kiev, and so on; everywhere there was the same sequence, everywhere the same executioners murdering Jews: police, *Wehrmacht,* SS, Waffen-SS, civilian administration, native collaborators.

It is documents and testimony like this that are the basis for the book by the American political scientist at Harvard, Daniel J. Goldhagen, who advances the thesis that the Holocaust was not the crime of a small Nazi clique but the deed of hundreds of thousands of normal Germans (and Austrians). They committed the murder of the Jews willingly, "joyfully," and not under compulsion or pressure of command; their motivation would be the destructive anti-Semitism that had settled into the heads of the German (and Austrian) people long before Hitler; they were a people of perpetrators acting from conviction.

Racial anti-Semitism was the very core of National Socialist ideology. Since the researches of the Viennese political scientist Raul Hilberg, we know that the process of destroying the Jews rested on support from all the pillars of the National Socialist system (party, *Wehrmacht,* bureaucracy, economy). But that also means that the Holocaust was not "sneaked past" the people by Hitler, Himmler, Globocnik, Eichmann, and a few SS rascals. It is certainly correct that only a few knew everything about the Final Solution, but only a very few knew nothing at all. Only a few public authorities and departments were exclusively preoccupied with the murder of the Jews (for example, Adolf Eichmann's staff; the personnel in the ghettos and in the gassing facilities at Auschwitz, Treblinka, Belzec, and Sobidor; or the members of the *Einsatzgruppen*), but nearly the entire German apparatus of repression in the east and the Balkans was involved at many levels in the war of annihilation following the attack on the Soviet Union in the summer of 1941.

The more detailed the research, the more frightening the total picture. The exhibition "War of Annihilation: Crimes of the *Wehrmacht* 1941–1944" has destroyed the legend of the "*Wehrmacht*'s clean hands" and demonstrated the *Wehrmacht*'s participation in the Holocaust; a case study about a police battalion during the Final Solution in Poland analyzes how ordinary men can turn into murderers of Jews. The disturbing thing about this is that the perpetrators came out of the center of German society, representing a cross-section of the "German *Volksgemeinschaft*." And questions must be raised about motivations and mentalities whenever we encounter in *Wehrmacht* soldiers' letters from the front every conceivable destructive anti-Semitic stereotype but not a trace of sympathy for the Jews: There is talk of "begging hyenas" and "the hostages of humanity," "filthy and fresh as cat shit," who all "need to go away or be neutralized"—"above all, the Jew must be eliminated." As an explanation Goldhagen offers the sensational thesis that the Holocaust was carried out as a "national project" by almost all pan-Germans, all of whom were in agreement with the eliminationist anti-Semitism propagated by the National Socialist regime. This analysis is one dimensional and certainly not tenable in its deterministic derivation. Neither the genocide of the Sinti and the Roma nor the willing complicity of Ukrainians, Latvians, Croats, and Rumanians in the murder of the Jews can be explained this way. In addition, Goldhagen reduces National Socialist racism to its most destructive and most awful chapter—the Holocaust—and suppresses the fact that the National Socialist racist utopia did not stop there but went on to include the elimination of all the handicapped and people with hereditary diseases and the sterilization of homosexuals and "biological undesirables."

Goldhagen's monocausal thesis of the pan-Germans' deeply embedded destructive wish cannot do justice to the destruction of the Jews. A centuries-old anti-Semitism as an integral part of the political culture was a necessary but not a sufficient condition for the Holocaust. Anti-Semitism in all its religious, economic, and racist shadings; obedience to authority; group pressure; fear; lacking the courage of one's conviction; career motives; enrichment; boundless feelings of power by the "master race"; or simply disinterest in the fate of the Jews—all these melted together into an amalgam that allowed the systematic implementation of the process of destruction to take place.

And yet this thesis must annoy us Austrians. For in practice, until March 1938 the anti-Semitic program of National Socialism hardly went beyond what the Christian Social elite in Austria had long been recommending. The anti-Semitic ground had been superbly prepared in Austria. The Nazis did not start a development; they completed one. The pogrom-like excesses against the Jews in the days of the *Anschluß* were home-grown and did not need to be ordered by Nazi officials of the German Reich. And as late as the start of 1945, local *Gendarmerie* members, *Volkssturm* men, and Hitler Youth members were murdering Hungarian Jews deported to the Mauthausen concentration camp out on the street.

Only with this generation has it seemed possible, in a more differentiated way, to deal with the involvement of the *Volksgemeinschaft* in the racist policy of destruction. The macro-crime of the Holocaust raises questions for our modern civilization and will continue to preoccupy this country, which has been clinging stubbornly to the myth of collective innocence, for a long time to come.

Originally published in *Profil 18* on April 29, 1996

TEN

SIMPLY A BAD BOOK

Eberhard Jäckel

T he world is unjust, the media world invariably so. In the United States there appear books of the highest caliber on German history, and hardly anyone pays them any notice. Last year alone, one came out on the Soviet occupation zone by Norman M. Naimark (*The Russians in Germany*) that counts among the best I have read recently; in addition, there is a wholly masterful diplomatic history of unification in 1990 by Philip Zelikow and Condoleezza Rice (*Germany Unified and Europe Transformed*); both were published by Harvard University Press, thoroughly researched, full of new insights, exciting to read. They get a few good critical notices but instigate no debates, which they truly deserve to have done.

Then along comes—from a professor at the university, not published by Harvard University Press—a failure of a dissertation, faultily researched through and through, and the media world quakes as if a comet hit it.[1] A dozen times newspaper editors have asked me what I think of Daniel Jonah Goldhagen's book. I tell them bluntly: It is not state of the research, it does not live up even to mediocre standards, it is simply bad. I say this with regret. For I recall the author as an intelligent, sympathetic young man. He visited me often while he was studying the documents in Ludwigsburg. He told me he was preparing a doctoral dissertation on the start of the shooting executions in the Soviet Union: These executions were the beginning of the murder of the European Jews; they were already the subject of a scholarly controversy (between Alfred Streim and Helmut Kraus-nick); the subject needed clarification. We had very intense conversations. Then it looked as though his question was not enough, and this led him astray.

The book is riddled with errors. Goldhagen relates that a Captain Hoffmann from Reserve Police Battalion 101, which murdered Jews in Poland, refused an order. He fails to mention that the story is already found in Christopher R. Browning's book *Ordinary Men*. Instead he emphasizes that Hoffmann and the other officers of the battalion were "not SS men, but ordinary Germans."[2] The distinction is not just questionable; in this case it is also wrong. Hoffmann had been a member of the SS since 1933. He was supposed to have sworn not to steal, not to plunder, and not to take goods without paying for them. This order, he wrote in a letter, injured "his sense of honor." Goldhagen reads into the letter that this restriction referred to Poles but not to Jews. In fact the order contained nothing of the kind. It was in line with Himmler's general directive to remain "respectable" while murdering.

As is well known, to the question of why and how the murdering took place, Goldhagen gives the answer that "the Germans" did it, willfully, en-joying it, and out of conviction—convinced by their centuries-old anti-Semitism. Supposedly they were all anti-Semites, Thomas Mann and Karl Barth just as much as Hitler and Himmler. Before he starts, Goldhagen an-nounces how "daunting" his undertaking is, that it has to be performed em-pirically and theoretically at the micro-, meso-, and macro-levels, and that almost everything done before has been done the wrong way, that, for exam-ple, scholars have held that the perpetrators were acting under pressure and would have been punished if they had not carried out the orders given them. But who in the world of scholarship actually maintains this? Goldhagen of-fers no proof. In reality it has been accepted for some time that the so-called command state of emergency could not be demonstrated in a single case. Goldhagen says that his book is the revision.

He further maintains that it is generally assumed that the Germans had by and large killed the Jews in gas chambers and that this technology had made the horror possible. In a note he refers (without a page citation) to Raul Hilberg's standard work. Hilberg, however, precisely categorized the deaths by cause and numbered the "open-air shootings" at 1,300,000. Gold-hagen wants to make a name for himself by disputing theses that nobody seriously put forward.

In Part One he tells the story of German anti-Semitism as a continuous escalation from, as he says, the "eliminationist" to the "exterminationist." This is the state of research as of the 1950s. It was then believed that the origins of the murder must be sought in an especially pronounced anti-Semitism. That Richard S. Levy has since ascertained a setback (he called it "downfall") of the anti-Semitic parties between 1903 and 1914, that Donald L. Niewyk[3] established that there was an abatement of anti-Semitism around 1928, that Shulamit Volkov reported on his investigations into continuity and discontinuity in German anti-Semitism since 1978—these facts do not appear in Goldhagen's account. He does not even mention these works (the standard bibliography is missing in his book). Now one can certainly dispute the results of previous research. But then one must certainly refute them and may not simply pass over them in silence. Goldhagen plucks out of the (mostly older) literature whatever suits his rhyme.

Goldhagen always refers to "the Germans" (the term occurs on practically every page, sometimes eight times). When he is not referring to all of them, he refers to "the vast majority." They wanted it, and this is how the situation progressed to the point of mass murder. No attempt is made to investigate different grades of anti-Semitism. A major problem of interpretation—that whereas traditional anti-Semites always had the German Jews in mind, during World War II it was the European Jews (of whom only about 2 percent were German Jews) who were murdered—is not even accorded a word. All Germans knew it, and they all wanted it. One wonders why the undertaking was secret.

Even if some Germans deplored the savagery because they feared revenge, Goldhagen concludes that they approved of it in principle. He treats his elder colleague Christopher Browning arrogantly. Browning, who scooped Goldhagen with his book, is incessantly and unjustifiably criticized. Karl Schleunes, who wrote a sophisticated book on the prelude to the Holocaust with the title *The Twisted Road to Auschwitz,* gets slapped with the sentence "The road to Auschwitz was not twisted."[4] Raul Hilberg, who has asked how the German bureaucracy overcame its moral scruples, is instructed that he has been assuming the bureaucracy had scruples,[5] whereas the fact was actually much simpler: There were no scruples, therefore no one had anything to overcome.

The book's main section deals with the police battalions and their cruelties. Here, as in the chapters on the death marches, Goldhagen manages to achieve some forceful passages. He wants to avoid the "clinical" perspective that restricts itself to numbers and place-names. He wants to convey the horror. He is right to do so. That is often neglected. But the main task of research is, after all, to explain, and Goldhagen neglects this task; the police battalions' place and share in things remain unclear.

The basic thesis naturally rests on the assumption that anti-Semitism was more intense in Germany than elsewhere. That this has also been argued, by George L. Mosse for example, does not even get a single mention. Comparisons are surely difficult, since the intensity of anti-Semitism can hardly be measured. But Goldhagen does not even look into the problem. Only once, at the very end (408), does he speak about it. With whom is he making comparisons? With Danes and Italians! Both cases have been carefully investigated. "Heroic" is the only word that occurs to him about the Danes, and he is not familiar with Jonathan Steinberg's careful analysis of Italian noncompliance. He does not mention that the Rumanians perpetrated a massacre in Odessa in October 1941 that was very similar to the one in Babi Yar.

Repeatedly Goldhagen says that one must view the Germans and their anti-Semitism before and after the Nazi period "anthropologically" (for example, 45). He thereby betrays his whole approach. Anthropology can mean different things. It is also a subfield of biology that investigates the innate rather than the acquired characteristics of humans. It gave rise to racial doctrine and, in turn, to racist anti-Semitism. Goldhagen gets suspiciously close to this biologistic collectivism, which is a method of passing judgment that is widespread in barrooms: People say "the French" are like that, just as anti-Semites say "the Jews" are their misfortune. Raul Hilberg occasionally tells this joke: One person says to another: "Yes, the Jews and the bicyclists." The second person asks: "Why the cyclists?" Says the first: "Why the Jews?" Like a lightning flash, the joke illuminates how completely empty-headed these judgmental generalizations are.

In all seriousness, it cannot be disputed that anti-Semitism was highly virulent in the Nazi era, and from the investigations on the SS intellectuals[6] we know that it was even more deeply rooted than had previously been assumed. But it cannot have been the only thing leading to that singular German mass murder, if only because there had been anti-Semitism earlier that did not have this effect. The path to Auschwitz was winding. Research has certainly not finished. It has, however, generated some results that one cannot just overlook with such a simplistic assertion. The book by Daniel Goldhagen is little more than a step backward to positions long since passed by; even worse, it is a relapse to the most primitive of all stereotypes. A capable young man, it seems to me, has gotten himself into the headlines, but at the same time he has robbed himself of any scholarly prestige.

A slightly different version originally published in *Die Zeit* on May 17, 1996

NOTES

1. Daniel Jonah Goldhagen, *Hitler's Willing Executioners: Ordinary Germans and the Holocaust* (New York: Knopf, 1996).

2. Ibid., 3.

3. Donald J. Niewyk, *The Jews in Weimar Germany* (Baton Rouge: Louisiana State University Press, 1980).

4. Karl Schleunes, *The Twisted Road to Auschwitz* (Urban: University of Illinois Press, 1980), 425.

5. Raul Hilberg, *Die Vernichtung der europäischen Juden* (Frankfurt am Main: S. Fischer, 1990), 385.

6. *Die Zeit,* no. 14, 1966.

ELEVEN

LIKE A THORN IN THE FLESH

Hans-Ulrich Wehler

W hen a contentious book with a provocative message has aroused lively, not to say passionate, controversy, it is desirable that any new contribution to the debate should strive to provide as sober and clear a cost-benefit analysis as possible. It is best, moreover, to attend first to the book's merits and achievements, before giving an equal airing to its faults and limitations. In the case of Daniel Goldhagen's book *Hitler's Willing Executioners* such a procedure is particularly advisable, since the response in the U.S. and German media to this 600-page study of "ordinary Germans and the Holocaust" has not only been rather speedier than that of the academic world—though scholarly authorities have also, uncharacteristically, been quick off the mark—but has also impaired the debate by promptly giving respectability to a number of stereotypes and misconceptions.

The enthusiastic welcome that the book has received from journalists and opinion makers in the United States is a problem in its own right, and we shall return to it later. But here in Germany there is no cause for complacency either, since the reaction in the public media has been far from satisfactory. With dismaying rapidity, and with a spectacular self-confidence that has frequently masked an ignorance of the facts, a counterconsensus has emerged. The book, we are repeatedly told, contains no new empirical data because everything of significance on the subject has long been known; nor does it raise any stimulating new questions. The book's empirical value is "close to zero," and the book's interpretation of the empirical finding is "naturally, pure nonsense." (These two quotations, representative of many others, come from Rudolf Augstein's commentary.) It would seem, then, that there is no need to waste any more time discussing the book than is needed to condemn it. The first of the two claims, however, is alarmingly selective, misleading, even false; while the second warrants, at the least, extended discussion.

The book has not merely—indeed, has perhaps not even primarily—reached an academic audience. (The academic experts, incidentally, have all been highly critical: for example, Omer Bartov, Yehuda Bauer, Christopher Browning, Norbert Frei, Raul Hilberg, Hans Mommsen, and Moshe Zimmermann.) It has had enormous public impact, re-igniting discussion of extraordinarily painful problems that are far from having been conclusively resolved. Even though there are valid objections to Goldhagen's work, we should welcome this, instead of automatically seeking to choke off all further discussion of the facts. And we ought also to be capable, in this country, of responding with greater calmness and respect to the moral indignation that has patently motivated the author.

There are at least six reasons why it is worth paying serious attention to parts of Goldhagen's empirical analysis and to some of the questions he raises. He presents three detailed case studies: of police units involved in the Final Solution, of labor camps for Jews, and of death marches undergone by Jews after the extermination and concentration camps had been broken up. Naturally these three topics have not been entirely overlooked in the extensive international research literature on National Socialism and the Holocaust. The outcome of this earlier research, however, can certainly not be said to be satisfactory.

1. With regard to the murder of Jews by *Einsatzgruppen, Sonderkommandos* [special units], SS brigades under Himmler's command, and numerous *Wehrmacht* units, the information at our disposal is now fairly detailed (though that has been the case, essentially, only since the 1980s). Those police units, however, that were similarly employed in the full-time daily work of mass murder have, to all intents and purposes, been the subject of only one previous study, Browning's comprehensive and precise analysis of a single police reserve unit, *Ordinary Men: Reserve Police Battalion 101 and the Final Solution in Poland* (1992). This is despite the fact that over a period of years about forty such police battalions were operating in Poland and Russia. One might assume that there would have been at least a handful of German dissertations or *Habilitationen* on the subject, but a search for them among the many thousands of historical studies that have been completed under the auspices

of German universities since 1945 will draw a blank. And yet there has been a superabundance of work in conventional political history, on subjects ranging from the War of the Spanish Succession to the diplomacy of the Wilhelmine era. Was Goldhagen not right to seek to make up for this deficiency? His work has been repeatedly compared with Browning's and found wanting, but we should remember that half a century had elapsed since World War II before Browning's exemplary collective portrait was published. Is everything really known, then? Sufficiently known to the many, not just to the specialized few? Is there really nothing left to be discovered? Chapters 6 to 9 of Goldhagen's book supply an answer to these questions.

2. Hitler's Germans set up over 10,000 camps for all manner of "opponents" of the regime: concentration and extermination camps with numerous ancillary branches, prison camps, ghettos, and labor camps. Many of these camps were exclusively for Jews. In Poland alone there were roughly 940 labor camps for Jews. Once again, a search for even a handful of dissertations on the subject will be in vain. The six large extermination camps, the well-known concentration camps, and the appalling *Wehrmacht* camps that housed millions of Russian prisoners of war have all been the topics of international research. But about conditions in the labor camps for Jews we really know very little, far too little—and the German-language research literature is particularly sparse. Is Goldhagen not right, then, to have pursued the matter, as he did in his Chapters 10 to 12?

3. There were about a hundred death marches westward when the concentration and extermination camps were abandoned, on Himmler's orders, in the winter 1944–1945 in advance of the arrival of the Red Army. If we make the conservative assumption that of 750,000 "inmates," at least a quarter of a million either were killed on the way or perished in some other terrible fashion (though the real figure may have been as high as 375,000), then we have to ask yet again: Where are the academic monographs analyzing these processions of apocalyptic horror? Is everything really known? Is it not understandable that Goldhagen should have wanted to do something to fill this gap, too? No one with a shred of feeling in his or her body will be able to read his Chapters 13 and 14 and remain unshaken.

4. The inferno of the gas chambers and the mass liquidations were preceded by a seemingly never-ending daily round of cruelty, in which women and children, the old and the helpless, were subjected to extremes of torment. Granted, we know that these tortures took place. But they are commonly discussed only in terms of the destructive operations of large, anonymous bodies that exercised an untrammeled reign of terror. Is Goldhagen not right to insist that we still need to explain cruelty on this mass scale?

Cruelty that arose quite suddenly and then lasted for many years, that involved many members of a once civilized nation, and that took on many different manifestations between the spontaneous pogroms of early 1933 and May 1945? Studying such behavior is psychologically very arduous, but the task is no less valid for that.

5. For the same reason, Goldhagen has set himself the goal of bringing individual actors into the forefront whenever possible. He has not monitored faceless groups like the SS, with their blind faith, or obedient executors of orders, such as the many *Wehrmacht* units that dealt out brutality and murder. Nor has he studied what Hannah Arendt called the "banality of evil," personified by such bureaucrats of the Final Solution as Eichmann, or the unrestrained fanaticism of demoniacal planners such as Himmler and Heydrich. Instead his professed aim has been to build up a more vivid picture of the hundreds of thousands of individuals who committed acts of wrongdoing. There is no guarantee, of course, that these individuals will emerge from behind the protective shield of their units. Browning's achievement, certainly, was to have broken through the armor of anonymity in this way. But that scarcely makes it right to brush aside Goldhagen's parallel attempt to give horror a personal face. The task is an extraordinarily difficult one, both methodologically and empirically, but its legitimacy is contestable.

6. The same applies to the question that has been ceaselessly debated since the 1930s: How deeply was anti-Semitism rooted in the thinking of millions of Germans, and to what extent did it make possible and foster the process that started with social discrimination and led, via psychological harassment, active persecution, and pogroms, to a comprehensive Final Solution? As a general principle, it is clear that *Weltbilder* [worldviews]—whether those enshrined in the great religions or the major political ideologies, those dominant in rural society, or those within the bourgeois business class—play a role in shaping mentalities and governing behavior. In the case of National Socialist genocide, however, the scope and influence of *Weltbilder* and, most especially, of the complex cross-currents created by their interplay with the material and nonmaterial interests and the concrete circumstances and constraints that jointly generate and sustain social action have not been definitively explained and are certainly not "known." These, of all matters, deserve precise and methodical further study. Those who are fortunate enough to know the answers in advance should perhaps be reminded of Hegel's famous dictum: "Once the realm of Appearance has been revolutionized, Reality does not persist any longer."

It will not do, then, simply to sweep this book aside—whether from the supposed heights of superior knowledge or at the promptings of a repressed desire to keep the horrors of the German past at arm's length. And yet when all is said and done, we cannot duck out of passing an unambiguous verdict on Goldhagen's central undertaking, his attempt to explain the Holocaust. The same steely passion that imbues his empirical case studies of the plunge into barbarism has induced him to do everything—absolutely everything—in his power to render his "explanation" untenable. Once again, six main points can be addressed.

1. Goldhagen's principal thesis is that anti-Semitism, based on an ingrained Christian hatred for the "murderers of Christ," has been endemic among "the Germans" since the Middle Ages. It penetrated the deep structures of German social mentality and became a central determinant of German thought and of all areas of German life, including the political culture. It became, in earlier parlance, an indissoluble ingredient of the German "national character." Even if anti-Semitism sometimes seems to disappear from Germany for fifty or a hundred years or so, we should not be misled: The underlying anti-Semitic mentality is continuously being reproduced by processes of socialization and is capable of being reactivated at any time. Moreover, by the early nineteenth century, if not earlier, "the Germans" had turned this fateful legacy into an "eliminationist" form of anti-Semitism, which led inevitably toward repression, removal, and ultimately "extermination." This uniquely German brand of anti-Semitism, culminating in the physical annihilation of the Jews, became, we are told, Germany's "national project." Every "ordinary German" harbored within his breast this mania for destruction. It was not the case, in other words, that Hitler and his dictatorial regime succeeded in gradually getting a sufficient number of Germans to participate in the Holocaust; far from it. The Nazis merely opened the floodgates, enabling "the Germans" at last to implement their "eliminationist anti-Semitism," their unique "project," with full and merciless rigor. From this construct of Goldhagen's, everything else follows. Why were there no protests against the discrimination suffered by the Jews during the "peaceful" first six years of the Third Reich? Because a yearning to discriminate had been present for centuries. Why were there no protests against pogroms such as the *Reichskristallnacht?* Because pogroms had also long been on the agenda. Why were there no protests against the Holocaust? Because the "eliminationist anti-Semitism" of all "ordinary Germans" now finally reached its fulfillment. None of these atrocities need astonish us, since "the Germans" were simply acting out their hatred of the "subhuman" Jews. And so on: In the light of this all-embracing explanation, every problem becomes a pseudoproblem.

2. What is going on here? Goldhagen's explanation is an act of unconditional intellectual surrender. Instead of attempting to construct a serious ex-

planatory model, he provides plain and simple demonization. In a bizarre new variation on the German *Sonderweg* thesis, "the Germans" are held to have been a pernicious offshoot of the human species since the Middle Ages. They alone were consistent and perfectionist enough to progress from anti-Semitism to a full-dress Holocaust. In effect—though Goldhagen clearly neither intends nor realizes this—the debate about National Socialism and the pursuit of genocide has received a clear racist twist. Not to put too fine a point on it, the same modes of thinking that were characteristic of National Socialism have returned in a new outward guise. For the "chosen people," who were to be obliterated, read "the Germans," qua degenerate incarnation of evil. The doctrine of collective guilt has been given a sorry new lease on life. And this form of racism in reverse, adamant in its rejection of any kind of effort at greater understanding, masquerades as would-be objective history of mentality. In fact it is a species of ethnocultural determinism; fixated on a monocausal explanation, it is an elevation of dogmatic, ideological history into myth. There is no attempt to address the complexity of historical situations. Nowhere is there any discussion of the long- and short-term factors that led to the rise of the Hitler movement, of the stages whereby dictatorship was consolidated, or of the ways in which anti-Semitic ideas were translated into action. Nowhere is there any discussion of the cumulative radicalization of German policy toward the Jews that culminated in the Final Solution. Nowhere is there any discussion of the links between the brutalization created by the First World War and that created by the second, notably in the Polish and Russian campaigns; of the connections between concepts of orders and obedience, authority and duty; of the distortion of reality; of the impact of specific circumstances; of group pressures; of the despotic power wielded by middling and petty authorities; or of the extent to which people could become acclimatized even to daily mass murder; and the list could go on. And where does Goldhagen's procrustean explanation leave the Federal Republic? If anti-Semitism is really so deeply dyed into the mental structures of "ordinary Germans" and if a century can easily slip by without any anti-Semitic irruptions coming to the surface, then presumably all the efforts to confront and break with the past that have been made since 1945 will have been doomed to failure. Well hidden at the end of the book, in a four-line note on page 582, we come across a tiny escape clause: There is, of course, no such thing as a "timeless German character," the author concedes; and in any case, after the "loss of the Second World War" German character changed "dramatically." Elsewhere, indeed, Goldhagen issues a form of apology, acknowledging the success of the Federal Republic in entrenching democracy and strictly outlawing anti-Semitism. These palliating statements, however, are profoundly at odds with the unyielding indictment that is constituted by the remainder of his 600-page book.

3. Why, Goldhagen asks, has the plain truth about the continuity of evil in Germany remained concealed for so long? Simply, he says, because it was quite unwarrantedly assumed that the Germans were one of the civilized nations of the West. The fact that National Socialist dictatorship and the policy of total war led Germans to commit unprecedented crimes against humanity was regarded as something exceedingly hard to explain. But if instead—taking a leaf from recent developments in cultural studies—we view the Germans in the detached way that a cultural anthropologist studies a distant aboriginal tribe, then we see at once that the Germans were different: They were never "like us." The proof—frightening in its self-righteousness— is that only the Germans, by virtue of their tradition, carried out the Holocaust. QED. The supposedly detached approach is actually an entirely circular mode of thinking, whose function is to underwrite a purely moralistic value judgment, not to promote analysis and understanding. The successes of Jewish emancipation, the cultural assimilation of Jews into the German educated middle class, their embrace of neohumanist cultural ideals—these were all illusions that generations of German Jews were foolish enough to believe were realities. How blinded they must have been, to have taken so long to see the writing on the wall!

4. Accounts differ as to whether Goldhagen's doctoral thesis, on which his book is directly based, received a prize for the best dissertation in the School of Government at Harvard or (as his publishers maintain) a similar prize awarded by the American Political Science Association. Either way, it was honored as a dissertation in comparative politics. And yet it is hard to think of a book that displays fewer of the virtues of the comparative method in history and the social sciences. It shuns comparison like the plague. For reasons that are not hard to understand, German anti-Semitism has been scrutinized more closely than anti-Semitism in any other country. Nevertheless, comparative studies of anti-Semitism across Europe before 1933 have been extensive enough to cast doubt on the alleged uniqueness of German history as a one-way street, and if one accepts Karl Schleunes's notion of a "twisted road to Auschwitz," then it becomes far from easy to decide which national brand of anti-Semitism was the most dangerous, the most rabid, the most likely to spread. Was it, to cite only a few examples, the poisonous strain that was prevalent in Hitler's own native Austria? Or the brutal tradition of pogroms found in Russia? Or the French variant (not confined to the Dreyfus Affair)? Or the anti-Semitism characteristic of imperial Germany (whether in its politically organized form or as it filtered down informally into society)?

Why were the international anti-Semitic conferences that were held before 1914 so well attended? Why did such large numbers of *Volksdeutsche* and SS volunteers from the occupied countries of Europe—the Luxembourgers in Reserve Police Battalion 101, Latvians, Lithuanians, Ukrainians, Rumanians— act as accessories to the German murder of the Jews? Sober comparative historical analysis can help to answer such questions. Goldhagen's assumption of a uniquely German form of depravity explains nothing.

5. Suppose, however, for the sake of argument, that we take Goldhagen's central tenet—that mass murder can be explained by reference to the character of one section of the human species—as the basis for generalizing to other cases. We are then led into a hopeless and dangerous explanatory dead end. Take, for example, the Turkish massacres of millions of Armenians: Instead of trying to provide an explanation in terms of a cluster of very varied causes and motives, should we simply give up and hand the job over to a young Armenian historian, so that he can then trace everything back to the centuries-old tradition of "Ottoman butchery"? And what is the application to the war in Kurdistan? Take the even more appalling decades of million-fold murder under the dictatorships of Lenin and Stalin: Instead of trying to provide an explanation in terms of a cluster of very varied causes and motives, should we simply give up and hand the job over to a young Ukrainian historian, so that he can then trace everything back to the centuries-old tradition of "Russian barbarism"? And what is the application to the war in Chechnya? Take the near-extermination of the North American Indians: Instead of trying to provide an explanation in terms of a cluster of very varied causes and motives, should we simply give up and hand the job over to a young Navajo historian, so that he can then trace everything back to the tradition of the American "killer," inaugurated when the Puritans first branded the Native Americans as "children of Satan"? And what is the application to My Lai? All historians are painfully aware that the rational explanation of mass murder has its limits. But a monocausal approach based on the deliberate, essentialist decision to stigmatize one section of humanity on ethnic, racial, and natural grounds as permanently evil is tantamount to a declaration of intellectual, methodological, and political bankruptcy.

6. By boxing himself into this corner—a tactic that has been hailed by his wildly cheering fans as a stroke of overwhelming originality—Goldhagen has contrived to successfully avoid even posing the main questions that arise concerning National Socialism and the Holocaust, let alone provide any answers that might have marked an advance on those that have been given before. What are these questions, with which historians have been struggling for the past half century?

How and why was a modern European state capable, in the middle of the twentieth century, of planning and carrying out the industrially organized mass murder of six million Jews, male and female, adults and children? Why did this happen in Germany, alone of all industrial and civilized states? Why did so many members of the elite groups in society cooperate? Why did the bureaucracy continue to perform so smoothly? Why did special units and regular troops commit murder with such efficiency and ruthlessness? Why did so many industrial firms, and the giant railway system of the Reich, play a part in the implementation of the policy? And why did a civilized nation give birth to the regime that was Hitler's dictatorship, supporting it or at least making an accommodation with it until the spring of 1945? Why did the members of this society either remain apathetic about the treatment of their Jewish neighbors or become hostile? Why did they seek to learn as little about mass murder as they could?

Nor does Goldhagen take into consideration the huge, complex edifice of National Socialist race and population policy—a submerged iceberg, whose full dimensions have become apparent only during the past decade and a half. "Hitler's willing executioners" did not murder only Jews, although that act of genocide was undoubtedly a unique event in world history. Millions of Slavic *Untermenschen,* Gypsies, homosexuals, and people with hereditary diseases or mental disabilities were also killed. The National Socialists pursued brutal programs of eugenics, euthanasia, sterilization, and "ethnic cleansing." The "advance planners of extermination" (in Götz Aly's phrase) had cold-bloodedly projected a "loss" of more than thirty million Slavs in the event that the *Generalplan Ost* [General Plan East], to say nothing of the *Generalsiedlungsplan* [General Land Settlement Plan], extending to the Urals, was carried out. Only the fact that the triumphal progress of Hitler's armies was turned into total defeat saved the Russians and other peoples from genocide on a colossal scale. Altogether, the National Socialist regime's planning and execution of its policy of extermination went even further, and was even more inhuman, than was assumed until the early 1980s. To repeat: The Holocaust was, for the reasons stated, mass murder of a unique kind. But is it proper, in a book of this sort, to gloss over so blatantly all questions of comparison?

It is more than merely irritating that Goldhagen finds it necessary to deliver impenitently arrogant strictures to all other historians who have written about National Socialism and the Holocaust for the sake of talking up the novelty value of his own book. (We shall make no mention here of the disastrous number of empirical errors he makes concerning the history of German anti-Semitism and the rise of National Socialism, nor of the pitiful single page he devotes to Hitler's seizure of power, nor of much else besides.) In a discussion at the U.S. Holocaust Museum and Memorial in Washington, D.C., in early April 1996, he explicitly endorsed the shrill fanfares of publicity that accompanied the book's publication, including claims [on the dust jacket] that he had produced "a work of the utmost originality and importance" that would "forever change our understanding of the greatest horror of the twentieth century." But Goldhagen's scholarship is actually an unashamed reversion to the state of play in 1950 (when the prevailing slogan was "From Luther to Hitler"), while almost all of the work that has been done by the leading scholars and thinkers of the present day is the target of his condemnation (for instance, studies by Uwa Adam, Martin Broszat, Raul Hilberg, Michael Marrus, and Hans Mommsen). Indeed, the more closely other such authors impinge on his project (as in Browning's case), the more harshly he judges them, to the extent of disputing their scholarly integrity and insinuating that they have an almost indecent degree of empathy with their subject matter. Equally instructive, however, is the fact that a large number of relevant works are not discussed by Goldhagen at all; clearly, their commitment to distinctions and nuances is incompatible with his reductionism (see, for instance, writings by Aly, Bartov, Bauer, Bein, Benz, Berding, Bock, Greive, Heilbronner, Kulka, Kwiet, Levy, G. Mosse, Poliakov, Puhle, Rührup, Schleunes, Schmuhl, Volkov, and Zimmermann).

The existence of such an unusually large and sophisticated body of scholarship should surely have given the supervisors of this dissertation pause; it should have been sufficient to knock on the head the whole concept of a nation as evil incarnate, bent on destruction. The whole purpose of having supervisory procedures in the academic world is to ensure that any new piece of work is empirically up to date and that its arguments mark a useful advance on the current debate and stand up to rational scrutiny. But as Yehuda Bauer, one of the grand old men of Holocaust research in Israel, has asked: Just what was going on at Harvard? Stanley Hoffmann, the first supervisor, is a brilliant political scientist; his field is France since the First World War and particularly since the second. Sidney Verba, the second supervisor, is also a respected political scientist, an expert in political development. The third member of the triumvirate, Peter Hall, is a specialist in political economy. The Harvard historian Simon Schama, whose encomiums grace the book's jacket ("phenomenal scholarship," "unavoidable truths," "will permanently change the debate" on the Holocaust), is a specialist in the early modern period, noted for his work on the Golden Age of Holland in the seventeenth century. None of these scholars is an expert on National Socialism and the Holocaust. They may have found Goldhagen's three case studies empirically convincing, but it is quite another thing for them to have countenanced his dismissive attacks on the real experts and, especially, his demonization of "the Germans." How would these scholars have reacted if a book with a similar range of shortcomings had been published in their own fields—even though the book had successfully undergone its academic rites of passage, had been awarded a prize, had been reprinted several times, and had been hailed as an earth-shaking achievement?

The episode raises the whole question of quality control in the academic world. The nonspecialist reader needs to be able to feel that basic monitoring mechanisms are functioning properly. A dozen years ago we had the case of David Abraham in Chicago and Princeton, in which there was a bitter controversy before criticisms of a slipshod piece of work on the fall of the Weimar Republic carried the day. Then in 1992 came the case of Liah Greenfeld, who, in a comparative study of nationalism in five countries, reasserted the uniqueness of German nationalism and portrayed the Final Solution as a built-in" outcome, the inescapable endpoint of a one-way journey from Herder to the Holocaust; this work was accepted and praised by illustrious figures from Harvard's community of scholars. And now, with Goldhagen, we have reached a new low. It is not amusing to witness yet another failure of academe's system of checks and balances.

The Goldhagen affair has not just been a dispute about historical interpretation and the preservation of scholarly standards; it has also taken on an indisputably political dimension. For some sections of the U.S. public, the book has been a quasi-scientific confirmation of deep-seated resentments and prejudices. The less familiarity readers have had with the nuances and qualifications of research, the more impassioned their approbation has been. Goldhagen cannot have been unaware of the existence of these emotions, and it tells us a great deal about his sense of responsibility as a politically conscious political scientist that he has been prepared to assist the media in the way that he has.

Above all, the international response tells us once again that Germans should be under no illusions: Even though fifty years have elapsed since World War II and the Holocaust, our past is still very much alive and capable of coming back to haunt us. Many people in Germany felt, at the time of the commemorations of 1995, that the past had been sufficiently discussed, or even "overcome"; certainly, that it had more than begun to "pass away." For the foreseeable future, however, it is not going to pass away, despite all proper attempts to historicize it: It has been too monstrous an interlude in human history.

And what of the response in Germany? Goldhagen has made things very easy for his critics by proffering an explanation and a style of argument that are so easily faulted. Judging from the treatment he has received so far, it is only too likely that the flimsy defences he has erected around his theses will be torn apart by the combined onslaughts of the experts. He has done immense damage to the cause of Holocaust research, both within the academic community and among a wider public. That does not mean, though, that we can summarily dismiss his empirical case studies or some of the important questions that he raises. His book cannot be simply written off as the arrogant, iconoclastic work of a young political scientist who thinks he is making a brand-new discovery with everything he touches. It will not do to say that his teachers should have got him to see the light by telling him that what is good isn't new, and what is new isn't good—however fair such a harsh indictment of his work would have been.

Several writers, seeking to take the edge off the controversy, have said that a repetition of the *Historikerstreit* of ten years ago is neither likely nor necessary in the present case because the requisite scholarly ammunition is lacking. The *Historikerstreit,* however, was not a matter of pure scholarship alone: It was first and foremost a dispute about fundamental political questions, conducted partly by means of historical arguments.

The political element in the treatment that Goldhagen's book has so far received in the German media lies in the dubious consensus that has emerged. Not only have the crudity and dogmatism of the book been repudiated—that response has been entirely appropriate. What is worrying is the way in which, at the same time, all sides have resisted attempts to conduct a substantive debate about the factual questions raised in Parts Three to Five of the book—which extend, it should be remembered, to 200 pages—as well as about important and as yet unresolved methodological problems; indeed, almost every plausible reason that has been advanced for treating the book seriously has been rejected out of hand. It is the quality of political debate in our country that is at issue here: Can we acknowledge the legitimacy of Goldhagen's challenge—and some heavily entrenched stereotypes and prejudices may need to be overcome before that happens—while nevertheless insisting firmly on the complete failure of his explanation? Is the answer really to consign his book to the bottomless pit, for being "too much for the majority of reunited Germans to take"?

Translated by Richard Deveson
Abridged version originally published in *Die Zeit* on May 24, 1996;
English translation originally published in *German History* 15, no. 1 (1997).

TWELVE

THE MENTALITY OF THE PERPETRATORS

Ingrid Gilcher-Holtey

T he book by Daniel Goldhagen is above all a methodological challenge to historical scholarship. Innovative investigation into the Holocaust, or relapse to the state of research from the 1950s and "the most primitive of all stereotypes," as Eberhard Jäckel wrote in *Die Zeit* on May 17, 1996? Daniel Jonah Goldhagen's study *Hitler's Willing Executioners: Ordinary Germans and the Holocaust* challenges the experts and the public. So far all the critics have overlooked the problem formulated by Daniel Goldhagen, the "sociology of knowledge approach" he takes up in the opening chapter of his book.

In journalism that may be excusable, but scholarly experts ought to deal intensively with methodological questions. For the analytical frame of reference delimits the object of investigation—rather like a slice of reality that can never be exhaustively conceived but can only be grasped and investigated by way of its analytic construction. What is going on with Goldhagen? What does he want to examine? With what kind of method is he proceeding?

At the center of his book the author places the structure of meaning, the behavioral dispositions, and the conduct-shaping mentality of the perpetrators who participated directly in the persecution and murder of the Jews, who murdered with their own hands. He wants to explain the Holocaust by uncovering the cognitive structure of the *causal agents,* the mentality of the killers. What motivated them? What empowered them to commit mass murder? Why and how could it happen that Christian morality's ban on killing was annulled?

The author is therefore not concerned with a new explanation of the political process that led to the annihilation of the Jews, to the industrialization of mass murder; he is not concerned with making another contribution to the dispute between "intentionalists" and "structuralists." He is seeking a new approach.

The anthropological glance that the author occasionally casts at his subject ensues from a mode of explanation used in the history of mentalities but previously not applied all that frequently to anti-Semitism and National Socialism. No doubt about it: The worldview and motivations of National Socialism's functionaries have been investigated. But the cognitive and mental structures of the "ordinary Germans" operating the machinery of annihilation have previously not been systematically researched. That is precisely the goal of Goldhagen's book.

His method is oriented around recent inquiries in cultural sociology that seek to apprehend the everyday thinking and habitual behavior of groups and individuals. How do basic ideological patterns, worldviews, and "images of the world" get carried over into schemes of thought and behavior that shape collective and individual conduct? To answer this, the social relevance of ideas is what should be analyzed. If one reads Goldhagen's study from this angle, then his controversial causal attribution exposes an innovative inquiry, and his theses compel confrontation with a heretofore insufficiently explored dimension needed to explain how the murder of the Jews was implemented and accepted: that of mental disposition.

Daniel Goldhagen directs attention toward the mentality- and conduct-shaping effect of "eliminationist anti-Semitism." He unfolds the problem from two sides: On the one hand, he sketches out the mental structure of "eliminationist anti-Semitism"; on the other hand, he investigates the practice of behavior structured thereby. The two investigations belong together, and they cannot be separated as many reviewers have suggested: If only the author had just published the empirical part of his study!

He is far from positing anti-Semitism as an "idea" responsible for the Holocaust, as Norbert Frei asserts in the *Süddeutsche Zeitung*. Goldhagen argues that only the internalization of the elements of anti-Semitism (like the image of the Jew or the attribution of characteristics stylizing the Jew on biological grounds into an enemy and the representation of evil) created latent schemes of thinking and perception as well as behavioral dispositions that permitted "ordinary Germans" to become persecutors and murderers of the Jews.

The habituation to modes of perception may be apprehended through historical analysis of socialization, through the deciphering of symbols in which stereotypical modes of perception get solidified, or through precise behavioral analysis. Goldhagen chose the first path. He attempts, like many historians of medieval and early modern mentalities, to derive collective schemes of thinking and perception from the behavior of individuals and groups.

Goldhagen does not thereby disregard the context of the actors, the totalitarian and repressive structures of National Socialism; instead he includes them as variables in his analysis of the processes of action. He apprehends the hierarchical command structures to which the perpetrators were subordinated, the social-psychological group pressure that subjected them to the expectation of conformity, and the possibility of putting themselves in danger by refusing an order. Meanwhile, in a manner as vivid as it is shocking, he shows in his analysis of the death marches that the perpetrators also killed without—indeed, against—orders. He demonstrates, in his reconstruction of Reserve Police Battalion 101's missions, that individuals who refused the killing order did not put themselves in danger and that their nonconformist behavior did not lead to their exclusion from the group.

But if command structure, group pressure, and self-endangerment cannot adequately explain the brutality and cruelty beyond the boundaries of National Socialism and its camp system, then (Goldhagen concludes) the motive of the perpetrators must lie in an internalized structure of dispositions to conduct and behavior that produced "eliminationist anti-Semitism."

How it became possible to transfer the ideology of anti-Semitism into a mentality-shaping behavior—that is something Goldhagen's study does not show. This would have required a longitudinal analysis of the mentality-shaping effect of anti-Semitism during the nineteenth and twentieth centuries. Such a study remains to be done; it would simultaneously clarify the causes underlying the weakness of that countermodel of German history[1] that lost out under National Socialism—the countermodel of a civil society based on human rights. Daniel Goldhagen's book is a methodological challenge—to push ahead, finally, toward a deeper historical debate on the mentality of German anti-Semitism and of National Socialism.

Originally published in *Die Zeit* on June 7, 1996

NOTES

1. Marion Countess Dönhoff, *Die Zeit*, no. 20 (1996).

THIRTEEN

THE RIGHT QUESTION

Ulrich Herbert

To be sure, Daniel Goldhagen's study *Hitler's Willing Executioners* is not a good book. It is full of errors and exaggerations. His main thesis—that the genocide of the Jews was a long-sought "national project" of the German people, who had already, for over a hundred years, been in the grip of an anti-Semitism aiming at extermination—is not tenable. The book draws a distorted picture of the development and significance of anti-Semitism in Germany. It takes the process leading from opposition to Jews through persecution of Jews and ultimately to genocide, a process influenced by a variety of factors, and reduces it to the unilinear development of one element: hatred of Jews by Germans. All of the historians in the field who have expressed their opinions thus far have criticized Goldhagen's work for being deficient in scholarship and a simplification. There is little that can be added to what they have said. This is no place for a debate or even for a *Historikerstreit.*

And yet the vehemence and unanimity of the criticism arouses a certain uneasiness, above all, when polemics are issued in Germany against the accusation of collective guilt. For this is a charge that Goldhagen does not even raise. And yet for all the exaggeration of its theses and the author's lack of analytical precision, the book does contribute to restarting (finally!) a public discussion that seemed to have been nearly forgotten in the last few decades and that does touch the core of this (now as ever) unbelievable past and the nerve of the German self-image: the questions of the extent and breadth of hatred toward Jews in the German populace and of the significance that should be assigned to anti-Semitism for initiating and implementing murder on a scale of millions. One of the most problematic side effects of the deficiencies and overstatements of Goldhagen's work is that they practically invite one to disqualify the entire inquiry as absurd and dubious along with the book.

Until well into the 1960s, it was not disputed that the anti-Semitism once raging in Germany was a major, quite possibly the decisive, factor initiating the National Socialists' policy of murder. However, there was little clarity about the precise extent and significance of anti-Jewish views, especially as they began spreading again in the 1880s, initially among the relatively small anti-Semitic parties, later among the nationalist associations that were rapidly growing in influence—from the Agrarian League to the Pan-Germans all the way to the Deutschnationaler Handlungsgehilfen-Verband. What was well known was how much support the radical anti-Semitic federations and parties were garnering in the years following World War I—organizations like the Deutsch-völkischer Schutz- und Trutzbund with its more than 200,000 members.

But it seemed as if this upswing in radical Jew hatred was only of short duration. Beginning in the mid-1920s, the theme apparently lost the public's interest; in the electoral propaganda of the ascendant National Socialists after 1930, anti-Semitism was situated rather peripherally.

And besides, there was an increase in the historians' reservations about whether such a direct connection could be established between the extent of anti-Semitic views among the German population and the initiation of the genocide. For there was radical anti-Semitism in other countries, too, even stronger than in Germany—as in Poland, the Baltic states, and the Ukraine—and also in France. The transition from persecution of the Jews to mass murder, it was argued, arose much more powerfully from the concrete historical situation. The war against the Soviet Union, the failure of the Nazis' gigantic expulsion and resettlement programs, and the National Socialist regime's built-in structural incapacity to conduct long-range policy and to integrate diverging interests—these were the decisive factors initiating mass murder. This analysis was persuasive, above all, because it put this horrible past back into the concrete political reality of the years 1938–1942 and placed the murder of the Jews in the context of other mass crimes of the National Socialist regime: the "euthanasia," the murder of the mentally handicapped, the "resettlement" and killing actions against the Poles, the German strategy of starvation and annihilation conducted against the population of the conquered Soviet territories and against others.

On the other hand, in this context and in this way the question of anti-Semitism's significance was never answered. The more we came to know about the structures of the National Socialist regime that promoted the initiation of genocide, the more certainly the perpetrators—the ones along the execution trenches as much as the ones at their desks in Berlin—faded into the background, along with their mental outlook and convictions, to the point where one could ultimately conclude that radical anti-Semitism was only a marginal phenomenon in Germany and was a factor ranking extremely low in the development of the National Socialist extermination policy.

There is no investigation that could conclusively inform us about the percentage of Germans who might have qualified as anti-Semites either before or after 1933 (just as we are really, contrary to what Hans-Ulrich Wehler believes, thoroughly ill informed about the spread of anti-Semitism during the Weimar Republic). There was a certain sediment of radical Jew haters, represented by the likes of the Nuremberg *Gauleiter* Streicher and the infamous anti-Semitic paper *Stürmer*. They were certainly not insignificant, but their pugnacious, often riotous appearance nevertheless ran up against occasional indignation among the public and even to a degree inside the NSDAP. After 1933 this group presumably experienced further growth among children and youth; and here, above all, is where support was garnered for the direct, pogrom-like riots against Jews, leading over and over again to excessive legal regulations and administrative measures such as we can observe most clearly in connection with the pogrom of November 9, 1938.

Far more important than the radical Jew hatred, on the other hand, was that form of anti-Semitism that was already widespread in the *Kaiserreich* and that received additional nourishment from developments during World War I and the postwar period but that did not manifest itself in open animosity or street brawls. Many in Germany were convinced that the Jews represented an alien element among the German people, that they possessed especially unpleasant characteristics, that they stood in alliance with the enemies of Germany from World War I, that they controlled the press, and that they had enriched themselves on the war as they had on the inflation and the economic crisis; and taking all the different shadings of animosity toward Jews into consideration, one cannot rule out the possibility that those harboring anti-Semitic sentiments already made up a majority prior to 1933. That applies, on the one hand, to the supporters and voters backing the NSDAP. To be sure, not all and maybe not even the majority of NSDAP voters were radical Jew haters, but they were certainly prepared to accept the deprivation of rights heralded for the Jews by the Nazi Party so long as they themselves were just offered bread and work. The German Nationalist People's

Party, too, was notorious for its transparent (and, on the party's right wing, even radical) anti-Semitism; and even in Stresemann's German People's Party (DVP) this view was not infrequently encountered; the situation was no different in the major military associations like the *Stalhelm* and, especially pronounced, in the Protestant church.

This was not a particularly fanatical, aggressive anti-Semitism. But it easily sufficed—for all the criticism of "exaggerations"—to make even radical action against the Jews acceptable, as long as it was managed not by the brawling rowdy anti-Semite but by the government and through "legal means." And to the extent that this acceptance spread, so, too, did the conviction grow that there must be just cause behind the persecution of the Jews, since anyone getting this kind of punishment could certainly not be entirely innocent. But it was a matter of indifference to most people in light of their own worries. The policy against the Jews—this is difficult to understand today—was not an important topic for the German population of the Reich. And not following up on the multitude of firsthand observations, reports, and rumors about what was going on with the Jews, not compiling them into a picture and drawing the obvious conclusions—this is exactly what characterizes the process of mental repression.

But prior to 1933 there were also countervailing forces—almost as strong as the anti-Semites themselves and ardently and openly fighting them— among the workers' parties, naturally, but also among the Catholic and left liberals. However widespread anti-Semitism may have been prior to 1933— whether present in 30, 40, or 50 percent of the population—it also encountered decisive rejection. And this, not least of all, was what gave the German Jews some hope that anti-Semitism was the remnant of a dark past gradually dying out.

This development is something we find throughout society during the Weimar years. But there was one arena in which a radical anti-Semitism achieved an early breakthrough and remained dominant through 1933 (and naturally beyond): the universities, that is, the very place in which was trained the generation that rose to positions of leadership in state and society during the National Socialist period and above all during the war years. As early as 1921 the Deutscher Hochschulring was setting the trend as a university-based association that most of the traditional student fraternities had joined and where, after a very short time, the most radical—meaning racially anti-Semitic—line had triumphed. In these years the Hochschulring won, on average, about two-thirds of the seats in student parliaments at German universities, where the Jewish Question was no marginal theme but at the very center of debate. The aim of the Hochschulring—to exclude students of

Jewish origin (not just of Jewish faith) from the Association of German Students and thereby to have the universities be the first state institution to break the rule of state citizenship and place the Jews under alien status—was, to be sure, rejected by the Prussian state. But in a plebiscite in 1927, with a high rate of participation, 77 percent of Prussian students decided in favor of maintaining the membership formula excluding Jews.

The type of anti-Semitism spreading here was radical and racist; at the same time, it was decidedly elitist and strictly opposed to "gloomy rowdy anti-Semitism." The Jewish Problem would be "solved" within a short time not by means of pogroms and riots but, rather, via laws regulating foreigners and via the expulsion of all Jews from Germany using measures of state—and it would be solved as radically as it would be solved "objectively," according to the widespread slogan. Individual confrontation with Jews was to be rejected. One should let oneself be guided not by hate and fanaticism, but by "science" and patriotism. Combating Jews was not a question of personal feelings but, rather, a "necessity derived from laws of nature."

The leadership of the security police and the SS, who ran the police and the *Einsatzgruppen* in the countries occupied by Germany after the war's outbreak, who were responsible for initiating the deportations and for the ghettoization that began in the autumn of 1941, and who were entrusted with the implementation of the Final Solution, was preponderantly composed of members of this very generation of university graduates—mostly lawyers combining cool professionalism and the conviction that what they were doing in accordance with the principle of the "*völkisch* worldview" was indispensable, necessary, and indeed, even ethically required to safeguard the interests of the German people. Here is where the connection between ideological "charge" and participation in genocide is more directly tangible; that is, precisely not among those who traditionally appeared as "anti-Semitic agitators," as fanatical Jew haters of the kind found in the *Schutzabteilung* (SA), in sections of the party, or in whatever environs anti-Semitic agitators were to be found but, rather, among the members of the new generation of elites who got the opportunity after 1933 to put their political utopias into practice in a manner previously not imaginable.

In recent years new investigations have appeared that make it clear, on the one hand, that support for the policies of the National Socialist regime among the German population was certainly quite a bit greater than had for some time been thought possible—although this popularity was related to approval for the National Socialist regime's war policy, an approval that climaxed with the victory over France, or also to approval for the measures suppressing marginalized groups like the Gypsies, homosexuals, or foreign forced laborers. On the other hand, new studies dealing above all with the implementation of mass murder against the Jews in certain regions show that the number of those who participated directly or indirectly in the National Socialist killing policy was far, far greater than the circle of those who wielded guns or sealed the gas chambers. Unlike in the Reich, the mass murder of the Jews in the occupied territories of the east was certainly no secret; too many civil servants in the administrations of the German occupation, representatives of the party and public authority, members of police and *Wehrmacht* units, personnel from economic staffs, industrial enterprises, railroad branch offices, and labor departments were involved or directly participating in the process of deportation, sorting, ghettoization, forced labor, or murder. From here the knowledge, or at least the suspicion, of mass murder spread; only a few days after the massacre of 10,000 Jews in Babi Yar near Kiev, they were talking about it at German officers' casinos in Paris.

So far we know only a little about the motives of those directly involved in committing murder. Here, as Ingrid Gilcher-Holtey has correctly pointed out, is where the focus of Goldhagen's investigative approach lies. And when Goldhagen points out that the killing of the Jews was not so much implemented against the resistance of the Germans but, rather, was accepted by those who came into contact with the killing, then one can only agree, especially in light of new empirical studies—and, indeed, this becomes truer the further eastward one looks. But existing studies as well as a large number of available sources seem to me, in contrast to Goldhagen, to reveal something much more like a multitude of motives. Opportunism played a role here, as did a widespread lack of positive, value-laden norms, fatalism and obedience to authority, sadism, and complete numbness. However, it also cannot be overlooked that most of the protagonists, if not all of them, were anti-Semites, even if apparently very different views could be concealed behind this concept.

But above all, the policy of genocide was certainly also understood as a climactic expression (legitimated by the state of emergency) of the very policy of war and conquest that was (for a long time, at least) supported by the majority of the German population. For the rationales behind mass murder were linked to the resolution of various dangers or threats that could be warded off by "liquidating" the Jews: the "cleansing of the hinterland" on the eastern front or the "roundup of partisan nests," the elimination of the black market or of diseases, the punishment of sabotage and of assassinations of German soldiers, or just the extermination of Bolshevism. Anti-Semitism found specific expression in the ways that persecution, suppression, and murder of Jews was justified on various utilitarian grounds and in the way the protagonists regarded as convincing the context that identified the Jews as carriers of Bolshevism, as disseminators of diseases, as spies, as partisans. In this way the genocide was linked to political, military, and policing goals and to population, health, and nutrition policies that commanded support (on patriotic grounds alone) even among those who believed their own outlook was remote from that of the National Socialists. However, to resist this would have required not indifference and withdrawal but, rather, explicit, value-laden rejection. But only a few were capable of this, especially when it came to Jews.

If one takes all the observations sketched here into consideration, a field encompassing very different forms of anti-Semitism becomes visible, forms that also get at different functions inside what occurred. For a major portion of the German population, above all for those who stood on the political right before 1933, one may indeed proceed on the assumption of a manifest anti-Semitism, without assuming, however, that this alone (or even primarily) shaped political orientation. This is something different from an age-old conviction aimed at the "elimination" of the Jews. But when this group's Jewish neighbors were hauled out of their homes and deported "to the east," it no longer possessed any kind of political or moral substance that would have kept it from putting up with, accepting, or supporting such measures; and this applied even more to those who were active in the service of the German occupation administrations after 1939 or 1941 and witnessed what was going on in occupied territories.

The radical type of anti-Semitism pushing for action was more discernable in relatively small groups, with two very different variants. On the one hand were the active, truly fanatical anti-Semites who pushed for immediate action and whose perspective was basically that of the pogrom. On the other hand was the group of young, academic radicals in the leadership of the National Socialist regime's terror and administrative apparatus, for whom mass murder signified an extreme—but under the circumstances approvable— variant of the deportation and expulsion policy and for whom racist anti-Semitism counted both as a motivating and radicalizing element as well as a legitimating factor.

One should not deceive oneself. The genocide against the Jews was certainly not committed by "the Germans" feeding on a centuries-old "eliminationist anti-Semitism" rooted in German culture. But a significant portion of the German population was indeed, along a graduated scale, keenly disposed against the Jews, and this attitude was undoubtedly of significance for the initiation and implementation of the genocide—for eliminating resistance, as a permissive factor loosening inhibitions, but also (and not least) as an independent motive with its own powerful thrust. The number of Germans who participated in the murdering probably does not go into the millions, but one has to proceed from the assumption of many tens of thousands. And the men in the leadership of the Reich Security Office, the SS, and the *Einsatzgruppen,* who more than anyone should be viewed as the core genocidal group, came not from the ranks of outsiders and marginal groups but from the center and from the leading strata of German society.

These contexts, however, will preoccupy us, the Germans, for a long time to come, quite apart from the debates and disturbances of the day. By contrast, the indignant, outraged rejection of a formula about the Germans' "collective guilt"—supposedly relaunched into the world (as it was after 1945)—proves to be just an escape into an accusation never made, a discourse of avoidance.

An abbreviated version originally published in *Die Zeit* on June 14, 1996

FOURTEEN

FAMILIAR TONES

Volker Ullrich

T he leaders of the historians' guild were furious. "The entire work strikes us as basically having missed the mark," thundered Golo Mann. It offers "essentially nothing new," chided Michael Freund, merely "the warmed-up Allied lie of war guilt in its crassest form," so that it is "stuck back in 1919." With "deep sorrow" and "concern for the generation to come," Gerhard Ritter dismissed the work out of hand, for it would darken "beyond all measure" the image of German history.

The criticism was applied in 1961 to a book by the Hamburg historian Fritz Fischer, *Griff nach der Weltmacht* (Germany's aims in World War I), probably the most important work of German historical scholarship since 1945 and a work that led to a fundamental revision of our views on the outbreak of war in 1914 and of German policy in World War I.

Conspicuously similar tones are being sounded in the debate about the book by Harvard assistant professor Daniel Jonah Goldhagen, *Hitler's Willing Executioners*. In light of the unanimity with which this book is being damned, however, it is helpful to remember just how much the eminent authorities themselves were in error in the early 1960s. Only ten years after the appearance of the Fischer book, a reviewer could assert with only a bit of exaggeration that Fischer's theses on the outbreak of the war in 1914 had "more or less become the public property of West German historical scholarship."

Presumably this will hardly ever be said about Goldhagen's book: His main thesis about the Germans' "eliminationist anti-Semitism" leaves him too wide open to attack. Still, this provocative study will transform our perspective on the Nazi era. For no prior historian has raised so sharply as Goldhagen the questions of participation by "ordinary Germans" in the Holocaust and of what drove them to their murderous deeds.

Just as Fischer broke with a stubborn taboo—the legend of Germany's innocence at the outbreak of World War I—so Goldhagen, too, touches on what is still a powerful taboo: the notion that the vast majority of Germans knew nothing about the murder of the Jews and did not desire it. If the findings of his empirical case studies should prove even halfway true, then a suspicion impossible to dismiss suggests itself. The Holocaust was not a crime bred in the sick minds of Hitler and Himmler and put into operation behind the backs of the populace; it arose from the center of German society and was everything from silently approved to energetically promoted by a large segment of the population. Herein lies the book's provocation, and the debate should be conducted on this point.

In contrast to the Fischer controversy, this time it is not the conservative guild leaders who feel particularly challenged but the social-liberal representatives of the discipline, like Eberhard Jäckel and Hans Mommsen. This is not surprising, for Goldhagen reminds these scholars, who have made enormous contributions to research on National Socialism, of omissions. In their highly learned disputes about "intentionalism" and "functionalism" (that is, about whether Hitler or societal structures were ultimately decisive), they have barely posed questions about the mentality and motivation of the "ordinary men" who practiced their murderous handiwork "on site."

For now we should simply await the German edition. Then the public will be able to form its own ideas about the quality of the research and the arguments of the critics.

Originally published in *Die Zeit* on June 14, 1996

FIFTEEN

DISCOMPOSURE IN HISTORY'S
FINAL RESTING PLACE

Andrei S. Markovits

STALE, REDUNDANT, AND—SUPERFLUOUS?

One of the most important and most widespread accusations against Gold-hagen is that the author is serving up material that has been familiar for a long time. This is true—for the victims. For them the torture and brutality of the German executioners is truly nothing new. They have to deal with the memories on a daily basis. This was exactly the feeling of those attending a meeting of Jewish survivors of the Holocaust this April [1996] in New Jersey: Goldhagen is only saying what all of us experienced firsthand.

However, I am not sure that Goldhagen's theses are just as familiar to the Germans. Their inexorably negative reactions lead one to suspect the opposite. Goldhagen has presented the German public with something new in direct and unadorned language. That the Germans do not want to read this and are incensed about being confronted yet one more time with their un-varnished past—that is another matter.

When there is something that one does not want to hear, one can always block it out by disputing its value and originality. This has happened at different levels in the German reviews of Goldhagen's book. For instance, in a piece contributed to both the *Süddeutsche Zeitung* (April 13–14, 1996) and the *Hamburger Abendblatt* (April 15) [Chapter 2 in this volume], the historian Norbert Frei said that Goldhagen's book is mostly based on secondary literature, a barely excusable sin in the historical scholars' guild.

The problem with Frei's objection, which has spread from Rudolf Augstein (*Der Spiegel,* April 15 [Chapter 4 in this volume]) via Peter Glotz (*Die Woche,* April 19) to Matthias Arning and Rolf Paasch (*Frankfurter Rundschau,* April 12), is that by being so consciously selective it amounts to calumny. One of the many strong points of the book lies precisely in the "breathtaking research [Goldhagen] lays out," as Josef Joffe writes in the *Süddeutsche Zeitung* (April 13), and in the "massive new material" that the author "brings to light." For Goldhagen's critics, however, even research in primary sources is not original enough. Frei downplays Goldhagen's efforts by referring to the "especially favorable source material" collected from 1962 to 1972 by "a dedicated prosecuting attorney's office in Hamburg" for a preliminary investigation of Reserve Police Battalion 101.

So? Is research with primary sources legitimate and original for Frei and other full-blooded historians only when it strikes gold after exhaustive searching in what were completely unknown archives, and only when it then brings something brand-new to light?

This brings us to the book that all Goldhagen's critics invoke: Christopher Browning's *Ordinary Men: Reserve Battalion 101 and the Final Solution in Poland.* Browning's study, like parts of Goldhagen's publication, rests on the documents of the aforementioned battalion named by Frei.

So? Can't such an important document about such an important event withstand two books? Is only the first publication allowed to be called "original"? Biographies of Mozart, Beethoven, Lincoln, and even Hitler are turned out as if by assembly line. Should we regard the entire body of Shakespearean research from the last few decades as wholly irrelevant and unoriginal, with the exception of the work of the Vassar College professor who was able, by means of computer analysis, to confirm Shakespeare's authorship of a previously unattributed poem? With respect to all this research, are we dealing with worthless stuff simply because we already know about every aspect of these men's lives?

By no means do I want to diminish the pioneering achievements of Christopher Browning. He is used by Goldhagen's critics to discount Goldhagen's equally enormous achievements, especially because it cannot escape the careful reader's notice that the two authors arrive at different interpretations of the same documents—something entirely legitimate when scholarship is at its best.

That Browning's version speaks more to most German readers is something I can understand quite well. This takes nothing away from the originality of Goldhagen's study. To me, as a political scientist outside the guild, it is indeed very surprising that this wealth of sources has until now been so sparingly researched, and only then by two Americans and not by a long line of German scholars.

Among the critiques of Goldhagen one also finds the plainly absurd. A few critics—in the lead here are Frei and, particularly caustic, Mariam Niroumand (*die tageszeitung,* April 13–14)—rank the infamous *Historikerstreit* of the 1980s at a higher scholarly level than Goldhagen's study. This is simply laughable given what the *Historikerstreit* consisted of: the publication in the *Frankfurter Allgemeine Zeitung* of an undelivered speech by Ernst Nolte, Jürgen Habermas's courageous response in *Die Zeit,* an essayistic volume bereft of any scholarly apparatus by Andreas Hillgruber (*Zweierlei Untergang*), and a series of what were certainly exciting—but hardly academic (because highly political and polemical)—publications in the daily press. By no means should the political significance of this debate be minimized, but its scholarly value approached zero.

No, Goldhagen's book *is* new, in its interpretation and the wealth of its material, in the directness of its language. Above all, it closes the shameful knowledge gap in German historiography whereby a great deal is known about the "desk perpetrators" of the Third Reich but frighteningly little is known about the executors of the Holocaust. As a major exception to this silence, one need only mention Herbert Jäger's *Verbrechen unter totalitärer Herrschaft* (crimes under totalitarian rule), which Goldhagen often cites.

One can and should subject Goldhagen's book to substantive criticism. But to disqualify it as unoriginal and stale, to offhandedly dismiss it as more akin to "chatter" than to "enlightenment," as Frank Schirrmacher does in the *Frankfurter Allgemeine Zeitung* (April 15) [Chapter 3 in this volume], testifies to intellectual indolence and moral dishonesty. This I had not expected from at least some of Goldhagen's German critics.

GENEALOGICAL EXCURSIONS, ANTI-SEMITIC TONES

In Peter Glotz's contribution to *Die Woche* we read the following: "The author, Daniel Jonah Goldhagen, son of a Jewish historian from Rumania . . ." In the *taz* (*tageszeitung*) the leader to Niroumand's review says: "The father of the author, Erich Goldhagen, survived the Jewish ghetto in the Rumanian city of Czernowitz and lost most of his family in the Holocaust." Likewise, Jörg von Uthmann in the Berlin paper *Tagesspiegel* (April 16) mentions the personal connection of Daniel Goldhagen's father to the Holocaust. And in other publications, too, we encounter Goldhagen's genealogy.

What is going on here? Since when are the family relations of the author presented to the public in book reviews? The subtext is clear: Goldhagen, the son of a father stamped by the Holocaust, naturally cannot write an objective book about the extermination of the Jews. At best the result may be understood as the son's revenge against the tormentors of his father. (Glotz and *taz*—leftists have suddenly turned into such great positivists? Strange. But especially on this topic, the most curious metamorphoses can happen.)

It gets even worse. Two journalists from the *Frankfurter Rundschau*, Matthias Arning and Rolf Paasch, reach the following conclusion in their excoriation of Goldhagen: "Thus far in the U.S. debate, just what and how much is really new has hardly been asked, since those doing the discussing here among themselves are mostly Jewish nonhistorians (substitute: journalists and columnists)." I will spare myself the task of giving a detailed reply to this infamous sentence; my University of California colleague W. Daniel Wilson has already done so (*Frankfurter Rundschau*, April 20). I should not want to be remiss, though, in making at least this passing remark: Among the German voices who are so zealously putting down Goldhagen's work may also be found those of many "nonhistorians (substitute: journalists and columnists)," including Jost Nolte from *Die Welt*, Rudolf Augstein from *Der Spiegel*, and Mariam Niroumand from *taz*, just to mention a few. Are columnists not authorized to take on historical subjects? This is a crude expression of an elitist mentality—and in the *Frankfurter Rundschau*, no less.

Naturally, things are different at *Der Spiegel*. Lately the columns of Rudolf Augstein have been promoted to a veritable showcase for his by-now-familiar anti-Jewish attitude. His article "Good Advice: Not to Be Had," which all but teems with anti-Semitic remarks and allusions, was the occasion for a reply in the *Süddeutsche Zeitung* (March 20) under the title "From the Poison Cabinet of Rudolf A." And just where is the rest of the German press? Is Herr Augstein sacrosanct, or does anti-Semitic language (with all its clichés like "some of my best friends are Jewish"—in this case it is Augstein's "former friend" Henry Kissinger) no longer even register?

What ensued was an attack by Augstein on Goldhagen, again dotted with anti-Semitic invective and allusions. Thus, naturally, we are once more confronted with the ubiquitous "Jewish columnists" of the United States, who obviously praise Goldhagen's book. Everyone knows Jews stick together through thick and thin. Then the U.S. doyen of Holocaust research—Raul Hilberg, who comes from Vienna and has carried out his life's work at the University of Vermont—is made into an "Israeli historian in this field." Israeli, Jew, what's the big deal? Hey, it's all the same. That Augstein should bestow on Goldhagen the appellation "handicapped historian" and even "sociologist," although he has never even studied sociology, counts as one of the least weighty defamations. What is meant is obvious: The sociologist (substitute: American Jew) is presumptuously and arrogantly playing the hangman toward the German people in a métier alien to his character; yet another act of Jewish aggression against the German people; yet another Jewish betrayal of the Germans.

Jost Nolte avails himself of flowery language in *Die Welt* (April 16 [Chapter 5 in this volume]). There we read: "Thereby is given unto the author not so much an understandable rage of *Old Testament* breath as . . . success" (emphasis added—A. M.). And the sensation stirred by Goldhagen's book "guarantees controversy for him and for his technique of simplification and generalization." Old Testament rage? Can one believe one's eyes?

GOLDHAGEN AND THE U.S. PUBLIC

One of Germany's (indeed, the world's) great historians, Hans-Ulrich Wehler, sees in the discussion about Goldhagen's book "in the United States a political matter, too, in which the situation of the Jews there is also at stake" (cited in a German Press Agency survey of April 20). What situation of the Jews is actually at stake? What "political matter" is involved? Does Wehler, like Frau Niroumand, believe that Goldhagen's success in the United States "appears as a useful protective shield [*sic*] against black activist Louis Farrakhan's anti-Semitic rhetoric of insinuation or also as a factor promoting identity formation at a time of dwindling religious ties"? Wehler wisely avoids spouting such nonsense as a reason for Goldhagen's success in the United States, but he does not shy away from charging Goldhagen with the use of "the darkest clichés."

Wehler underpins his accusations more precisely in a philippic in *Die Zeit* (May 24 [Chapter 11 in this volume]) in which he "structurally" attributes to Goldhagen's epistemology the same "modes of thinking that were characteristic of National Socialism." Thank God that we are only dealing with "modes of thinking" in Goldhagen's case, since if he had tanks then the German people would surely be reduced to a third of its current constituency. Wehler's objection gets even sadder in that he not only ascribes Goldhagen's theses to a mixture of his academic incompetence, undefined thirst for vengeance, a more or less unadorned racism, and youthful arrogance but also to the failure of the purported guardians of academic excellence— namely, Goldhagen's dissertation committee, made up of Stanley Hoffmann, Sidney Verba, and Peter Hall. Not only does Wehler reproach these men for professional incompetence and intellectual negligence in the supervision of Goldhagen's work, but he also accuses them of being responsible somehow by proxy for "another failure of academe's system of checks and balances" in the United States: David Abraham, Liah Greenfeld, "and now . . . a new low" in the case of Daniel Goldhagen! And again it is the Jews!

In addition to passages colored by anti-Semitism, one finds among the critiques of Goldhagen a proper dose of contempt for "the intellectual condition of a society [the United States is meant—A. M.] that regards such theses [Goldhagen's—A. M.] as intellectual progress" (Frank Schirrmacher, *Frankfurter Allgemeine Zeitung,* April 15 [Chapter 3 in this volume]). That anti-Americanism in Germany has traditionally closely accompanied anti-Semitism as a spiritual traveling companion is hardly surprising. Still, it is amazing what a condescending tone German critics of the book have bestowed upon its reception in the United States.

Hardly ever is it mentioned—or if it is, then only with disdain—that Goldhagen's doctoral thesis, the basis for his book, was awarded the highly coveted and prestigious Gabriel A. Almond Award of the American Political Science Association in 1994 for the best dissertation in the broad field of comparative politics.

I have never had the honor of belonging to the jury for the Almond Award. Therefore I cannot give watertight testimony from firsthand experience to the selection criteria used in awarding this prize. But I have been the member of a jury for another association prize not quite as prestigious as the Almond. Based on the conscientious and detailed work of this other body, I can say with reasonable certainty that the evaluation by the Almond Award committee is very rigorous: multiple readings of the nominated dissertations, preparation of a list of the ten or twelve best theses in a collective procedure, solicitation of reviews by outside experts in a blind review process, a second evaluation of the thesis by committees usually made up of three to five members after receipt of the outside evaluations. And only then is the award granted. The professionalism and the seriousness of the procedure are beyond doubt. And there can be no talk of superficiality in the U.S. reception of the Goldhagen book.

Of course, it is asserted that the study has gotten positive reviews exclusively from Jewish publicists and journalists. This is—in every single respect—demonstrably false. For example, the volume was severely but—since substantively—fairly criticized by Jewish historians and intellectuals like Omer Bartov (an Israeli, Herr Augstein!) in *The New Republic* (April 29), a magazine dominated, as is well known, by Jewish intellectuals.

Hardly anyone subjected Goldhagen to a more rabid scolding than the American Jew Jacob Heilbrunn, a figure previously conspicuous in the Federal Republic for his especially sharp anti-German position. His tirades against Goldhagen were immediately honored in the German press with two publications (*Der Tagesspiegel,* March 31, and *Die Woche,* April 19).

On the other hand, renowned non-Jewish historians and Germany experts like Volker Berghahn, Dietrich Orlow, and Gordon Craig have by and large given the Goldhagen book very favorable mentions, although these reviewers—as did others—articulated substantive criticism. Thus Volker Berghahn in the *New York Times Book Review* calls the book a "tour de force" and compares it in significance with Hannah Arendt's *Eichmann in Jerusalem.*

Dietrich Orlow, to be sure, criticizes the book in the *Boston Globe* (March 24), but he still comes to the following conclusion: Goldhagen's study "is the most detailed analysis of the activities of [the *Ordnungspolizei*] we are likely to have for some time, and the author's narrative of these units' activities will indeed force us to rethink the distinction between Nazis and 'ordinary Germans.'"

And, finally, Gordon Craig ends his, on balance, positive review in the *New York Review of Books* (April 18) with this thought: Goldhagen's "reflections on the camp system as a central element of the Nazi revolution are incisive, and his extensive research on the various genocidal agencies should be a model for future scholars working on the Holocaust." (Strangely, Craig's observations for the German public [*Die Zeit,* May 10] came out in a much more mixed tone.) Augstein denies Craig any right to decide on the book: "Craig is a profound authority on Germany and a highly regarded historian. However, one cannot call him an expert on the Holocaust." But Augstein, of course. . . .

It says something about the level of the German discussion that the religious-ethnic origin of the reviewers must be mentioned in order to clarify the slanders and insinuations that have so far befallen Goldhagen's study. (As long as we are already on this unpleasant but defining theme of the debate: It has occurred to me that, until now, the book has mostly gotten favorable mention in Germany only from authors of Jewish descent like Josef Joffe, Julius H. Schoeps [*Die Zeit,* April 26, Chapter 8 in this volume], Gertrud Koch [*Frankfurter Rundschau,* April 30/May 1], and Micha Brumlik [*Frankfurter Rundschau,* May 10].)

One would think that the ascriptive characteristics of the participants in scholarly discussions would hardly qualify as relevant parts of a substantive debate. This does not appear to be the case with the German reception of the Goldhagen volume. Thus, for example, many critics mention Goldhagen's youth—he is, after all, thirty-six—and choose disparaging terms like "junior professor" as a professional designation.

Questioned about this (to my way of thinking) dubious phenomenon, one editor of an esteemed German daily paper said that, in the postmodern era, it should be permitted "to call things by their name and not let oneself be made to feel insecure because of some traditional taboos." As early as the mid-1980s, Hilmar Hoffmann, at that time director of the Theater am Turm and today director of the Goethe Institute, characterized approaches like this as the "end of the closed season." Germany 1996: *Intellectual postmodernism meets old-fashioned anti-Semitism.* A feast for the eyes!

If Goldhagen's book offers nothing new, delivers only polemics and empty chatter, and maliciously defames the Germans, wherein lie the reasons for a scholarly work enjoying such phenomenally successful sales in the United States, Great Britain, and Ireland, where it has been on the best-seller list for weeks? In the case of the United States, not a few German critics will surely point to the purported Judaization of the public in this gigantic country and the supposed strength of the Jewish lobby in the culture industry. But what about Great Britain and Ireland? In both cases, U.S. cultural (or just general) imperialism could be trotted out. Or the global Jewish conspiracy, which is anyway related to U.S. imperialism, at least in this particular intellectual milieu in Germany.

SIMPLIFICATION OF THE GERMAN NATIONAL CHARACTER?

Every negative criticism of the Goldhagen book also contains the assertion that Goldhagen simplifies the Germans' character. No doubt about it: Goldhagen puts the ideology and values of a historically anchored exclusionary and annihilationist anti-Semitism—he speaks of "eliminationist anti-Semitism"—in the center of his explanation not only of the regime that conceived and carried out the Holocaust but, above all, of the executions in the field.

According to Goldhagen, this frightful form of anti-Semitism, of Jew-hating without bounds, is deeply rooted in German history. I think that Goldhagen, instead of singling out the culture of German annihilationist anti-Semitism, should have spoken of this as something European or even Christian. This widening of the horizon—which I would prefer—hardly negates Goldhagen's analysis of the German situation. The fact that there was this kind of anti-Semitism in Poland, too, in the Ukraine, Hungary, the Baltic states, almost everywhere in Europe, diminishes German guilt not a whit. The *Zeit* piece by Julius H. Schoeps (April 26 [Chapter 8 in this volume]) reveals how deeply and deadly the anti-Semitic germ was anchored in German political culture and why the path "from character assassination to mass murder" did not have to be an especially winding one.

Goldhagen makes it clear that this especially virulent form of anti-Semitism embodied a necessary but not a sufficient condition for the Holocaust. Without the structural boundary conditions of a highly modern industrial state and the violent potential of the German *Wehrmacht,* the culture of annihilationist anti-Semitism could never have led to those mass murders that Goldhagen holds up graphically and brutally before the reader's eye in a clear language bereft of any academic euphemism. It was the synthesis of these factors—anti-Semitism and German power—that facilitated the Holocaust.

Goldhagen's argumentation about eliminationist anti-Semitism and its development in Germany is classically cultural-institutional. By no means is it racial-characterological or biological-genetic, as his German critics almost without exception, including Erich Böhme in the broadcast "Talk im Turm" (April 28), charge him with. Only a downright mean-spirited reading could come to this conclusion.

Goldhagen explicitly declares that structures and institutions arose in the postwar Federal Republic and in today's Germany that would never permit a culture of eliminationist anti-Semitism to emerge and that force its latter-day relics offside in politics. But Goldhagen's hard-working critics will not even allow him credit for this. The clearest protest comes from Peter Glotz, who accuses Goldhagen of having composed a crude, deterministic book about the German psyche and national character as an explanation for the Holocaust. But he also attacks Goldhagen for letting postwar Germans off the hook: "Completely absurd that Goldhagen generally absolves the Germans of today. 'They have reeducated themselves.' If it were only as simple as that! . . . It is certainly true that for decades no country has lived out its hate so perfectly as the Germans at the time of National Socialism. But the womb out of which that crept is still fertile—in Yugoslavia, Rwanda, Afghanistan, Chechnya, among the Hamas extremists, in 15 of the world's hot spots."

Only not in today's Germany; that is precisely the point. There, acts of horror like the ones that occurred in the name of an earlier Germany—and that still happen elsewhere—are unthinkable. I am sure that Daniel Goldhagen would also concede this point. But in his obdurate zeal to render this a bad book, Glotz adopts the absurd point of view that the changes in contemporary Germany spring solely from Goldhagen's wishful thinking. Glotz finds all his examples *elsewhere*. He thereby achieves just one thing: a relativization of the Holocaust, but without refuting Goldhagen's thesis about the institutionally created and culturally perpetuated anti-Semitism of that Germany that did make the annihilation of the Jews possible.

To make a long story short: Daniel Jonah Goldhagen has written a brilliant book about the most delicate and until today most incomprehensible portion of recent German (but also European) history, which—in spite of countless fifty-year anniversary celebrations, in spite of majestic speeches by

Herr von Weizsäcker then and Herr Herzog now—is far from having been processed and which, in spite of more efforts in the same vein, cannot be laid to rest. Closures are apparently harder to achieve than most Germans would like.

Since Goldhagen's message does not suit the Germans, some of them went to work to discredit the messenger and his book as quickly and permanently as possible. A serious debate about Goldhagen's book has so far been lacking in Germany. I very much hope there will be one, maybe when the German edition of the book comes out in August from Siedler Verlag.

Monika Ziegler, editor of New York's German Jewish paper *Aufbau,* asserted in the "Talk im Turm" broadcast that the German criticisms of Goldhagen have not been based upon a proper reading of the book. She was rebuked by Frank Schirrmacher for making such an "imputation." I cannot resist registering a similar suspicion to Frau Ziegler's. Certainly the book was read, but there are readings and then there are readings.

The German edition will provide a broader public with the opportunity to give Goldhagen's work the attention due it. It remains to be hoped that the massive defamation and calculated discrediting of his study that swept through the German media in April and May has not, a priori, prevented debate. The educated German public deserves better than what it has been offered up to now.

Originally published in the
Blätter für deutsche und internationale Politik, June 1996

SIXTEEN

THE FAILURE OF THE CRITICS

Daniel Jonah Goldhagen

n a few days, on August 6, 1996, the German edition of my book *Hitler's Willing Executioners: Ordinary Germans and the Holocaust* will be published. Contrary to what many in Germany have been led to believe by those who have defamed it, it is not a polemic about German "national character" or "collective guilt." It is a scholarly investigation that offers a new interpretation of the Holocaust, and as several German commentators have suggested, it opens up areas for discussion that have too long been neglected in Germany and elsewhere. Its two related principal parts consist of a wide-ranging study of the German perpetrators of the Holocaust, namely, the men and women who knowingly contributed to the slaughter of Jews, and a reexamination of the character of anti-Semitism in Germany before and during the Nazi period.

The book shows that the German perpetrators were ordinary Germans coming from all social backgrounds who formed a representative sample of adult Germans in their age groups; that not a small number but, rather, a bare minimum of a hundred thousand Germans and probably more were perpetrators; and that these ordinary Germans were, by and large, willing, even eager executioners of the Jewish people, including of Jewish children. It also shows that the eliminationist anti-Semitism that moved these ordinary Germans was extremely widespread in German society during and even before the Nazi period. The basic eliminationist anti-Semitic model held that

Jews were different from Germans; that these putative differences resided in their biology, conceptualized as race, and were therefore immutable; and that the Jews were evil and powerful, had done great harm to Germany, and would continue to do so. The conclusion drawn by Germans who shared this view was that Jews and putative Jewish power had to be eliminated somehow if Germany was to be secure and prosper.

When Hitler came to power, he was therefore, first, easily able to mobilize many ordinary Germans in the utterly radical persecutions of the 1930s—which all Germans knew about and against which little principled dissent existed—and then to call upon them even for the extermination of the 1940s. He could do so because even though most Germans, on their own, had certainly never considered acting upon the radical implications of their views of Jews, all the Nazis' eliminationist anti-Jewish policies had as their foundation this widely shared, preexisting model of the nature of Jews. The German perpetrators of the Holocaust were motivated to kill Jews principally by their belief that the extermination was necessary and just.

Though my book treats other themes, this is its core argument, an argument that is grounded in extensive research on the perpetrators, particularly on their own testimonies as given to the authorities of the Federal Republic during postwar legal investigations and trials. It is the perpetrators who tell us of their own voluntarism in the slaughter, of their routine brutalities against the helpless Jewish victims, of their degrading and mocking of the Jews. It is they who tell us of their boasting, celebrations, and memorializations of their deeds, not the least of which are the many photographs that they took, passed around, put in their albums, and sent home to loved ones. This record of the perpetrators, their own words and photographs, much of which has never been used before, forms the empirical basis of my book and its conclusions. As the member of one police battalion, speaking after the war for himself and all his comrades, testifies: "The Jew was not acknowledged by us as a human being."

To my surprise, months before the publication of the book's German edition, a firestorm of reactions and criticism erupted over it in Germany. Although any number of reviewers have responded favorably and responsibly to the book (even when they have expressed certain disagreements), much of what many critics have written either has a tenuous relationship to the book's contents or is patently false.

Some of the outright falsehoods include these: There is nothing new in the book, as I have done little original research; I put forward a monocausal and deterministic explanation of the Holocaust, holding it to have been the inevitable outcome of German history; I am making a "racist" or ethnic argument about Germans; and I am charging Germans with collective guilt. None of these is true. Yet the widespread currency that they have gained in Germany compels me to devote this discussion to dispelling these and other false notions instead of to the serious historiographical issues from which the critics have diverted the German public.

The critics fail with their attacks upon my book in the most fundamental ways, not the least of which are these baseless charges. The critics suffer a general failure in their avoidance of the central issues. They are derelict in their specific obligations as critics. The principal individual charges that they do put forward are hollow. And the general positions that they adopt regarding Germans' roles in the persecution and extermination of the Jews are not only untenable but also implausible. I will take each of these up in turn.

Thousands of books, monographs, and articles have been written on Nazism and the Holocaust. Yet the questions of why many tens of thousands of ordinary Germans from all walks of life, Nazis and non-Nazis alike, killed, tortured, and degraded Jews with zeal and energy and why only a minuscule number availed themselves of the opportunities to withdraw from the unimaginably gruesome killing fields and slaughterhouses of European Jewry have scarcely been broached by historians. Most would agree that these are questions of great importance and that no explanation of the Holocaust can be called adequate if it does not contain intellectually satisfying answers to them. Yet those who search for such answers in the writings of my academic critics, such as Norbert Frei, Klaus Hildebrand, Eberhard Jäckel, Hans Mommsen, and Hans-Ulrich Wehler, indeed, in the writings of nearly all historians of this period, will be disappointed. These eminent scholars not only fail to answer these central questions, they do not even ask them (Christopher Browning is a notable exception). What is more, when confronted by a book that provides answers to them, they—no differently from the derogatory journalists and other commentators, such as Matthias Arning and Rolf Paasch, Rudolf Augstein, Peter Glotz, Jacob Heilbrunn, Fritjof Meyer, Gulie Néeman Arad, Mariam Niroumand, Jost Nolte, Frank Schirrmacher, Jörg von Uthmann, and others who have also never done any extensive research on the perpetrators—respond with a fury that brings to mind those who seek to squelch someone who has violated a deeply held taboo. This critical chorus made up of historians, commentators, and journalists, often repeating the same transparently false charges, treats my book as a pernicious tract that ought to be consigned to some Index Librorum Prohibitorum.

The critics frequently assail my book not with reasoned, factual arguments, not in keeping with scholarly conventions, but with ad hominem attacks, sometimes spiced with anti-Semitic and anti-American allusions. My book, it is said, is a mere political pamphlet that is "stale" and contains nothing but "dark clichés" and old anti-German hat. Its value is "close to zero"; I am "devious," supposedly driven by a putative urge to avenge the suffering of my father. One reviewer suggests that I am as intellectually aberrant and morally reprehensible as the notorious Holocaust denier David Irving. Another likens my views to those of an obscure American Jewish pamphleteer, Theodore Kaufmann, who in 1941 proposed that all Germans be sterilized. (As Hersch Fischler demonstrates in the July *Konkret,* Meyer in his calumnies against me has stooped to employing and reproducing in the pages of *Der Spiegel* false Nazi propaganda about Kaufmann.) The general polemicizing manner and tone of any number of my critics has led Hanno Loewy to use the phrase "foaming at the mouth."

My book obviously goes against the grain of the critics' outlooks and of the existing literature on the Holocaust. It does so by shifting the focus of the investigation of the Holocaust's perpetration away from impersonal institutions and abstract structures directly onto the actors—onto the human beings who committed the crimes and onto the populace from which these people came. This forces people to come to grips with the most central, trying, and perhaps troubling questions of the Holocaust.

My book acknowledges the humanity of the actors in a specific manner that others works do not. It eschews the ahistorical, universal social psychological explanations—such as the notions that people obey all authority or that they will do anything because of peer pressure—that, against so much evidence, are typically and reflexively invoked when accounting for the perpetrators' actions. Instead it recognizes that the perpetrators were not automatons or puppets but people who had beliefs and values about the wisdom of the regime's policies, beliefs and values that informed the choices that each individual and that they collectively made. Indeed, my analysis is predicated upon the recognition that each individual made choices about how to treat Jews. It therefore restores the notion—against much of the literature on the Holocaust—of individual responsibility. My book also takes seriously the real historical context in which the German perpetrators developed their beliefs and values about the world, beliefs and values that were critical for their understanding of what was right and necessary in the treatment of Jews. For these reasons, it is imperative to learn as much as possible about the German perpetrators' views of their victims and about the choices that they made, as well as about the views of Jews that were generally present in their society.

This leads to two sets of questions central to the understanding of the Holocaust, questions that are posed in *Hitler's Willing Executioners* but that have not received the concerted discussion that they deserve. The first set is about the perpetrators: What did they believe about Jews? Did they look upon them as a dangerous, evil enemy or as innocent human beings who were being treated unjustly? Did they believe that their treatment of the Jews was right and necessary? The second set of questions is about Germans during the Nazi period: How many were anti-Semites? What was the character of their anti-Semitism? What did they think of the anti-Jewish measures of the 1930s? What did they know about and think of the extermination of Jews? A striking aspect of the literature on the Holocaust is that, with some exceptions, these central questions about the mentality of the actors are not addressed directly, systematically, or thoroughly. The questions, particularly those about the mentality of the perpetrators, are often barely raised at all and if raised are answered in a perfunctory manner, without the careful presentation and weighing of evidence that other topics receive. Indeed, any work that fails to answer these questions cannot plausibly claim to explain the perpetration of the Holocaust.

Any critic who does not address these questions with systematic counter-evidence and argument is avoiding the central issues. The critics, as Ingrid Gilcher-Holtey points out in her review, do not take up the challenge to investigate the perpetrators' mentality. Almost none of the critics even proposes any answers to the relevant questions regarding the perpetrators. The very few who do simply list unilluminating clichés ("ideas of obedience," "group pressure," "dullness," "nothing but beer drinkers and card players," and so on), many of which were first postulated before significant research had been done on the perpetrators. These and other concepts (such as careerism, conformism, bureaucratic perfectionism) have been mechanically slapped onto the perpetrators like labels without their applicability being sufficiently investigated; for decades they have substituted for knowledge, have hindered in-depth empirical investigation into the perpetrators' motivations, and have kept the perpetrators at a safe, comfortable arm's length away.

The failure of the critics to engage the contents of my book and to address the central historical questions of this period is striking, illuminating, and not accidental. No critic whom I have read has carried out the basic, specific obligations of a serious critic, and almost all have neglected to perform even one of them. These obligations include telling the reader of the author's purpose; presenting his or her general approach; discussing the findings, explanations, and conclusions; and should the explanations or conclusions be found wanting, putting forward ones that better account for and accord with the facts—aspects of which I will now address.

The purpose of the core investigation of my book is to uncover and explain the perpetrators' pattern of actions, that is, the pattern of their choices. This enterprise, which is informed by the methodology of the social sciences, should be recognized as the primary explanatory task when studying the perpetrators. I am able, for the first time, to adopt this purpose because, unlike the existing accounts of the perpetrators, I accept the premise upon which it depends, namely the recognition that individuals are responsible agents who make choices. Because this is its purpose, my book begins with a reevaluation of the explanatory task, which includes the assertion that until now those who have written about the Holocaust have specified it incorrectly.

It is not just the killing that needs to be explained but also something that others have not recognized: the virtually limitless cruelty that the perpetrators inflicted upon their victims and that was a constituent feature of the Holocaust, as central to it as the killing itself. As the testimonies of survivors consistently attest and as the killers with their testimonies themselves confirm, the perpetrators brutalized Jews in the extreme. They beat them wantonly, degraded and mocked them, and forced them to perform all manner of debilitating and dangerous amusements, which they often called "sport." This brutality, which had no utilitarian purpose, was among the German perpetrators—and this needs to be emphasized again and again—well-nigh ubiquitous, inflicted by the overwhelming majority of those who held power over the Jews. To beat and degrade Jews was, among their German keepers, the norm. As one former perpetrator attests: "Schlägereien waren im Lager an der Tagesordnung [Beatings were a part of the daily schedule in the camps]."

Why were the Jews not put to death in the same manner that common criminals were executed? Why did ordinary Germans not act as modern hangmen do, who are required to administer death in a prescribed quasi-clinical manner, swiftly, without torment, and with minimum pain—indeed, in the manner in which the ordinary Germans who killed the mentally ill and others in the so-called Euthanasia Program made efforts to kill? By contrast, the ordinary German perpetrators of the Holocaust routinely sought to inflict the maximum pain on Jews. This and much other evidence from the Nazi period and from other historical instances of mass killing show that such great cruelty is not integral to the task of killing; rather, the frequency, character, and intensity of perpetrators' cruelty vary greatly with the perpetrators' conception of the victims. Even if Germans had not killed millions of Jews, the amount of sustained, inventive, wanton, and voluntary cruelty and degradation that they inflicted upon the Jews would be seen as one of the great crimes in history and would in itself demand an explanation. Yet no historian has thought it necessary to put this phenomenon at the center of his or her study.

My emphasis on the perpetrators' cruelty is fundamental in three respects: It shows that any explanation of the perpetration of the Holocaust that leaves out this constituent feature is fundamentally inadequate. It shifts, in the language of social science, the dependent variable, namely what kinds of actions and outcomes must be explained. And it drives the central task of the book, namely, to explain the actions of the perpetrators. My assertion about the centrality of the perpetrators' cruelty, my respecification of the explanatory task, is foundational; it is essential both for assessing the character and conclusions of my study and for how we conceive of the Holocaust. Yet, with one exception, my book's critics give no notice of it, and none of them ever grapples with its implications.

Not just my purpose but my approach is also laid out explicitly in *Hitler's Willing Executioners*. This includes my assumptions, my methods, my interpretive framework, the nature of the available data, and how I reason to my conclusions. Indeed, there are many explicit and implicit methodological challenges to the conventional ways of conceiving, studying, and explaining the phenomena at hand. In order to provide an explanation that accounts for the many facets of the Holocaust, I have examined and integrated three levels of analysis: the actions of individuals, the character of institutions of killing, and the overall course and character of the program of extermination. I have examined in detail different institutions of killing (police battalions, "work" camps, death marches, and, more generally, the revolutionary institution of the camp), each of which reveals different features of the Holocaust, by combining in-depth case studies with broader empirical analyses of the general features of each institution.

The critics respond as if it is insufficient that I have written a wide-ranging study of the perpetration of the Holocaust. Although the critics' own works contain no methodologically rigorous comparative study—and this is generally true of literature on the Holocaust in general—many of the critics suddenly deem extensive comparison to be necessary for my book and therefore decree it to be self-disqualifying on this ground. It is true that my book is not a work of systematic comparison with other genocides, which is no surprise because my book is about the Holocaust. Yet what the critics do not mention is that I attend both to comparative features internal to the Holocaust (the Germans' differential treatment of Jewish and non-Jewish victims, the different institutions of killing, and the actions of different perpetrator groups) and to comparisons between the Holocaust and other genocides. Not only are these issues brought up at relevant points of the analysis, but the book includes about fifteen pages devoted explicitly to aspects of the comparisons. I would agree that a variety of kinds of methodologically rigorous comparative studies should be undertaken. Yet the central comparative issues that I do raise—including the features of the Holocaust that make it singular and how my explanation does account for them in a comparative perspective—are not even acknowledged, let alone discussed, by my critics, who pretend that there are no such discussions.

My book is carefully and transparently constructed upon a complex series of methodological considerations. It is based on a multiplicity of observations from a variety of different types of sources. Yet many of my critics say or suggest that the readers should believe otherwise. They ignore that mine is a rare study of the Holocaust that incorporates into its interpretations the insights and theories of the social sciences; that in it an entire chapter is devoted to the exposition of a new framework for analyzing anti-Semitism; that in a methodological appendix I discuss the interpretive problems involved in evaluating the testimonies of German killers of Jews and set forth the prescriptions that I have devised and adopted for this and for my study in general. The critics not only fail to take up the challenges of my discussion of issues of method or theory but also write as if such issues are not discussed in my book and are not important. They disparage and dismiss my complex book as simplistic.

Those who adopt this posture may be confused in believing that a simple explanation means a simplistic study. Many horrific and complex outcomes have simple causes. The complexity of the specification of the problem and of the manner of its study, on the one hand, and the complexity of the answer or explanation, on the other, are logically unrelated. Simple explanations are not to be rejected merely because they are simple or with a wave of the hand and the statement that "we know that things were much more complex." My book is a challenge to much that "we" supposedly know, so the appeal to conventional wisdom is no retort. The call for complexity is often the refuge of those who find certain conclusions unpalatable. And if some want to deem my explanation, as opposed to the character of the study, simplistic, then they must demonstrate that a better one exists.

It is on this point—regarding a third general task of any critic, to assess my findings and my explanation of the perpetrators' actions—that the critics' failure is perhaps most glaring. They say that my explanation is wrong without providing any coherent alternative and without themselves even presenting, let alone accounting for, all the different facts and kinds of evidence on which my explanation is based and which any rival explanation would need to explain. (This also is true of their attacks on my interpretation of anti-Semitism in Germany.) Not a single critic even attempts to account for the perpetrators' cruelty and its specific features; not a single critic (even among those who acknowledge that I have demonstrated this) provides any alternative explanation of the great voluntarism and zeal of the perpetrators; not a single critic even acknowledges, let alone offers an alternative explanation, the multiplicity of actions shown to require explanation. Critics charge me with being dismissive of the work and explanations of others, a charge that is at best misleading. What the critics do not say is that far from being dismissive of them I demonstrate that the conventional explanations—the ones that the critics themselves sometimes, without any substantiation, invoke—cannot account for the actions of the perpetrators and the other central features of the Holocaust to which they pertain.

Indeed, I show how all the conventional explanations suffer from a slew of disqualifying conceptual and empirical problems, including a common flawed analytical structure that their proponents assume without ever justifying—which is that the perpetrators did not believe that the slaughter was just and necessary and therefore that it must be shown how men could be induced to kill against their will. The book's second to last chapter ("Explaining the Perpetrators' Actions: Assessing the Competing Explanations") is an over-forty-page examination of the rival explanations' capacity to account for the findings, point by point. Not a single critic even mentions this assessment. It shows that the only way to account for the perpetrators' actions, as well as for the distinctive and comparative features of the Holocaust, is by recognizing that ordinary Germans were motivated by a virulent form of anti-Semitism that led them to believe that the extermination of the Jews was necessary and just. The other explanations, it demonstrates, are conceptually untenable and, most important, are definitively belied by the facts. Some of the critics put forward some of the explanations in criticism of my conclusion. They do so without any acknowledgment of my considered treatment of these same explanations and without any arguments for why they still hold in the face of all the falsifying evidence. This practice is astonishing.

As this discussion suggests, the critics have not even addressed, let alone come to grips with, the issues at the heart of the book, which is about the perpetrators. Instead they have directed their fire overwhelmingly at my account of anti-Semitism in German society. Many act (without saying so explicitly) as if showing that I am wrong about German anti-Semitism would mean that they and the readers need not deal with my treatment and conclusions about the perpetrators. Although I stand by and will vigorously defend my account and interpretation of German anti-Semitism, it should be stated clearly that this stance of the critics is intellectually untenable. Even if some were to conclude that I am not entirely correct about the extent and character of German anti-Semitism of that time, it does not follow that this invalidates my study and my conclusions about the material at the heart of my book—about the evolution of the program of extermination, about the nature of the institutions of killing, about the perpetrators and their motives, and about the character of the Nazi revolution. The central part of the study, about the perpetration of the Holocaust, can stand on its own logically and must be confronted directly by any honest critic.

Turning now to my account of anti-Semitism: I argue that an eliminationist form of anti-Semitism had already become extremely widespread in Germany in the nineteenth century. By the time Hitler came to power, the model of Jews that was the basis of his anti-Semitism was shared by the vast majority of Germans. That is why Hitler succeeded with frightening ease in accomplishing the task that he had proclaimed in one of his earliest speeches (August 13, 1920) of converting Germans' hitherto inactive anti-Semitic sentiments into a genocidal impetus: "Our task must be to awaken, whip up, and foment the instinctual feelings toward Jewry among our people to the point where they join that movement which is prepared to draw conclusions from those feelings," and that conclusion, he intimated elsewhere in the speech, ought to be the death penalty for that "parasitic people."

My conclusions about German anti-Semitism and my conclusion that Hitler, the often astute diagnostician of the people whom he would come to lead, was right in his own assessment follow from my reconceptualization of the nature of anti-Semitism, which the critics do not bother to mention, and a new synthesis of the existing literature on German anti-Semitism. My assertions about the reach of anti-Semitism in Germany before the Nazi period is supported by the works of some of the most distinguished scholars of anti-Semitism (who are cited repeatedly in the notes, though they and the nature of German anti-Semitism before 1933, curiously, are almost never discussed in depth by others who write about the perpetration of the Holocaust). Where I depart from some of these distinguished scholars is not over the extent of anti-Semitism in Germany but over its content and nature. This is also true regarding the Nazi period itself, for which the evidence that anti-Semitism permeated German society is overwhelming. As Ian Kershaw has concluded: "To be anti-Semitic in Hitler's Germany was so commonplace as to go practically unnoticed."

The critics denounce my conclusions as if they are outlandish, as if they are not grounded in the evidence and supported by a clearly articulated theoretical model, and as if there had not been extremely widespread and virulent anti-Semitism in Germany, even though many of the most prominent scholars of German anti-Semitism have drawn similar conclusions about its extent in Germany. Pointing to the existence of institutions whose leadership was formally opposed to anti-Semitism, such as the large Social Democratic Party, is no evidence that their supporters were not anti-Semitic. Workers and others could vote for the Social Democratic Party, for example, because of its economic program even though their eliminationist anti-Semitism was not shared by the leadership of the party. Any student of voting behavior knows that individuals' attitudes on single issues cannot be inferred from their votes. As the Social Democratic Party's own report from 1936 lamented: "Anti-Semitism undoubtedly has taken hold in broad spheres of the roots of our people . . . the general anti-Semitic psychosis also has an effect on our comrades." Still, it should be said that the existing data regarding anti-Semitism in Germany are less than ideal, which means two things: that legitimate disagreements can exist about its extent and nature and that the conclusions one draws depend greatly on the methodology and interpretive framework being employed. It is precisely for the latter reason that I, unlike my critics, explicitly lay out my methodological and interpretive approaches. But whatever exact conclusions might be drawn, the data cannot possibly support any view that denies that anti-Semitism was widespread in Germany during the Nazi period, that the images put forth of Jews in the public sphere were hallucinatory in content, that much of the anti-Semitism that existed in Germany was virulent, and that many wanted to eliminate Jews, even by utterly radical means.

As this discussion shows, the portrait of my book that its critics have given the German public is greatly skewed owing to their failure to reveal and discuss its central features. Yet the critics' still more damaging technique has been to actively misportray the book's contents and character. It is to these misportrayals that I now turn.

It is hard to believe that anyone could make the charge that there is nothing new in the book. This claim is no less false than the charges made on many specific points (which space limitations constrain me from exposing), such as Jäckel's assertion that I begin the book by erroneously stating that Captain Wolfgang Hoffmann was not an SS man. I write not that he was not in the SS but that the men under his command were not. Anyone who checks the book about this (in this case the very first paragraph of the Introduction) or any of the other attacks upon my book discussed here will be struck by the discrepancy between its contents and what the critics assert are its contents. I have already suggested a number of ways in which the book is novel. These include the new interpretations that the book offers and my use of much new source material—even the critic Wehler acknowledges this, chides other critics for denying it, and wonders aloud why German historians have not themselves done similar investigations.

To add one example here, until now no one has discussed seriously the number of people involved in the genocide. Neither Browning nor Frei nor Hilberg nor Hildebrand nor Jäckel nor Mommsen nor any of the other critics have given a serious estimate of the number of Germans involved. As far as I know, none of them has even raised the issue in his own writings as an important one. (Some of them might object that they have not written on the subject, but it is they who put themselves forward here as the experts with the final word.) The critics do not bother to inform the readers that I am the first to discuss the numbers (and the problems of providing an estimate); nor do they convey to the readers the significance either of the findings or of the fact that we have had to wait until 1996 to learn one of the most elementary facts about the Holocaust. For the critics to discuss accurately just this, let alone the many other issues that they ignore or misrepresent, would be directly to belie one of their central lines of attack, namely, that it has all been said before and that there is nothing of value in my book. It will become apparent to anyone who chooses to read the book how disingenuous this claim is.

The Holocaust emanated from Germany and was therefore principally a German phenomenon. This is a historical fact. An explanation of the Holocaust must obviously ground the Holocaust as a development of German history, which, it is worth noting, other treatments of the perpetrators, like Browning's, do not do. It should be recognized, however, that the Holocaust was not—contrary to what some critics pretend that I say—the inevitable outcome of that history. Had Hitler and the Nazis never come to power, then the Holocaust would not have happened. Had there not been an economic depression in Germany, then the Nazis, in all likelihood, would have never come to power. The Holocaust, like the Nazis' own ascension to power, was historically contingent. Many developments had to occur—developments that were not inevitable—for the Holocaust to happen.

No adequate explanation for the Holocaust can be monocausal. Many factors contributed to creating the conditions necessary for the Holocaust both to be possible and to be realized. Most of these factors—such as the facts that the Nazis gained power, that they crushed internal opposition, that they conquered Europe, that they created the institutions of killing and organized the slaughter—are well known, so, as is explained in the book's Introduction, I do not dwell on them. Instead the book focuses on the motivational element of the Holocaust, and it argues that the will to kill Jews derived, both for Hitler and for those who implemented his murderous plans, principally from a single, common source, namely, a virulent anti-Semitism. How the anti-Semitism was mobilized and found expression depended on a host of other factors—material, situational, strategic, and ideological—and these are discussed in depth, especially in the analysis of the evolution of the regime's anti-Jewish policies and of the character of Jewish "work" during the Nazi period. The regime and the perpetrators produced complex and sometimes even seemingly inconsistent policies and actions toward Jews. This occurred precisely because they were acting upon their anti-Semitic animus within political, social, and economic contexts that often placed practical restraints upon their actions and because in formulating and implementing their policies they naturally took into account the other practical and ideological goals that they were simultaneously pursuing. Explaining the Holocaust and its many features requires, therefore, attention to many factors other than anti-Semitism. Yet whatever the influence of such factors was upon the formation and implementation of the Nazis' anti-Semitic program, the source of the will of the Nazi leadership and of the ordinary Germans who executed the policies to persecute and kill Jews derived not from these other factors but principally from the actors' common anti-Semitism.

The Holocaust occurred in Germany because and only because three factors came together: First, the most committed, virulent anti-Semites in human history took state power and decided to turn private, murderous fantasy into the core of state policy. Second, they did so in a society where their essential views of Jews were widely shared. Third (a factor that I will not elaborate upon here), only Germany was in the geo-military situation to carry out a genocide of this sort. Had any of the three factors not obtained, then the Holocaust would certainly not have occurred as it did. The most virulent hatreds, whether it be anti-Semitism or some other form of racism or prejudice, do not result in systematic slaughter unless a political leadership mobilizes and organizes those who hate into a program of killing. So without the Nazis, and without Hitler in particular, the Holocaust would not have occurred and anti-Semitism in Germany would have remained relatively dormant. But without a broad willingness among the ordinary Germans to tolerate, to support, and even, for many, first to contribute to the utterly radical persecution of Jews in the 1930s and then, at least for those who were called upon, to participate in the slaughter of Jews, the regime would never have been able to kill six million Jews. Both factors were necessary. Neither was, on its own, sufficient. Only in Germany did these two factors come together.

This also makes clear why the extent and substance of anti-Semitism in other countries is not relevant for explaining why Germany and Germans perpetrated the Holocaust. However anti-Semitic Poles, French, or Ukrainians were, a regime bent upon exterminating Jews did not come to power in their countries. People's anti-Semitism or other kinds of virulent prejudices alone, when not harnessed to a state policy of violent persecution and killing, do not produce genocide. For this reason, the critics are wrong when they assert that a comparative analysis of anti-Semitism is necessary for explaining why anti-Semitism had such catastrophic consequences in Germany but not elsewhere. Both conditions—an anti-Semitic populace and a regime bent on mass annihilation—were necessary, which means that neither was alone sufficient, to produce the Holocaust. Therefore the obvious absence of one of the necessary conditions in other countries (a regime bent on mass murder), means that there is no need, within the scope and for the purposes of this book, to investigate the degree to which the other condition (virulent eliminationist anti-Semitism) was present. This is so obvious that it makes one wonder how it is possible that many of the critics could make this demand. It should be said, however, that the existence of such anti-Semitism elsewhere in Europe does explain why the Germans found so many people in other countries who were willing and eager to help them kill Jews.

The critics routinely point to the complicity of non-Germans in the Holocaust, as if showing that there were anti-Semites elsewhere either would somehow prove that the widespread anti-Semitism in German society had nothing to do with moving the German perpetrators or would somehow make me wrong to focus my study on the German perpetrators. The first conclusion simply does not follow. Regarding the second, as I have already said, the perpetration of the Holocaust was principally a German phenomenon. What one can say about Germans—that is, "no Germans, no Holocaust"—cannot be said about any other national group. Do we really have to argue as to whether the Holocaust emanated from Germany?

My book never invokes or even hints at any ethnic, racial, or biological notion of Germans; in no sense does it posit anything about some eternal German "national character"; in no sense is it about any essential, unchangeable psychological dispositions of Germans or anything as nebulous as "the German nature." All of these notions are inventions of the critics—which they cannot ground in the text—and they are notions that I reject categorically. In stark and direct contrast to the critics' imputations, I repeatedly and emphatically make clear in my book that my argument focuses on the beliefs and values that existed in Germany, that were part of German political culture as it was then constituted, and that informed the Germans' response to the anti-Jewish measures of the Nazi period. To say that most Germans were anti-Semites in the 1930s is no more racist than to say that most Germans today are supporters of democracy. Both are empirically based, accurate generalizations about most, though not all, Germans. Indeed, the charge that I am tainting the Federal Republic could not be farther from the truth. As I have said in numerous interviews, political cultures change and evolve, as has German political culture during the Federal Republic. The Federal Republic has seen both an enormous decline and transformation in the character of anti-Semitism and a concomitant development of a genuine democratic ethos, each of which is explicable using the same framework I use to explain why so many Germans were anti-Semitic in the nineteenth and first half of the twentieth centuries. We can at once decry the anti-Jewish beliefs and actions of many, though not all, Germans during the Nazi period and applaud the political and cultural achievements of the Federal Republic and its citizens. Is this not obvious?

"Collective guilt" is an indefensible notion that I reject categorically and to which my book owes nothing. Only individuals who have themselves committed crimes can be held guilty for them. Against "collective guilt," my book restores the notion of individual responsibility to the actors and shows that individual guilt was far more widespread than many have supposed. Those who taint my book and my name with the delegitimizing and inflammatory concept of "collective guilt"—which everyone knows to be a red flag for many Germans—never substantiate their defamation with textual evidence. They cannot, because my book does not even raise issues of judging guilt and innocence; I do not raise them precisely because they do not belong to the scholarly enterprise of explanation. (For a further discussion of my views on the subjects of guilt, generalizing about Germans, and the changed character of the Federal Republic, people should read the preface that I have written for the book's German edition.)

On the subject of my identity and alleged motives: They are irrelevant to the evaluation of the book. Many of the same critics who fail to acknowledge, let alone discuss, the many issues of method and interpretation that I put forward in the book, who fail to address the central questions of the period, let alone provide coherent explanations where mine are deemed wanting, pointedly mention my Jewish background and that my father is a survivor, the obvious effect of which is to delegitimize me as a scholar by saying explicitly or implying that a Jew is too afflicted to write in a scholarly manner about the Holocaust. (For a withering analysis of this and some of the other pamphleteering, polemical strategies adopted by the critics, see Andrei Markovits's article in the June *Blätter für deutsche und internationale Politik* [Chapter 15 in this volume]). Two publications, *Der Spiegel* and *Der Tagesspiegel*, have presented entire articles containing laughable though defamatory psychologizing about my father and me and about my motives for writing the book, even though neither author has ever met me, spoken to me, or knows anything of substance about me. Heilbrunn, who merely expresses in the crassest and most blatant form what others insinuate about my father or about my background, writes in *Der Tagesspiegel* that I have been "brain-washed" by my father. I kid you not.

Suppose every time I wrote about the work of a German scholar, I insinu-ated, by mentioning aspects of his or her background, that he or she might not be able to adhere to scholarly principles. Suppose I pointed out, for example, that a scholar's father had served on the Eastern Front where Ger-mans were slaughtering Jews openly by the tens of thousands or had been a member of the Nazi Party or the SS; suppose I mentioned that the scholar in question had himself been exposed to the virulent anti-Semitism of the Nazi period, had been in the Hitler Youth, or himself might have yelled, "*Juda Verrecke.*" Imagine the outrage that would ensue. Yet when it comes to the Jew Goldhagen, conjuring up the specter of my identity and background is permissible and even deemed by some to be necessary. All those who insinu-ate that Jews in general or, because of my background, I in particular cannot write in a scholarly manner about the Holocaust do so without blinking an eye at the implication that, however such considerations might apply to Jews, they would also apply to Germans who themselves or whose parents had lived through the Nazi period—and perhaps in spades. Their one-eyed vision is stunning. Every decent person should respond to this disgraceful aspect of the discussion of my book by demanding that scholars and other commentators discuss scholarship, not each other's backgrounds, identities, and alleged character and motivations. In writing my book I have made everything that I have done transparent precisely so that other scholars can take issue with every aspect of my research and argumentation. It is to the book's contents and methods that commentators should confine themselves. Anyone who discusses my background, identity, or alleged character and motivations is clearly not engaged in scholarly inquiry and unwittingly be-trays that his is not a reputable scholarly voice in the discussion.

Such is the nature of the principal attacks by those, historians and non-historians alike, who have written, preemptively, before the book's appear-ance in German, in a manner that would convince German readers that they should denounce the book without reading it. With their egregious misrep-resentations, the critics cast into doubt their sobriety in constructing their seemingly more reasonable arguments. What Ulrich Herbert writes in the final sentence of his response to my book [Chapter 13 in this volume] about one of these disingenuous lines of attack could be said about all the others: "By contrast, the indignant, outraged rejection of a formula about the Ger-mans' 'collective guilt'—supposedly relaunched into the world (as it was after 1945)—proves to be just an escape into an accusation never made, a discourse of avoidance."

I will return now to the central themes of the book: the perpetrators and German anti-Semitism. The critics charge me with putting forward outrageous conclusions, yet it is their positions that appear, upon even a little reflection, dubious in the extreme. Regarding the perpetrators: My position is that those who, uncoerced, chose to mock, degrade, torture, and kill other people and to boast about, celebrate, and memorialize their deeds did so because they hated their victims, held them to be guilty, and believed that they were right to treat them in these ways. The position of all those who say that I am wrong is that people who acted in these ways did so even though they did not hate their victims, held them to be innocent, and did not believe that they were right to do so. Hans Mommsen, one of the prominent scholarly critics, wrote in a recent paper "that the machinery of murder was not fueled by sadistic hatred or racial fanaticism so much than by bureaucratic perfectionism and subalternity."[1] Compare Mommsen's utterance, which is emphatically belied by a vast body of documentary sources, to the testimony of a German policeman serving in the Cracow region, who recounts that his compatriots "were with few exceptions eager to participate in the shootings. For them it was a party." He also makes it clear that these genocidal executioners were not value neutral bureaucrats but virulent anti-Semites motivated by their genocidal beliefs: "The hatred directed toward the Jews was tremendous. It was revenge." In the face of the perpetrators' voluntarism, their torture, their zeal and energy in killing Jews, their celebrations to mark the deaths of Jews, and the testimony of the perpetrators themselves to all of these, what do empty phrases like "bureaucratic perfectionism" have to do with the reality of the Holocaust? What does it have to do with the reality of the ordinary Germans in Police Battalion 309 wantonly rounding up and then burning to death over 700 defenseless Jews in the great synagogue of Białystok? In a remark uncharacteristic for the alleged bureaucratic mindset, one of the genocidal killers exulted: "Let it burn. It is such a beautiful little fire. It is fun." What does "bureaucratic perfectionism," with its antiseptic air, have to do with the reality of the virtually boundless, unnecessary, collective suffering of the Jews at the hands of the ordinary German perpetrators who, as one survivor puts it, "always came to us with whips and dogs"?

The oddness of the critics' view of the perpetrators is set in sharp relief when seen from another perspective. When people think about any other mass slaughter or genocide, including the recent genocide in Rwanda, the slaughters in the former Yugoslavia, the Turks' genocide of the Armenians, or the Khmer Rouge's murders in Cambodia, people naturally assume that the killers believed that what they were doing was right. (Indeed, in these and other instances of large-scale mass slaughter, such as the murders in the Soviet Union or the massacre of the Indonesian Communist Party, it is recognized that the two necessary genocidal conditions that I mentioned earlier—a perpetrator group that hates the victim group and a political leadership bent upon mass killing—have been present.) The only perpetrators of genocide or mass slaughter about whom people routinely assert the opposite, namely, that the perpetrators did not believe that they were right to kill, are the German perpetrators of the Holocaust. This odd, singular stance itself cries out for an explanation, which might be demanded of all who propagate it. I am saying that, in this one sense, the German perpetrators were like the perpetrators of other mass slaughters. It is the denial of this—against so much evidence—that is curious and that should be controversial.

Why, it might be put to all the critics, has the fact that no German perpetrator was himself ever killed, sent to a concentration camp, jailed, or punished in any serious way for refusing to kill Jews not been at the center of every discussion of the Holocaust? I had already written an article on this in 1985 (many critics erroneously claim that on this point I simply follow Browning, whose book appeared in 1992), and before me Kurt Hinrichsen in 1971 and Herbert Jäger in 1967 had demonstrated this historical fact. In my book I show for the first time that the German perpetrators of many units knew that they did not have to kill because their commanders informed their men that they could exempt themselves from killing without suffering retribution. The men themselves tell us so in their postwar testimony. That the perpetrators were able to exempt themselves from the killing, which is perhaps the central fact about the perpetrators of the Holocaust, is absent from almost every single work ever written on the Holocaust. What does this say about the quality of the work regarding the perpetrators, the likely verity of their authors' explanations of the perpetration of the Holocaust, and the analyses of the critics, almost all of whom themselves have failed to confront these and other central facts?

It is significant that among the appreciative readers of my book are survivors of the Holocaust. In person and in numerous letters and telephone calls they tell me that my portrayal of the actions and motives of the Germans who lorded over them in the ghettos and camps, who killed their families, who dragooned them while they were toiling as slaves is the most accurate of all the scholarly analyses that they have read. They affirm that the ordinary Germans with whom they came into contact or observed were, with exceptions, not mere obeyers of orders or coldly uninvolved executioners, as so many historians have argued; the perpetrators were bristling with boundless hatred of Jews, subjecting them to harsh and cruel treatment, mocking them, and killing them with gusto. Indeed, this is the common theme of the vast body of books, memoirs, and testimonies of the survivors.

One of the serious omissions of much of the historiography of the perpetration of the Holocaust is its failure to draw on the accounts and testimonies of the victims. Slaves and victims of violence and repression are indispensable witnesses to the actions of their oppressors and tormentors. They can tell us whether their victimizers acted eagerly or reluctantly, with relish or with restraint, whether they abused their victims verbally or performed their tasks with detached taciturnity. No historian would dare write of the conduct of American slave masters without drawing on the available accounts of slaves. Yet many historians of the Holocaust and of Nazism—as can be seen in their writings, including those of Browning, Frei, Hildebrand, Jäckel, Mommsen and all the rest of my critics—rarely, if ever, listen to the voices of the dead Jews speaking to us through their surviving diaries or to the voices of Jewish survivors recounting the manner of their treatment at the hands of the ordinary German practitioners of the Holocaust. As my book reveals, the respective accounts of the survivors and of the perpetrators—both of which I use extensively—regarding the cruelty of the perpetrators actually often reinforce one another.

My critics' position on the topic of anti-Semitism in Germany also seems difficult to defend. I am maintaining that in Germany, a country where there was such a vast outpouring of institutionally supported and propagated public eliminationist anti-Semitism, with virtually no institutionally supported, positive public image of Jews available, many shared this view of Jews and that their beliefs informed what they were willing to tolerate and do when called upon by the Nazi regime. Even surveys of Germans conducted in face-to-face interviews by the U.S. occupation forces in 1946, when Germans must have feared that expressing anti-Semitic beliefs could conceivably have placed them in difficulty—and which therefore surely greatly underreport the extent of anti-Semitism in Germany—reveal how widespread was a ferocious, eliminationist anti-Semitism. (In one survey 61 percent of Germans were willing to express views that classified them as racists or anti-Semites. Another 19 percent received the classification of nationalists.) The critics are maintaining that—in a country where anti-Semitism was so widespread and intense and against so much evidence, which is presented in my book and in the works of many others—most Germans were immune to eliminationist anti-Semitism, the anti-Semitism did not substantially influence Germans' attitudes toward Jews and the persecutions, and the anti-Semitism had little to do with the perpetrators' actions. This would be akin to maintaining that the official, public antiblack racism of the U.S. South before the Civil War was not shared by most whites and that it had little or no influence upon whites' (even slave masters') attitudes toward and treatment of blacks. Who would believe such nonsense about the U.S. South? Whose position regarding anti-Semitism in Germany should be controversial, mine or that of the critics? Let the readers choose.

I have used this space to reintroduce to the German public a book that has been falsely introduced by others and subjected to a quantity of discussion and degree of misrepresentation prior to its German publication that may have no parallel in the history of the Federal Republic. I have therefore not engaged the more serious historiographic issues that many reviewers have raised or hinted at, such as what percentage of the perpetrators refused to kill Jews, what the distribution of motives was among the perpetrators, how widespread and what the character of anti-Semitism was in Germany at various times, how to interpret the extent and meaning of dissent and opposition to the regime's policies, what various types of comparisons reveal, and whether the different eliminationist measures (forced emigration, ghettoization, and killing) can rightly be seen to be on a continuum. These criticisms engage important issues that I hope will spur further investigation and discussion. These themes—unlike the red herrings discussed here such as my background, collective guilt, German national character, or monocausality— pertaining to the conceptualization of the issues and the problems of explanation are the sorts of issues that everyone should be discussing. I do not agree with the criticisms that have been made on these points and think that convincing answers can be given; many of them are already provided in the book. But even if the critics are right on these points, this would lead only to amendment and qualification of some aspects of my study, not to its refutation. For these reasons I will let them be for now. What is more, the very raising of these issues and the widespread discussion that my study has already provoked underscores its value.

The time to publicly engage these specific issues of historiographic evidence and interpretation, many of which require detailed argumentation, is after interested people in Germany have had a chance to read the book themselves and to consider its contents more soberly. If people believe that my brush strokes are too broad—whether about the extent and character of anti-Semitism in nineteenth-century Germany, about the attitudes of Germans toward the various eliminationist policies of the 1930s and 1940s, or about my methods of generalization—then they should not denounce and reject in its entirety a book that treats a wide array of themes but should endeavor to demonstrate that they can draw the strokes more precisely. Indeed, if my book is as colossally wrong as the critics would have people believe, then why have the critics not addressed its central issues and refuted its major conclusions with overwhelming evidence—something that their claims would suggest they should be able to do easily and conclusively? And since the critics have shown that they are unable to do that, then why do they not take up the challenge to engage the serious historiographic issues and, where my views are deemed to need revision or qualification, to provide interpretations grounded in the evidence that they consider to be superior?

With the intention of furthering responsible, thorough, and sustained discussion of the issues that my book has raised, I will soon be coming to Germany. Discussions—which should be confined to the calm, sober, and scholarly treatment of methods, weighing of evidence, and presentation of arguments—will take place before the German public in many fora, including in a number of public symposia with other scholars around the country and on television.

Readers might naturally be wondering two things: Is it possible that so many have so thoroughly misrepresented my book? And if they have then why, do I think, has it occurred? To the extent that the second question is about motivation, it is not mine. Frankly, I am in no more privileged a position to know what has moved my critics to craft attacks that are patently false than is anyone else. And I care far less about why my critics have chosen to write in this manner than about the veracity of their positions and the probity of their critiques (to which their motives, however interesting, are irrelevant), which are what is at issue. That is why I have confined myself here to showing that my critics have shirked their general responsibility as critics and have failed to be convincing with the particular positions that they have set forth. I will add here only this thought: The book's new perspectives, questions, and interpretations and its use of the methods and insights of the social sciences in a field populated overwhelmingly by historians would, if persuasive, require many to abandon fundamental positions that they have long held. It would not be surprising if it is precisely the novelty of the book, and also the frankness with which the book confronts central yet sensitive issues, that have produced so much misunderstanding and controversy.

Still, this does not answer the first question: whether my critics' misrepresentations could be so widespread and egregious; this is a question that, however powerful my retorts may be, might still be lurking in the minds of readers. The best I can do now is to echo Volker Ullrich's admonition at the end of his June 14 article, which concluded *Die Zeit*'s two-month series on my book with a powerful critique of my critics [Chapter 14 in this volume].

Before people judge, they should read the book: "Then the public will be able to form its own ideas about the quality of the research and the arguments of the critics."

Originally published in *Die Zeit* on August 2, 1996

NOTES

An altered version, entitled "Motives, Causes, and Alibis: A Reply to My Critics," appeared in *The New Republic* on December 23, 1996.

1. Hans Mommsen, "Schuld der Gleichgültigen," *Suddeutsche Zeitung,* August 8, 1996.

SEVENTEEN

WHAT WERE THE MURDERERS THINKING?

Interview with Daniel Jonah Goldhagen by Rudolf Augstein

AUGSTEIN: Professor Goldhagen, you have become famous in the Western world within a very short time on the basis of a single work. Over the last few days your book *Hitler's Willing Executioners* has now become available in a German edition, too. But already many of your German colleagues have raised a storm of protest against (among other things) your thesis that the murder of the Jews was a "national project" of the Germans.

GOLDHAGEN: I could have put it differently. The destruction of the Jews would not have been possible without the participation of a large number of persons from all strata of German society. These persons were mobilized by the government and were active in a large number of institutions. Whether we call this a "national project" or not does not alter anything substantial about this continent-wide killing enterprise or about the interpretations and conclusions of my book.

AUGSTEIN: It sounded as though you meant an undertaking of the German people planned well in advance, even before Hitler.

GOLDHAGEN: I can't agree with this interpretation. But if it sounds that way, then I would rather dispense with the formulation; it doesn't change any of what happened. Naturally, there was no poll taken in 1938 or 1939: "Do we want to do it?" But according to my investigations, one can say that the model of thinking for what later became the Holocaust, the image of the Jew as an enemy, existed among many Germans and went back a long way.

AUGSTEIN: Still, it may be hard to find almost anyone in Germany willing to come to terms with this kind of generalization. A good week ago in *Die Zeit* you published a long, egocentric article, which, to put it frankly, I regret because you presented your opponents with just the thing they hold against you.

GOLDHAGEN: I can't go along with your impression that the article was ego-centric. I was extremely surprised at the personal and professional reaction to my book and at the kind of discussion surrounding it, to which I then had to respond. None of the critics has so far convincingly clarified what is wrong with my generalizations. Every historian has to generalize. I can— and I do this in the book, too—explain my methods.

AUGSTEIN: And with this set of tools you want to explain the Holocaust it-self. Isn't the heavy grumbling perhaps in response to your attempt to under-stand what has been deemed unfathomable?

GOLDHAGEN: The Holocaust is not inexplicable. I agree with Max Weber, who said that in order to explain an action, we first have to understand what motives played a role and how the actors saw their deeds. Even if it becomes very difficult in the case of the Holocaust to uncover the motivating forces, I believe that it is possible in principle. That is why I turned to the question of what thoughts and feelings moved the murderers.

AUGSTEIN: There's no question but that an anti-Semitic potential was pre-sent as early as 1932–1933, especially among students. But many Jews, ab-surdly enough, reacted to the shameful Nuremberg Racial Laws like this: "Now we finally know where we stand; earlier and elsewhere, too, we've been in dire straits."

At that time we advised our Jewish acquaintances: "Get out of here, what's keeping you here?" "No," they said, "now we see what we're dealing with, and it's not so awful for us personally, either." By their own account, they also misevaluated the Reich pogrom night [*Kristallnacht,* of 1938— Trans.]. I believe it registered in many people's minds (perhaps even the ma-jority's) as a depressing event—not just in Hannover, where I lived at the time. It had only one single advantage: It convinced a great many Jews that they had to get away after all.

GOLDHAGEN: The Nuremberg Laws certainly weren't welcomed by the Jews or regarded in any way as desirable.

AUGSTEIN: Of course not.

GOLDHAGEN: Some might have calculated that arbitrary violence against them would decline somewhat. On the whole, however, many Jews still hoped that Hitler would not last. Certain outbreaks of violence also really did subside. But that didn't really improve things.

Nor can I share your interpretation of *Kristallnacht* in 1938. Violence against Jews, as we know, created some uneasiness among many Germans. But the question is: Why? Of course there was some sympathy for the Jews when next-door neighbors were attacked. That type of action—SS men in the streets beating up people, smashing windows, burning down synagogues—was initially bewildering. But the records show that there was almost no resistance to the National Socialist doctrine that the Jews were somehow to blame and deserved punishment.

AUGSTEIN: You write in your book that the majority of those who looked on as synagogues were burned were supposedly thinking that it served the Jews right. How can you prove that?

GOLDHAGEN: The absence of evidence is evidence itself. Where principled rejection is missing. . . .

AUGSTEIN: . . . doesn't amount to the same thing as the prevalence of principled agreement; quite apart from whether anyone could even have expressed principled disapproval under a totalitarian regime. Certainly there were organized events where the people said, "This serves the Jews right." Totally clear. Only, it was so obviously criminal and insane in every respect that the people were more disconcerted than enthusiastic.

GOLDHAGEN: Your assertions about dissenting opinions and about how much disapproval was expressed are untenable. There is a large number of explicit, recorded protests against different measures, including persecutions—but not in the case of the persecution of the Jews. For comparison's sake, take the so-called *Fremdarbeiter* [alien workers—Trans.]. In their case, there were lots of "violations of the law" by ordinary Germans who were then punished in exactly the same way as they would have been for statements friendly to Jews or hostile to the regime. With respect to the Jews there is almost nothing corresponding to this.

AUGSTEIN: As a young American who grew up in a democracy, you cannot imagine what conformist pressure—in its worst form, moral cowardice—could be like, certainly not during the Hitler dictatorship. Later we had the terror of the dictatorship *and* the terror of the war.

GOLDHAGEN: The widespread view that National Socialist Germany was ruled by naked force like Stalinist Russia is wrong. Not every dictatorship rests mainly on terror. There are popular dictatorships. In spite of its repressive, police-state character, the National Socialist dictatorship enjoyed great popularity, and Hitler was an acclaimed charismatic leader. The essential features of his policy, including the persecution of the Jews, were welcomed by most Germans, certainly in the late 1930s. That Hitler was so extolled proves that many Germans didn't feel terrorized.

AUGSTEIN: But to go back to the beginning. In his book *Why the Heavens Did Not Darken,* Professor Arno Mayer, with whom you are certainly acquainted, goes so far as to say that Hitler came to power not because of but in spite of his anti-Semitism. For a while after 1933 he didn't have complete power. He only got this once old Hindenburg was dead, who always looked out for the Jewish combat veterans and no longer for anything else. Hitler demonstrated what he was capable of in that he murdered his *Sturmabteilung* (SA) comrades. That was naturally something that the people took note of.

GOLDHAGEN: All the more remarkable, then, that this murderous character and brutality didn't lessen general approval of Hitler.

AUGSTEIN: But here's how it was: The citizenry thought—I learned this from my father—"Now the regime is on a better path, now the hooligans have been killed." Hardly anyone was interested in the Jews back then. Then along came the draft, anti-Versailles. That got a lot of people excited. In 1936, during the Olympic Games in Berlin, the French came marching into the stadium with the embarrassing Olympic salute that looked like the Hitler salute—nobody had told them that the Nazis always march this way: again, a big success for Hitler.

Today it's no longer so easy to appreciate that the majority of the populace back then was on his side, and one didn't worry about the Jews. Besides, of course, at this time Goebbels had postponed the Jewish question for as long as possible. We didn't learn anything about the disgusting crimes of the Gestapo and of Gauleiter Bürckel during the Austrian *Anschluß.* And it goes on like this. If Hitler had died then, as Joachim Fest writes, hardly anyone would have hesitated to call him one of Germany's greatest statesmen. But then he wanted to have his war, as did his generals, the military elite—though for other, irrational reasons.

GOLDHAGEN: Without a doubt. Hitler wanted to fulfill his worldwide, grandiose, murderous, racist aims. For him, the war provided an opportunity to solve the so-called Jewish problem.

AUGSTEIN: Yes, without Operation Barbarossa, no Holocaust.

GOLDHAGEN: Hitler's determination to kill existed long before Barbarossa. The attack on the Soviet Union provided him with the necessary preconditions for implementing his will. In this operation many, even if not all, of the military leaders voluntarily took part in the murder of Jews. But what happened with the German army is noteworthy: Almost overnight the old code of honor was gone, at least in the east. If you had told the German generals in 1916, "In twenty-five years you will all be voluntarily helping to massacre Jewish men, women, and children by the tens of thousands," they would have said you were insane.

AUGSTEIN: But then how did it come to this change of attitude? I think that Hitler as a person gets short shrift from you. If he had told Reinhard Heydrich "As of today no more Jews will be allowed to die," Heydrich would have implemented everything he was told. Himmler writes in May 1940—the Nazis were then at their apex—that, based on his deepest convictions, it would be un-Germanic and impossible to exterminate an entire people. How were other ordinary Germans supposed to think that something like this could be possible?

GOLDHAGEN: Because in Germany it had been acceptable for a long time to contemplate the political and then the racial elimination of the Jews. It wasn't a question of whether but of how it would happen: place them under alien law, deport them, or exterminate them. This was, in any event, a mental option familiar to most.

AUGSTEIN: Really? On November 15, 1942, the resistance groups of the Jews in the Warsaw ghetto sent a declaration to the Polish government in exile in London telling them how fatal it was that most Jews didn't believe they would be killed. This was exactly the attitude in Germany, too.

We had Jewish acquaintances in Hannover at that time. We could speak completely openly with them. They said: "It's clear to us that there is going to be a war." We said: "Yes, there'll be war." The response we heard was: "But it's completely clear that we Jews will then suffer more than you." "Yes, that's probable, that's how it is." Then they said: "But we have a slim chance of coming back. Please, take our Lovis-Corinth pictures. When we come back later on, or when one of us comes back, then give us half a share." We replied: "Unfortunately, that's something we can't do. The war will be lost, and we don't want to be found in possession of Jewish property." That was the attitude then. The people didn't believe that the Nazis would murder the Jews.

GOLDHAGEN: Of course this wasn't foreseen by most people because there had never been a genocide like this. But when it took place, the sources show, a great many Germans approved of the radical persecution of the Jews. Even among those opposed to Hitler there were many anti-Semites, and the persecution of the Jews was not a major stimulus to their resistance. So the question pertaining to the Germans is not whether there was any animosity toward Jews but, rather, what kind and degree.

AUGSTEIN: The Germans were so thoroughly demoralized by Hitler's skill that the feelings many had at the time—namely, this won't do, either—could hardly be articulated. This could only be done by an institution, not by an individual.

GOLDHAGEN: Certainly, there was a lack of leadership for the resistance.

AUGSTEIN: In my school, for example, all the teachers were nationalist, including National Socialist. They also wanted the war, but there was one thing they didn't want. I still remember this exactly. After the night of the pogrom, the Latin teacher came into class and said: "We're not going to look outside. What happens on the street is not our business. We're going to write up a class exercise, and I will explain every single vocabulary word except *et,* 'and.'" That was his manner of resistance.

GOLDHAGEN: Resistance would definitely have required leadership—from the churches, for example. But there would also have had to be a lot of people who could be mobilized. We are really more in agreement than it sounds: In 1932 there was a large anti-Semitic potential that Hitler and the Nazis could then exploit, amplify, and extend. Individuals could achieve very little, to be sure.

You—as almost everyone has until now—are assuming that there was a will, but not a way, to resistance. But in my book I show that there wasn't even a widespread will to protest. There is virtually no evidence for this, though by contrast there is plenty of evidence of support for the regime's extermination policy.

AUGSTEIN: . . . as one would expect in a dictatorship. Take just one of your examples: You declare that the Germans, most of the ordinary Germans, approved of the deportations of Jews. The deportations were even popular. You support this with a single scene on a streetcar. Then you say: "Hardly anyone could have had any illusions about the fate of the Jews. But didn't the deportees themselves have illusions about what awaited them?"

GOLDHAGEN: I'd say, "Of course": It was clear that a nasty fate awaited them. What was suspected or feared by whom isn't decisive for interpreting peoples' reactions. Take the police battalions that became death comman-dos: When they were ordered to kill Jews, they did it willingly and zealously although many knew they could refuse. Christopher Browning, in his book *Ordinary Men,* also emphasized that they could have refused to kill. As an explanation, Browning offered a kind of group pressure. I show that this doesn't suffice to understand the psychology of the perpetrators.

AUGSTEIN: What does one need, in your opinion, to understand them?

GOLDHAGEN: Most of all, what I want to do is redirect attention toward the real actors—whether they killed Jews without feeling or passionately, whether they rejected or approved of the murder of the Jews. I want to create a frame-work for analysis. And then I also indicate reasons. One of these is: Most of the people who participated in the Holocaust believed they were doing the right thing. The perpetrators acted in the first instance neither out of coer-cion nor out of obedience to authority, neither as a result of social pressure nor out of self-interest; nor did they act out of bureaucratic shortsighted-ness. What was decisive was that they shared a virulent anti-Semitism that was present in all of German society.

AUGSTEIN: . . . which you, as many of your critics have angrily written, see as having been in operation for hundreds of years in Germany. It can't be true that anti-Semitism brought Hitler to power. In the last free elections—not the ones that took place under Hitler—58 percent of the people, and with the DNVP [the Nationalists—Trans.] even over 66 percent, were still voting for parties that were not aiming at the killing of the Jews.

GOLDHAGEN: Of course, not all those who voted for the Nazis were voting for violence, much less for violence against Jews. They voted for order, for the restoration of German power, for economic strength, and so on. But I think what's more fundamental is that Hitler, the paranoid anti-Semite, was viewed by many not as a madman but as a politician to be taken seriously.

AUGSTEIN: But only by a portion of the population. . . .

GOLDHAGEN: . . . but, it became apparent, cutting right through a cross-section of society. The mental world of many Germans at that time was completely different from our own. Although there were certain exceptions, this is something one can generalize. There was no publicly supported alter-native to the received image of the Jew, not even going way back.

AUGSTEIN: There was lots of anti-Semitism, but officially the Jews had a good position. The author of the Weimar constitution, Hugo Preuß, was a

Jew. There were several cabinet ministers who were Jews. During the war there was the armaments commissar Walther Rathenau, who, later on when he was foreign minister, was murdered, certainly above all because he was a Jew. Who would have been able to prevent Rathenau from becoming the Reich's chancellor?

GOLDHAGEN: Okay, for all the anti-Semitism that also existed in the Weimar Republic and the *Kaiserreich,* its impact on Jews was much different from its later impact because no government tolerated outbreaks of violence against Jews. Verbal attacks were as far as things went. But in spite of this, that doesn't mean that the venomous concept of the Jew was not around for a long time.

AUGSTEIN: Since when?

GOLDHAGEN: Since before the nineteenth century. Most Germans were anti-Semites—not in the Nazi meaning, of course—as heirs to medieval Christian anti-Semitism.

AUGSTEIN: We know that Martin Luther was a rude fellow, an especially awful person. But what tells you that most Germans were supposed to have been anti-Semites?

GOLDHAGEN: I'm not saying that the Germans would have followed a Hitler in 1750, only that there was an antipathy against Jews, as there was throughout the rest of Europe. No one disputes that. Only with the Enlightenment and industrialization, with modernity, did anti-Semitism develop differently in individual countries. In most cases it became milder, except in eastern Europe. In the Germany of the nineteenth century it developed the racist-biological foundation.

AUGSTEIN: . . . but not solely in Germany.

GOLDHAGEN: Not solely, but Germany gradually turned more and more into the center.

AUGSTEIN: Why, then, did we have so many good relations between Germans and Jews in Germany? Germany was actually the country where it was easiest to assimilate, and that's exactly why your critics don't understand why we of all people should have been the center of anti-Semitism in the middle of the last century. A whole lot of believing and nonbelieving Jews sat in the *Reichstag.* One can't say that Germany was more anti-Semitic than other countries. The critics had to read out of your book the wicked resurrection of an anti-Semitic German national character.

GOLDHAGEN: Of course there's no such thing as an unalterable German national character.

AUGSTEIN: The ugly German after all.

GOLDHAGEN: To make it absolutely clear: Germany's political culture today is substantially different, by 180 degrees, from the prevailing German political culture around 1933.

AUGSTEIN: At least we hope so.

GOLDHAGEN: There's no doubt about it. Who wouldn't be convinced that the vast majority of Germans today are in favor of democracy and believe in democratic institutions?

AUGSTEIN: I wouldn't be so sure.

GOLDHAGEN: Now we're exchanging roles.

AUGSTEIN: Of course something has changed. Recently a debate took place in the British House of Lords. The lords said that the Germans should finally cease staring at their past and start directing their view forward. They shouldn't let themselves be impressed by Lady Thatcher, who doesn't understand any of this. I found that strikingly comical. But it is clear that an anti-Semitism of this kind cannot repeat itself. That's ruled out.

Today people ask themselves how to comprehend the horrors of war and genocide, like what happened only a short while ago in the former Yugoslavia.

GOLDHAGEN: There have already been frequent debates about comparisons like this in Germany. Of course historians have to compare—not in order to relativize the Holocaust but, rather, to understand it better. The events in the former Yugoslavia are large-scale massacres, but not genocide.

AUGSTEIN: Whereas Hitler, after he returned from the war, wanted to drive out all the Jews, to the extent he could get his hands on them, though in reality he wanted to murder them. But then I ask myself if he really believed that the Jews started the war. He couldn't have believed this. It's so insane.

GOLDHAGEN: I think so. The Jews were a metaphysical adversary, the originators of everything evil. He made them responsible for the situation in which Germany found itself. In his eyes this then compelled the start of the war. This is how he thought. And there's a second major difference from Yugoslavia. Whatever gruesome things the Serbs and Moslems have done to each other, the situation was different from the Holocaust because the Jews were an imaginary adversary. There was no real conflict. Why should poor Jews in rural Russia have any cause to go to war with Germany?

AUGSTEIN: But hardly any of the Germans thought that way. That was all Nazi propaganda, and that's something you've written, too. "International Jewry controls Bolshevism"—those were Hitler's obsessions.

GOLDHAGEN: But this imaginary evil was not something only Hitler believed in. Those who carried out his orders believed in this, too.

AUGSTEIN: If the Holocaust, committed by Germans, remains so singular, why have you recently called for revoking this uniquely German law against popular incitement [a hate speech law—Ed.]?

GOLDHAGEN: During the early years of the Federal Republic, one might have maintained that such restrictions were necessary. But is this the right policy forever? In general I believe that as much free speech as possible should be allowed.

AUGSTEIN: I was always against this law.

GOLDHAGEN: Ultimately governments are more powerful and societies stronger when all views are allowed to be represented. Conversely, one ban makes a second easier. To be sure, if the law were revoked now, a lot of ugly things would come to light. But on the whole we'd find that the vast majority of people in Germany would regret such racist views, that they would emphatically raise their voice against them, and that the few agreeing with such views would meet with contempt.

AUGSTEIN: What makes you so confident?

GOLDHAGEN: The manifest, profound changes that have taken place since the war. Let me say one more thing: Yesterday I was sitting outside in the pedestrian zone in Hamburg having a bit to eat. I looked around: young Germans, boyfriends and girlfriends. People going shopping and taking walks. I thought: What do they have to do with the past, what do they have in common with that? Nothing. If I had been sitting in Boston, I could have observed completely similar people. Young people like this shouldn't have to feel permanently tortured by the past.

AUGSTEIN: The routine commemoration days don't do much anymore for lots of people. What would normality in dealing with the past look like?

GOLDHAGEN: I'm almost in agreement with the people in the British House of Lords. They surely didn't mean that young Germans should simply forget what was—the Holocaust may not and will not be forgotten. But they shouldn't have to feel tormented any longer.

AUGSTEIN: Professor Goldhagen, we thank you for this conversation.

Originally published in *Der Spiegel* 33 (August 12, 1996)

EIGHTEEN

ON THE BROAD TRAIL OF THE
GERMAN PERPETRATORS

Kurt Pätzold

H
e has made it hard on himself, for sure, this Daniel Jonah Goldhagen. Here he is, appearing before a circle of experts, telling them that their previous research and interpretations were carried out in an "empirical vacuum" and that they have shown a "complete lack of interest" in serious questions. And he should not be surprised when people react by shaking their heads, especially when he offers them a "completely new perspective," a "radical revision" of previous views.

Nevertheless, the indignant reaction of the German members of the guild to the book by the American historian Daniel J. Goldhagen, *Hitler's Willing Executioners,* is surprising. For one thing, they all live in a society, after all, that forces them daily to distinguish between the advertisement and the products. What is the source of this lack of self-control? Injured vanity and rage over ignorance may play a role. Maybe it was also crucial that critics of this book reacted in the first instance not as specialists but as "Germans." Be that as it may . . . .

First and foremost: That the book by the American sociologist and historian is now available in German translation should be taken as an opportunity for many here at home to broaden their knowledge and reconsider their ideas about the murder of the European Jews that emanated from Germany and was committed by Germans. This demands more than careful reading. What the author has presented after extensive research, above all in the files of (West) German judicial archives, will not only ask questions of some for the first time and of others again. It can also awaken feelings that one could claim to recognize in current political arguments in Germany. The book demands that one take sides. It arrives here at the right time; one need only consider the rampant excuse already thought up by the chief defendants in Nuremberg to extricate themselves (and not just mentally) half a century ago: "The others, too."

Goldhagen has set out on the broad trail of the German perpetrators who committed the crime. He ascertains that their number—of the perpetrators, confederates, and accomplices—is significantly larger than has been assumed (although—as happens frequently—he does not distinguish between common public awareness and scholarly findings). He has filled out our picture of how the atrocity occurred by the way he has portrayed the role of guards in the camps, in the police battalions working for the *Ordnungspolizei,* in the commandos accompanying Jews on the death marches.

He is not the first to approach any of these topics. Without a doubt, however, he is correct in noting how neglected and belated scholarship on perpetrators has been. It should suffice to remind ourselves that—thanks to Wolfgang Benz and his international working group—we have for years been in possession of an energetic investigation into the number of Jewish victims of the Holocaust but that no comparable work on the murderers has even been tackled. Now as ever, the German media's everyday shorthand for this atrocity (as well as for others) has been to attribute it to the "Führer" (Hitler's orders, crimes, goals, and so on).

In brief: In those sections where he reconstructs the unprecedented criminal events, Goldhagen's book does more than other portrayals to force those contemporaries of the German fascist dictatorship who are still alive to ponder the question: What kind of people were we then? And the mass of Germans born afterward must ask: Who were they, our ancestors? In either case what might well follow is the difficult self-examination in which one asks how far anyone may actually have come from the spiritual and emotional condition of one's contemporaries or ancestors. (In several interviews, incidentally, Goldhagen has asked this question of the Germans and has attested to their having become completely different people, so that they no longer require laws against fascists.)

So far what has excited most of the protest has been Goldhagen's monocausal explanation of the actions of the participants. The Germans were "viciously eliminationist anti-Semites," and they were already that way before January 30, 1933. In fact, he does not allow for any important distinction between the spiritual makeup of Hitler and the "many" or "overwhelming majority of Germans"—although he obviously knows about the existence of "anti-Semitisms."

The "Führer" found "the Germans" already ripe for the murder of the Jews. It was, therefore, easy for him and his accomplices to mobilize this mass of the ready and willing as soon as he saw the appropriate time approaching. According to Goldhagen, it was completely a matter of chance who the specific persons were that drove the gas wagons, massacred with rifles and pistols at the ravines, operated the gas chambers in Auschwitz, watched Jews perish in the ghettos. The Germans were all prepared to be murderers.

This is hardly what one could call reconstructing history in time and space. Whatever does not fit into this picture the author has simply left aside or marginalized. For this reason, even in the initial discussions about his book in the United States, it was objected that the motives of the killers could not be reduced to a single factor. But since one cannot precisely establish each and every motivation and their mixture does not lend itself to qualification, the dispute over motives is bound to have a long life. The dispute is by no means—as it might appear—of an academic nature. Under historical circumstances of revolutionary macro- and microsocial conditions, people can change their modes of behavior very rapidly. The next time Goldhagen comes to Germany, he might encounter this, perhaps in conversation with sociologists who are dealing with changes in the behavior of people from eastern Germany over the last six years. And these are changes taking place under the completely "ordinary" pressure of capitalist relations, not inside a fascist dictatorship.

To be sure, the book's author has barely dealt with the overall history of that dictatorship. What should one think about statements that Germany was supposed to be surrounded—indeed, walled-in—by hostile powers in 1933? This is what one could read and hear from Hitler and Goebbels. Although Goldhagen postulates that the Holocaust cannot be explained by anti-Semitism, that is just what he does. He endlessly instructs the reader that the murder of the Jews was the "center of state power," the "decisive characteristic" of the regime, its "central" and "characteristic feature," and finally a "specific central feature of all of German society" in those years. He really believes that Hitler actually wanted nothing more than to create a world without Jews in order to fulfill his "private murderous fantasy." Only in passing is there any mention of the war, of the "revanchist promises" with which the rulers took power, of undesignated "other areas of policy," of "proposals" for the transformation of Europe corresponding to the "ideals" of Hitler and his accomplices.

Kurt Pätzold

The imperialist plan for military victory—fulfilled but ultimately defeated—and the racially motivated murder of Jews, Slavs, Asians, and Gypsies is something that Goldhagen is unable to put into the context where they both belong. Indeed, he regards such racial murder as nonexistent. To him, the war—this, too, of course, is not his discovery—appears only as a recognized, sought-after, and exploited opportunity to kill the Jews. Goldhagen also once again reheats the legend that the measures for killing Jews had priority, to the point of displaying his ignorance regarding military requirements. Where reference is made incidentally to military preparations and war, we find fantasies: The Jews could not be murdered before 1939, for Hitler might then have prematurely risked a war, and they could not be killed around 1939–1940 because the USSR would have broken the Non-Aggression Pact.

The messy picture of the German fascist dictatorship's essence that Goldhagen offers and the nearly complete neglect of actual social interests that achieved influence in German society in the years between 1933 and 1945, have thus far hardly come into the sights of critics here at home. Maybe this is still to come. For only from this perspective might there come an answer to the question that is directed to the "why" of the genocide against the Jews. Goldhagen has only seen one of its aspects and has directed attention to the question of why perpetrators were "found." The other question is why they were "sought"—and not only in the interest of fulfilling a "private" outlook on the world.

Originally published in *Neues Deutschland* on August 17–18, 1996

NINETEEN

THE UNIVERSE OF DEATH AND TORMENT

Götz Aly

E verything Daniel Jonah Goldhagen tells us is true—and yet it is only the tip of the iceberg. Goldhagen relates the story of the murder of the European Jews from the necessarily narrow perspective of those who did not sit behind desks but took part directly. He inquires into their individual, social, and cultural programming, into the significance of a specific, "eliminationist," and ultimately "exterminationist racial anti-Semitism." "No Germans, no Holocaust" is his succinct conclusion.

Three compact, well-researched, well-formulated sections form the empirical heart of the study, taking us into the "universe of death and torment." They provide examples of so-called ghetto clearings—that is, of the extermination of whole Jewish communities within a few hours—by units of the *Ordnungspolizei,* of despairing death in the camps set up to exterminate arrested Jews through senseless labor tortures, and of the death marches of concentration camp inmates in the last months of the war. These took place on the verge of impending German defeat, were committed in plain sight of all, and claimed at least 250,000 lives.

Goldhagen bases his information mainly on thousands of interrogation records collected by concerned prosecutors and criminal justice officials between 1962 and 1972. Their efforts excited little public attention at the time, rarely leading to trials and even less frequently to adequate judgments by criminal courts. At least, however, the investigators succeeded in documenting the well-nigh "endemic cruelty." Goldhagen is one of those—along with Hans-Heinrich Wilhelm, Ernst Klee, Dieter Pohl, and Christopher Browning—to bring these findings to light. It is true that such secondary sources are replete with omissions, shameless lies, and nonsensical rationalizations; nevertheless, overall they allow us, in a way perhaps otherwise impossible, to come close to knowing what actually happened—assuming one accepts the author's methodological maxim: "To discount all self-exculpatory testimony that finds no corroboration from other sources."

Page after page, he describes how "ordinary Germans" became murderers of Jews, spontaneously, without any special preparation or indoctrination. Normally, they were blue- or white-collar workers in the most varied fields; older heads of households formed a clear majority in police reserve units. Only a minority belonged to the Nazi Party, and very few to the SS. They represented no specially created, carefully chosen elite of racial warriors but the average member of German society at the time. The same was true of the concentration camp guards. "They were thrown together by chance by place and time," by the employment office or a heart problem that made them unfit for military service. "Nothing indicates that any attempt was made to examine the 'fitness' of these men for their future genocidal activities," is Goldhagen's well-founded conclusion. In Poland a German doctor drew the anatomy of the human neck in the sand, marked the spot they were supposed to hit, and off they went.

This study contradicts the still-common image, defined in part by Hannah Arendt, of the cold-blooded killing machine who simply carried out the instructions dictated to him, merely stamping, countersigning, or turning on the gas. But recourse to the proverbial blind Prussian obedience is no explanation. Nor is the theory that the murder of the European Jews could only be achieved through a modern division of labor because only such fragmentation was capable of overcoming the traditional limits of conscience. Goldhagen rightly insists upon the complete freedom of each individual to decide and refuse. Not a single German who refused to kill a Jew was demoted, sent to a concentration camp, assigned to a suicide mission, or sentenced to death.

On the contrary, such orders commonly included an offer that "anyone who did not feel up to the upcoming task could come forward." This occurred only in exceptional cases. Those who did so were neither taunted nor pressured; rather, they were treated with consideration. They were given different duties, often back home. There were always others willing to take over the murders—the "proven pragmatist" Himmler could soon be sure of that. Men were generally eager for the job, as shown, for example, on a November evening in 1942 in Łuków, Poland, when musicians and performers from the Berlin police department came to entertain Reserve Police Battalion 101: "They also learned of the forthcoming shooting," according to witnesses, "and offered, even pleaded emphatically for permission to participate in the execution of these Jews. This strange request was granted by the battalion." This means voluntary mass murder as a social pastime and a thrill—and without orders.

The book shows concretely how good the perpetrators felt before, during, and after their "operations"; how they humiliated, beat, and tortured defenseless people and then shot them in the back of the neck without the slightest hesitation; how the men posed before their living or dead victims, laughing into the camera, bloodthirsty, sadistic, and lascivious. After they had done their day's work, they celebrated with a "death banquet" for the Jews, went to bed with their lovers, or wrote home faithfully that these snapshots and extermination anecdotes would someday be "extremely interesting to our children."

The guards who patrolled the walls of the Warsaw ghetto decorated their recreation rooms with an illuminated Star of David and a board on which they kept track of the number of Jews they had killed. Goldhagen reminds us that German police officers, who in everyday life directed traffic and were supposed to act as "friends and helpers" (the slogan, still in use today, was crafted in Himmler's propaganda workshop), spent June 27, 1941, in Białystok. First they murdered the patients in the Jewish hospital; then they drove at least 800 Jewish men, women, and children into the city's main synagogue, locked them in, surrounded the building, set it on fire, and shot anyone who tried to jump out the windows. "Let it burn, it's great fun," commented one member of the master race who took part. This on only the sixth day of the eastern campaign, in a city taken without a fight, making the "progressive brutalization of war" obsolete as an explanatory argument.

The book publishes the names and pictures of the newly married, pregnant officers' wives who watched a massacre with obvious enjoyment; it describes German Red Cross nurses who did the same, as well as a scene from early 1945 in a city in Lower Saxony: "We asked for food. At first they thought we were German refugees. The SS man who accompanied us shouted, 'Don't give them anything to eat, they're Jews!' And so I got no food. German children began to throw stones at us." The guards who in April 1945 drove some 600 emaciated Jewish women through the Bohemian forest gave the bread meant for the starving people to the hens, before their eyes; they hated, tormented, and murdered to the very end, against Himmler's express orders, which had been delivered by courier on the second day of the march.

They admitted all these facts during later interrogations, showing as little re-morse as, more recently, SS Officer Priebke showed before a military court in Rome. His rigid self-righteousness is typical of an entire generation. They shared a basic assumption: "The Jew was not acknowledged by us to be a human being."

If this had continued, a Polish author wondered in 1973, "Who knows how many diaries and memoirs would have been published by now in Ger-many with titles like 'I was in the Political Department of Auschwitz Concen-tration Camp' or 'I Exterminated 600,000 Enemies of the Third Reich' or 'Buchenwald—Maidanek—Mauthausen: The Battle Stations of a Loyal SS Man.'" The beginnings of this could certainly be seen: In the autumn of 1941 the propaganda ministry distributed a brochure entitled "German Soldiers See the Soviet Union." It contained soldiers' letters home from the Eastern Front, cost twenty pfennigs, and was published in an edition of two million. In it, a Private Heinrich Sachs wrote of the "end of this race": "A separate chapter is the fact of how the Jewish question is currently being solved with impressive thoroughness, to the enthusiastic applause of the local popula-tion." Future Free Democratic Party member Wolfgang Diewerge had cen-sored out the "descriptions of atrocities with a sexual element." Goldhagen does not quote the authors who published such things long before he did, just as he ignores or dismisses the work of some who have made observations simi-lar to his. This may be the result of a certain monomania that is perhaps un-avoidable when dealing with this subject, but it hardly diminishes the value of the book.

It is wrong of Ulrich Raulff to claim that Goldhagen has arranged the "aesthetic of a horror film," linking pornography with atrocity and accom-plishing a "step into the horror business" (*Frankfurter Allgemeine Zeitung,* August 16, 1996). This verbal tirade was logically followed by a call for "seri-ous historiography." That is ridiculous. The book attempts to portray histori-cal events that border on the indescribable, and as Martin Broszat remarked in 1979: "For the language and reflection of historicity, accustomed to the exalted ideas of history, mass executions and gas chambers are a 'stylistic in-consistency' of history."

Goldhagen creates the necessary detachment with the help of frequently moralistic interjections and occasional sarcasm. For example, he speaks of a Jew who screamed with cold and was therefore shot: "The only kind of warmth a Jew could expect from this man was the cold grave. The cremato-rium was unavailable." To me, such slipups are understandable. In any case I am grateful for his attempt to relate something that is difficult to relate. I know many of the details from the files and from scattered serious literature, and I could add countless details, but I rarely write about them—the documents render me speechless. An example is the following story of the P. family of Metgethen, Königsberg, which I removed from a finished manuscript in 1988.

Hans P. headed a local *Sicherheitsdienst* (SD) branch in the small Yugoslavian town of Kragujevac. In March 1943 he ordered a raid on an inn in which Communist meetings were supposedly held, but he found no indications of such meetings. Perhaps in anger over the miscalculation, perhaps for other reasons, P. then shot the innkeeper and lied in his report that she had attempted to escape. A few days later, a young woman came to his office either to report a hidden weapon or to denounce her landlord (the reason is unclear). In any case, P. tortured the twenty-two-year-old, raped her over several days and nights, and finally let her go. The Belgrade SS and police court found out about this arbitrary act, which was counterproductive even from the Nazi standpoint ("unnecessary emergence of resistance"). It convicted P. of murder and rape and sentenced him to ten years' imprisonment. "Dear Mama," wrote the prisoner to his wife, "You know what I did," and he continued, "Because of that stinking Serbian wench, who would have been shot anyway in eight days, a German family is thrown into misfortune." Charlotte P. included the letter in a petition for a pardon that she sent to Himmler. He did not commute the sentence, but he made it less severe; he also made sure the family, now indigent and deeply in debt, was taken care of. But this only lessened their difficulty; the husband had not been pardoned, let alone rehabilitated. In this situation, Frau P. wrote to thank the *Reichsführer* and added a macabre request. She told him of her healthy son's progress and about her well-developed daughter. But about her youngest child, four-year-old Rüdiger, she wrote: "He suffers from the effects of a severe cerebral infection. The doctors, especially Professor Bamberger[1] at the university clinic, whom I visited at the recommendation of Gauleiter Erich Koch, are of the opinion that his illness is incurable. I hope, however, that I will be able to give my seriously ill child significant relief one day." Nine days later, Koch wrote to Himmler, "I spoke quite openly with Frau P. about the case. She would be grateful if the child could be brought to one of your 'clinics' and freed from his suffering." Himmler responded immediately and passed the information to the department in Hitler's Chancellery responsible for murdering handicapped children. Rüdiger P. became a victim of the so-called Children's Euthanasia Program.

I came upon this abyss of German family history—sketched here as briefly as possible—during my research into the "euthanasia" murders. I filed it together with a copy of a decision by the Munich SS and police court against Max Täubner, an aircraft engineer. Although the story of the P. family remained in my memory, I had completely forgotten this old judgment, with the markings on it I myself had made—I could have sworn, until the Goldhagen debate led me to look through my files, that I'd never read anything of the sort.

Although it involves completely different people and places, the content is exactly identical to a description in *Hitler's Willing Executioners*. The court had jurisdiction over Täubner because he had headed an SS workshop. The sentence was also ten years' imprisonment because, according to the court transcripts: "The defendant is a fanatic enemy of the Jews. At the beginning of his assignment in the East, he resolved to 'take care of' 20,000 Jews." With no orders, "on his own," Täubner and his people carried out two mass shootings in September and October 1941, more or less as follows: "SS Unterscharführer Müller, who did not belong to the defendant's unit but had his permission to take part in the shootings, tore children from their mothers, held them in his left hand, shot them and threw them in the ditch."

The court conceded that these cases involved "more or less systematized forms" of execution, but in the next town, there were "terrible excesses." "SS storm trooper Wüstholz (one of the defendant's subordinates) told the Jews to beat each other to death; they were promised that the survivors would not be shot. The Jews did in fact beat each other, though not to death." So Täubner took part in the beatings, had individuals shot behind a house, had one hanged, and had others buried in the ruins of a wooden house that still others were forced to pull down. While taking a short break from the murders, Täubner (married, father of three children) "played the song 'You're crazy, my child!' on the harmonica." All of this he had photographed: "These are pictures that record the worst excesses; many are shameless and disgusting. The prints were developed at two photo stores in southern Germany, and the defendant showed them to his wife and friends."

The SS and police court saw this as a serious violation of the duty of secrecy and convicted this man in 1943 for that and, in addition, for "excesses" that "violate discipline." In its decision, the court explained:

> The defendant is not convicted for the Jew operation as such. The Jews must be exterminated; none of the dead Jews is any loss. The defendant should have told himself that the extermination of the Jews is the task of commandos created especially for the job, but it should be held in his favor that he may have thought he had the authority to participate in the extermination of Jewry. True hatred of Jews was the driving force behind the defendant's actions. However, he allowed himself to get carried away into cruelties unworthy of a German man and SS

leader. It is not the German way to employ Bolshevik methods, even in the necessary extermination of the worst enemies of our people. The behavior of the defendant borders alarmingly on this. The defendant allowed his men to fall into such brutalization that they, under his leadership, behaved like a wild horde.

As I said earlier, I do not normally write about these things. Instead, I am interested in the processes of political opinion formation that led to the Final Solution: the planning centers, the organizers of resettlement. My research is fixed, like that of Hans Mommsen or Raul Hilberg, on the multifarious power structures of the Third Reich, things about which Goldhagen has only the barest knowledge. Subjectively, such an approach creates distance; it allows one, in studying the documents, to ignore or read highly selectively the things laid out in *Hitler's Willing Executioners.* This occurs—at least for me—not out of "seriousness," but out of self-protection. Certainly the cool, analytical eye of the forensic doctor, detached from emotion, contributes—sometimes decisively—to the solution of a crime, but at a trial it is also necessary to speak of the maliciousness and vileness of the offenders and of their general and specific motivations.

Goldhagen believes he has found the "explanation and theory of the Holocaust." This is out of the question; he cannot accomplish this with such a consciously one-dimensional, extremely deterministic approach. While the old literature gave us Hitler the "intentionalist," pressing for genocide from the start, Goldhagen's book gives us "the Germans" as the great intentionalists. They were just waiting for war, he maintains, because it finally "provided the opportunity" for them to carry out what they wanted anyway: the extermination of the Jews. The author does not always really seem to believe this himself—for example, when he talks about how the terrorist camp system "transformed" the personnel's "mental and moral substance," or when he somewhat absurdly writes: "The Germans wanted nothing less than for the Jews to suffer and die; and they worked to prohibit all social connections between Germans and Jews." Victor Klemperer provides a more exact description of the monstrous combination of government prescriptions and contradictory personal behavior, though even he quickly realized: "I become more and more convinced that Hitler really is the spokesman for almost all Germans."

Nevertheless, the book, if read with critical sympathy, adds to our knowledge. This is entirely true of the empirical sections, and to a certain extent it is also true of the controversial central thesis. It poses questions not only about the hundreds of thousands of immediate participants in these deeds and the millions who knew about them but also about the character of Nazism. Nazi Germany was a dictatorship, certainly, but one based on the consensus of the great majority, a consensus that was constantly renewed. Neither before nor after did such a high degree of harmony exist in Germany between the people and their leadership. And every historian in this field knows how much is glossed over, how much inaccuracy is often present, when issues of guilt and responsibility are obstinately addressed with concepts such as "Nazis" or "fascists," "the regime," or, tortuously, "the dignitaries of the Third Reich."

And one more thing: The greater the precision with which structurally oriented research exposes the political motivations behind the transition from deportation plans to the practice of extermination, the clearer it becomes that this practice was at first experimental. The initiators remained skeptical for months whether their project could really be put into practice. Hitler abruptly stopped the euthanasia murders on August 24, 1941, because popular sentiment could be "inflamed" by it "in this critical phase of war" (Goebbels); but the German leadership must, in the succeeding months, have been convinced that the barely hidden beginnings of the genocide of the Jews had no effect on the great majority of the German population or even—as I suspect—that they had an integrational effect. This fatal certainty was the result of the first (positive) experiences with the murder commandos, the soldiers' letters, and the absence of even the slightest semipublic protest. Only as a result of this unconcealed, indirectly clandestine agreement or shoulder-shrugging indifference did the certainty grow, in early 1942, that the Final Solution of the Jewish Question could be carried on and the test phase ended. This well-grounded thesis stands in contrast to Daniel Goldhagen's hermetic superintentionalism. But it brings a new and different intensity to the question of the responsibility shared by many Germans.

Translated by Belinda Cooper
Originally published in *Süddeutsche Zeitung* on August 28, 1996;
in English in *Yad Vashem Studies* 26 (1997)

NOTES

1. Philipp Bamberger was a famous professor of pediatric medicine who later practiced in Heidelberg.

TWENTY

BURDENS OF PROOF

Jeremiah M. Riemer

T his past April, after Christopher Browning had finished delivering a scathing attack on Daniel Goldhagen's new work *Hitler's Willing Executioners* before an audience at the U.S. Holocaust Museum and Memorial in Washington, D.C., Goldhagen took the podium and thanked Browning for accurately representing what he had written in his book. Had the Holocaust museum event been organized as a debate between these two scholars who have done extensive research on the "ordinary" killers of European Jewry, the audience who followed the rambling podium discussion from the auditorium or on the public affairs cable channel C-SPAN might have had the opportunity to learn something from the encounter. As it happened, the Holocaust museum's format allowed Goldhagen too little time to deal with the serious questions of evidence, method, and explanation raised by his work *and* (it must be added) by that of his chief scholarly "rival." Instead time for serious discussion was crowded out by side issues like the originality of Goldhagen's research or by such entirely bogus problems as the supposed arrogance of youth and the alleged provinciality of U.S. education. Hovering uncomfortably over the forum was an openly articulated suspicion that there must be something fundamentally wrong with scholarly findings published by a commercial press with resources to publicize an author's claims to insight. As Goldhagen's rebuttal ran up against its desperately brief time limit, the author said he hoped the audience would not take it as disingenuous of him to suggest that a fuller defense of his ideas might be gained by actually reading the book.

The Washington debate turned out to be a preview of the book's subsequent reception in the German press and much of the historical profession on both sides of the Atlantic. From late April through July, as I followed the Goldhagen debate, I got the impression that German reviewers and my American colleagues in the German studies community were reacting to a book that was very different from the one I had read.

The book I had read was a thoughtful, carefully argued, and meticulously documented investigation into the behavior—and, moving from behavior, into the motivation and mental outlook—of Germans who murdered Jews half a century ago. Its brief history of nineteenth-century anti-Semitism was sketchier than I would have liked, but it also struck me as adequate to the author's explanatory task and consistent with the findings of such authorities as Werner Jochmann and Jacob Katz. The book's vivid accounts of the killings were unrelentingly hammered into the reader's consciousness, yet they reminded me of the American sociologist Barrington Moore's admonition (in a critique of systems theory) that social history is about what people do to each other. Goldhagen's insistence on designating the perpetrators as "the Germans"—on the grounds that we also call U.S. soldiers who fought in Vietnam "the Americans"—sounded like a logical usage of language. Two things left me unsatisfied at the end of my reading: The book seemed to raise as many problems of interpretation (about evidence, causality, and comparison) as it answered. And the richness of its focus on human agency seemed paradoxically matched by an absence of politics. Yet at the same time Goldhagen employed a scholarly apparatus (of references to the existing literature and of reflections on difficult methodological choices) in a way that left the curious reader with an opening to explore his doubts about the thesis of *Hitler's Willing Executioners*.

This openness to genuine controversy—as opposed to "provocation with an eye on outrage" (Augstein's favorite quote from a *Frankfurter Rundschau* article)—has largely been lost on the reviewer's guild. The invitation to debate has been overlooked both by the adulatory voices in the U.S. press that preceded the Holocaust museum debate and the offended German feuilleton writers who followed. With the partial exception of the series in *Die Zeit*, Goldhagen's claim to have initiated a paradigm shift in Holocaust scholarship has not been taken seriously. The U.S. commentators have been insufficiently aware of how novel it is for a Holocaust *scholar* (as opposed to a victim) to emphasize anti-Semitism. Germany's gatekeepers of opinion have been put off by the author's presumptuousness to tread on (in their view, to retread) four decades of well-laid research turf.

To much of the German press it has seemed as though Goldhagen were really writing about Germany today, or about the "eternal German," and not specifically about the very different Germans who set out to destroy the Jews of Europe sixty years ago. Several historians have faulted Goldhagen for not making established research agendas on *related* topics—such as how the genocide was planned or how the Nazis came to power—central to his study of the perpetrators. (Without apparently noticing the contradiction, they have also criticized his reliance on secondary literature to give these neighboring themes the brief attention he realizes they deserve.) Only Ingrid Gilcher-Holtey (in *Die Zeit*) has bothered to mention the "methodological challenge" raised by Goldhagen's decision to put the killers' mental outlook in sharp relief while relegating other aspects of German history to the background. Although Goldhagen undertakes the effort to clarify his research strategy at every step—to explain, for example, why he believes that multicausality may be important in accounting for the Nazi regime but not in accounting for the perpetrators' actions or why the comparative analysis of anti-Semitism has limited value for explaining the Holocaust—most readers of the German press would gain the impression that provocation rather than elucidation is the author's goal.

The charges leveled at Goldhagen by German historians and journalists come down to two: that he is engaged in damnation and simplification. He is simplifying German history, the indictment reads, by treating the Holocaust as though it was a "national project" signifying for Germans something like what socialism meant to Stalin—anti-Semitism in a single country. Other factors—other peoples' anti-Semitisms and other German motives—are blocked out. Aspects of German political culture apart from the emergence of "eliminationist anti-Semitism" in the nineteenth century are neglected. Though it is reasonable to wonder why Goldhagen insists that "a monocausal explanation does suffice" to elucidate the self-motivation of "ordinary Germans" (in contrast to the multifaceted pressures operating on Browning's "ordinary men"), it is also striking that his explicit methodological rationale for so insisting has been largely ignored. In characterizing Goldhagen's research method, Augstein takes British critic Paul Johnson's insult "sociobabble" a step further by hurling it against Goldhagen the "*Überzeugungstäter*" (he is also called "*Scharfrichter*" and "*Henker*" in *Der Spiegel*) ["perpetrator out of conviction," "hanging judge," and "henchman"—Ed.]. But even better-informed critics with more civil tongues have missed the opportunity to discuss their interpretive differences with Goldhagen. They dismiss him as an interloper onto territory already claimed by established historians whose own methodological choices are not questioned. The discrediting of Goldhagen's credentials coupled with the automatic bonus awarded to Browning has meant that neither scholar's perspective on how to evaluate the motives of the killers has received the scrutiny each deserves.

For the fact of the matter is that any research strategy for evaluating evidence about some of the twentieth century's worst crimes is bound to be fraught with difficulty. Goldhagen is one of the few—maybe the only—scholars to have indicated what may be wrong with Browning's methodology. Browning excludes victims' testimony entirely from his book *Ordinary Men* on the grounds that contact between the Jews in Polish towns and the police battalions who rounded them up for slaughter was too fleeting for victims' testimony to carry much weight. Yet Goldhagen has uncovered meaningful statements from victims speaking to the killers' zeal and cruelty, and he also claims to find instances of perpetrators' statements taken at face value by Browning that turn out to be contradictory or deceitful. Goldhagen's complete exclusion of self-serving testimony from Germans confronting possible war crimes charges raises another set of problems. He believes no explanation can be adequate that fails to account for both the breadth and variation of the perpetrators' behavior. Specifically, this means trying to understand why Germans often displayed a special cruelty toward their Jewish victims, why they often struck mocking, proud, or boastful poses over defenseless old Jewish men or were eager to hunt down Jewish women and children hiding in forests, why Jews (unlike, say, Poles) were not valued as slave labor but were worked or marched to death. Frank Schirrmacher of the *Frankfurter Allgemeine Zeitung (FAZ)* entirely misses what is contestable about this approach when he compares Goldhagen's schematization of Nazi-era attitudes toward non-German "racial" groups to a computer program and faults the author for making history too automatic. The real problem is not simplification but a different appreciation of complexity. For most historians of this subject, complexity is all on the side of the perpetrator's purported motives (or of the process leading to the genocide), whereas the range of the killer's behavior tends toward the monochromatic. (Depersonalized accounts of the killing—with social theories to match—mirror this tendency.) For Goldhagen the priorities are more or less reverse. Combined with the author's insistence on discrediting exculpatory testimony, his priorities favor a highly leveraged explanation in which one factor (anti-Semitism) carries the burden of proving extremes of behavior.

Goldhagen does not ignore the motives that other Holocaust scholars consider important. When he discounts or rejects such factors as peer pressure, stress, or "apathy," it is always after painstaking consideration of what these mental states actually mean. (There is a brilliant note on how the ad-jective *"teilnahmlos"* [unsympathetic—Ed.]—frequently used to characterize the perpetrators' attitude toward their victims—has a completely different behavioral and moral meaning than *"gleichgültig"* [indifferent—Ed.]) His main point is that no account of the Holocaust is plausible if it fails to appreciate that most of the perpetrators believed it made sense to kill Jews. Where Goldhagen thinks most of the killers stood on the scale that ranged from devotion to acceptance of the eliminationist assignment is a point he could stand to clarify. Yet more than any other work on the subject, *Hitler's Willing Executioners* takes seriously Max Weber's insight that accepting the legitimacy of authority is more than a matter of following orders. No German was ever severely punished for refusing an order to kill Jews, and the officer in charge of the infamous Reserve Police Battalion 101 explicitly offered anyone under his command the opportunity to excuse himself from killing duty. At some level even the Nazi authorization for genocidal murder was *internalized* by those who carried it out. At the Holocaust museum Browning accused Goldhagen of denying the perpetrators' humanity, and he is certainly correct in identifying the issue at stake. Most Holocaust scholars think that the humanity of Germans in that era is best fleshed out by historicizing the situation and the system in which they found themselves. Goldhagen believes in doing justice to their humanity by ascertaining their beliefs. He thinks the range of the perpetrators' behavior and the cultural setting of the killing fields point not to a coercive, depersonalized moral vacuum in which men could anesthetize their scruples about killing defenseless human beings (the conventional wisdom among Holocaust researchers) but to a rich social life empowering ordinary Germans to express and act upon their view that killing Jews (perceived as harmful to the German people) was just.

The highly leveraged stress on anti-Semitic beliefs to explain acts of dedicated genocide may leave out grey areas of conduct by the perpetrators. It also sometimes makes it seem as though *Hitler's Willing Executioners* is a work of political science without politics. Even though Goldhagen emphasizes the centrality of Hitler, a reader can get the impression that the Nazi regime did not matter much as a force for mobilizing public opinion against Jews. Previous German regimes (Weimar and the *Kaiserreich*) seem to count because they inhibited Germans from acting on eliminationist beliefs about Jews. But Goldhagen's version of the Nazi dictatorship does not seem to have the same importance for promoting anti-Semitism; it *relies* on popular anti-Semitism more than *cultivating* it. Reviewing *Hitler's Willing Executioners* for the U.S. weekly *The New Republic,* Israeli historian Omer Bartov cites an episode to illustrate his criticism that the regime might have mattered more than Goldhagen thinks. On one of the death marches in 1944, villagers (presumably German) offered food to starving Jews, although the Germans in charge of the marches (obviously closer to the regime than the villagers) prohibited this friendly gesture. Bartov sees "ordinary Germans" on both sides here, with proximity to the regime determining anti-Semitic behavior. Goldhagen emphasizes the voluntaristic character of the death marches, whose organizers disobeyed an order from Himmler (certainly closer to the heart of Nazi power than anyone) to stop killing Jews while he negotiated with the Allies.

Goldhagen's critics may think that his sketchy treatment of political mobilization by the Nazis reduces Hitler's system to a mere pretext for letting Germans do to Jews what they had longed to do under two previous regimes. Yet practically no one uses a like measure of historical concreteness to test Browning's *Ordinary Men,* which speculates on how psychological lab experiments or personality surveys conducted in other places and times may be applied to a German police battalion in occupied Poland. Browning concludes his book by pondering whether any one of us might have behaved the same way under these circumstances. Yet neither this abstract reflection nor any of the many other attempts to conceptualize the Holocaust using general theories of modernization or the "authoritarian personality" has been attacked as "ahistorical" so fervently as have Goldhagen's effort to place the Shoah in the context of modern German history.

Even though a uniquely German undercurrent of relativization flows beneath the torrent of criticism against *Hitler's Willing Executioners,* the accusation that the author simplifies has not been the property of any single country. On this point historians in the United States and Israel have lined up against the book as well. National sensitivity is reflected much more in the second charge against Goldhagen's "provocation": that he aims at damnation. Many German critics apparently think that Goldhagen has consigned all of their countrymen to a special circle in hell. Damnation and simplification meet in the frequent charge that Goldhagen is turning the wheel of historiography back to the 1950s, when a didactic literature dominated the protean subject (hardly yet a "field") of Holocaust commentary (not yet "research"). Anxieties about U.S. perceptions of a unified Germany and its role in the world seem to fuel the German misperception that Goldhagen is interested in condemning a Teutonic psyche. There are versions of this misapprehension on both the left and right. Nothing could be further from the truth than Frank Schirrmacher's belief that Goldhagen wants Germany bound to its historical *Sonderweg* for all eternity. (*Die Welt* reviewer Jost Nolte's mythopoetic declaration that Goldhagen has created a German Sisyphus is a variation on this theme.) Writing in *Die Woche* Peter Glotz refuses to believe Goldhagen's statement that his book is not a thesis about national character. Then he goes on to mock the American social scientist's optimistic view that postwar Germans have successfully reeducated themselves and (in a masterpiece of relativization, as Andrei Markovits has pointed out) to cite crisis hot spots from Bosnia to Rwanda as the really troublesome examples of genocide *outside* Germany's borders. Whereas the German right may worry that the eternal *Sonderweg* will tie Volker Rühe's hands, the left often concludes that throwing up one's hands about evil around the globe is the appropriate response to the genocide in Germany's own past.

So far as I can tell, there are no clear-cut implications for postunification Germany's domestic or foreign policy in Goldhagen's book. It will not settle what Germany should do about Bosnia or refugees. The only obvious moral imperative to be derived from *Hitler's Willing Executioners* is that each country must counter racism and anti-Semitism with powerful popular counter-images and broad institutional supports protecting all its citizens' rights. In the Dreyfus Affair supporters of the Republic staked the identity of France on the cause of a wronged Jewish officer, during the 1960s liberal Americans stirred out of a century of inaction to redefine their legal system in defense of blacks and other minorities, and citizens of the Federal Republic have also associated themselves with the unfinished revolution in human rights. Germany's political class has often given the concept of *"streitbare Demokratie"* [contested democracy—Ed.] too narrow—too exclusively parliamentary or executive—a construction. But even if some founding myths of the Bonn republic (notably, that Germans needed Art. 20 GG [the constitutional clause empowering citizens to disregard unlawful orders—Ed.] to get the requisite backbone for resisting state-sanctioned injustice) are *not* corroborated by Goldhagen's book, its author has no quarrel with either the framework or the broader civic culture of what he calls postwar Germany's political "conversation."

Goldhagen the American should be taken seriously when he says that Germans today—unlike the Germans of fifty years ago—are "like us." He does not say that Germans changed overnight (the 1946 opinion poll he cites indicates how alarmingly high anti-Semitic feeling remained just after military defeat). Yet anti-Semitism in Germany today is more like anti-Semitism in the United States, though with the important caveat that the eliminationist program carried out in the Nazi era hovers like a legacy over any new outbreak of German intolerance. I do not know if it is easier for an American to accept that dramatic changes in mental outlook like those analyzed by Goldhagen can really take place. The most burdensome historical legacy of the United States is slavery. Racism remains an ever-present factor in U.S. poli-

Jeremiah M. Riemer

tics. Yet in my lifetime I have witnessed how the character of U.S. racism has profoundly changed. It is no longer socially acceptable for even the most reactionary public figure (such as Pat Buchanan) to articulate beliefs that were considered axiomatic in the U.S. South when I was a child. Southerners then believed that civilized life depended critically on segregation, that the virtue of innocent white women was continually threatened by oversexed black men, and that it was understandable or even desirable that black people seeking the right to vote be murdered along with the "nigger-loving outside agitators" who aided their cause. Federal judges and troops (the U.S. South's equivalent of the postwar Occupying Powers) had to intervene at public schools and universities before the South could "reeducate" itself to the point where the Olympics could be brought to Atlanta by associates of the man who symbolized the struggle against racism. Although Auschwitz inspired the burning of a synagogue in Lübeck as surely as the legacy of U.S. apartheid gave someone the idea to burn black churches, this is no reason to confuse past with present.

The Goldhagen debate is not about the burden of one country's past but about the competing burdens of many history scholars' proofs. Unlike his admirer Elie Wiesel, who persists in seeing the Shoah as an ineffable phenomenon beyond belief, Goldhagen believes the German genocide against the Jews can be explained in terms of its perpetrators' beliefs. His aim is analytical, not theological judgment. Only reviewers who insist on reading hidden meanings into *Hitler's Willing Executioners* will feel the "rage of Old Testament breath" imagined by Just Nolte in *Die Welt* or suffer the "*Scharfrichter's*" vengeance caricatured by Augstein. The book is not a call for judgment on collective guilt. It is an invitation for readers to examine the evidence and judge for themselves.

A much shorter version translated into German and
published in *die tageszeitung* on August 29, 1996

TWENTY-ONE

THE THIN PATINA OF CIVILIZATION:
ANTI-SEMITISM WAS A NECESSARY,
BUT BY NO MEANS A SUFFICIENT,
CONDITION FOR THE HOLOCAUST

Hans Mommsen

The attention that Daniel Goldhagen's prize-winning book *Hitler's Willing Executioners* has garnered—above all in the United States, but in other Western countries as well—teaches us that the emotional after-effect of the German murder of the Jews still lingers after decades. The book itself, which consciously aims to provoke, does not actually justify the debate that has flared up anew. It plainly lags behind the current state of research, rests on broadly insufficient foundations, and brings no new insights to bear on answering the question of why it became possible for an advanced and highly civilized country to relapse into barbarism, into the systematic liquidation of millions of innocent human beings—here, primarily, of Jews.

The emotional burden carried by any attempt to explain the Shoah had already fully erupted on the occasion of the 1960 Eichmann trial in Jerusalem, when Hannah Arendt coined the controversial phrase "the banality of evil" in her report on the trial and rejected the allegation of the court—but also of the majority of research at the time—that the murder of the Jews was primarily the result of a strategy of destruction planned in advance. She drew serious opposition when she asserted that anti-Semitism represented only one factor in the implementation of the genocide.

And indeed, the overwhelming view of public opinion worldwide was that Hitler had planned the destruction of the European Jews from the beginning and exposed his program step by step until it was finally realized under the conditions of the war. It was equally unquestioned that significant segments of German society, especially the members of the functional elites, must have known to some extent or other about the systematic destruction of the Jews.

Likewise research scholarship was convinced that the systematic destruction of European Jewry definitively went into action on July 31, 1941, when Hermann Göring gave Heydrich the assignment of initiating the "Final Solution of the European Jewish question"; research scholarship assumed that only Hitler could have given such an order. This is doubted by the majority of researchers today, especially as we are dealing with an instruction that Adolf Eichmann had drafted for Göring and that the latter had merely signed (quite apart from the fact that the instruction referred to measures on the "Jewish question" to be undertaken after the war).

There is also widespread agreement that there was no formal order to initiate the Final Solution. Likewise, prior to 1940 the regime had set no long-term goal beyond the forced emigration of the Jewish segment of the population, and this goal became more and more hopeless in the course of the Reich's eastward expansion, which multiplied the number of Jews living under German rule.

After preliminary stages in subjugated Poland, it is only with the activation of *Einsatzgruppen* A and D in occupied Soviet territory (and here only from late summer 1941 onward) that actions to exterminate the Jewish population (including women and children) are employed in a manner signifying a qualitative shift. Research puts these in the context of Himmler's visit to Russia and of the euphoric hopes for victory in which he also shared, which led him to increase by more than twentyfold the personnel available for extermination measures and also to enlist for this purpose the services of the police battalions employed in the region behind.

The turning point suggested here does not correspond to the instruction first issued in October–November 1941 by Gestapo chief Heinrich Müller preventing the emigration of Jews from occupied French territory to Morocco. This measure was still connected with the shifting reservation projects that the population planners under Himmler and the Reich Security Main Office (*Reichssicherheitshauptamt*) envisioned, including the Madagascar Plan, the plan for a reservation near Lublin, and finally the plan for the yet-to-be-created polar sea district.

Even at the time of the Wannsee Conference, the solution that was finally found in March 1942—simultaneous mass liquidation in Auschwitz and the construction of extermination camps—was not yet an agreed-upon objective, although there continued to be ambivalence about the principle of "extermination through work" that Odilo Globocnik was practicing in eastern Galicia and the *Generalgouvernement*. The turning point toward a pan-European Final Solution was represented by *Aktion Reinhard,* the step-by-step liquidation of Jews in the *Generalgouvernement,* after the various reservation solutions came to nothing as a result of the war's unanticipated course.

The latest research delineates an interaction between local and central actors leading finally to the formation of a consensus among all participants that Jews in German hands were to be liquidated. Not only ideological motivations but also invented material and psychological predicaments were decisive. Thus it was the assurance given to the Soviet Union that hundreds of thousands of ethnic Germans from the Baltic countries, from Volhynia, and from Bessarabia would be resettled in the Warthegau and other regions of east central Europe that gave the decisive push toward deporting the Jewish population and creating ghettos in the *Generalgouvernement.*

The complexity of these events has caused historians of the Holocaust to exercise great caution about making generalizations. On the one hand, field research (extended in recent years to include eastern Europe) has shown that it was not just the SS and the narrower terror apparatus of the regime but also the *Wehrmacht,* the Foreign Office, considerable portions of the domestic and general administration, the police agencies, and the German Reichsbahn railway that were implicated in the policy of murder.

Today it can be stated as fact that the program of murder could not have become reality without the active support of portions of the functional elites, even if the majority of them have never answered for the murderous consequences of their deeds, whether for reasons of psychological repression, political naiveté, or moral indifference.

Those who participated in the deportation of the Jews and in their social isolation and dispossession or who were the immediate beneficiaries of the same also cultivated vagueness or ignorance about the implementation of a criminal program. For example, in his studies of the German railway workers responsible for the transports to Auschwitz, Raul Hilberg had to state that they mainly went about their business of conveying the Jews to the death camps without thinking about it. And Christopher Browning's epoch-making study on the Hamburg Reserve Police Battalion 101 shows that the members of this unit (which participated directly in the destruction of the Jews in the occupied Soviet Union), although not primarily disposed toward anti-Semitism, were nonetheless by no means merely coerced to go about their murderous work.

This led Browning to the formulation "ordinary men," since this group's social composition was not significantly different from that of the population as a whole. We get a different argument from Goldhagen, who on the basis of the same material—but with less interpretive profundity—imputes fanatic anti-Semitism as motive and delight in sadistic violence against Jews (which there was in individual cases) to all the men of the police battalion. He modifies Browning's phrase and speaks of "ordinary Germans," whom he makes generally responsible for what happened. He counts a million Germans among the narrow circle of the executioners, which represents a misleading application of Ulrich Herbert's estimate of the direct and indirect participants in the deportations.

One can commend Goldhagen for having persistently worked out that the implementation of the Holocaust was the work of an astonishingly large number of persons and that the secrecy was not complete. It is just as undeniable that the crimes were also not (or not to the full extent) perceived by the majority of the population, and it is hard to reduce the social-psychological causes for this to a common denominator. Attempts to quantify the actual number of those who shared in the perpetration and knowledge of the crimes, by contrast, are of secondary importance and only aggravate the problem of collective repression, a problem related to insufficient information. Likewise it may be doubted that a widespread knowledge of the crimes would have triggered publicly relevant protest from the populace. To this extent, Goldhagen's attempt to draw conclusions about the nation as a whole from the number of active executioners is methodologically of little help, especially as it can only be a case of making estimates without empirical support. In order to explain how the process of extermination took place—which is the matter at hand, and not primarily attributions of guilt—it makes more sense to analyze more closely the middle level of the executioners, meaning the "desk perpetrators," whose mentality was shaped by bureaucratic perfectionism, and this—contrary to Goldhagen's assertion—has been abundantly if not exhaustively done.

At the same time, the argument over Goldhagen's book touches on the question of what weight should be assigned to anti-Semitic attitudes, as well as to other factors in the history of mentalities. It is indisputable that the general anti-Semitic climate stirred up by Goebbels's propaganda (along with the threat facing those who tried to speak up for Jews or help them)—as well as the strong anti-Semitic currents among members of the Eastern peoples, especially Ukrainians and Lithuanians—laid the groundwork for the systematic Holocaust.

Likewise, there can be no doubt that the latent anti-Semitism within the

German upper stratum's goal of dissimilation, which was especially widespread in the military and civil service during the *Kaiserreich,* considerably increased this stratum's corruptibility in the Third Reich. Thus the general population followed without noticeable objection Hitler's equation of Jewry with Bolshevism and his call for a "race extermination war" against the Soviet Union.

The real thrust toward the Holocaust, however, emanated from the fanatic anti-Semites, who even inside the party constituted a minority of 20 percent at most but who found prominent spokesmen in Hitler and Himmler and especially among the Nazi satraps. After the early resignation of Justice Minister Gürtner and in light of the ministerial bureaucracy's readiness to leave the "Jewish question" as a field of activity to the NSDAP, these radicals did not have to reckon with any sanctions. The minority of fanatical racist anti-Semites, constantly encouraged by Hitler and urged on by hopes of recognition from the dictator, represented the real dynamic moment, which continuously restarted the regime's characteristic "cumulative radicalization." Logically, a constellation came about where, as Martin Broszat has described, "propaganda had to be taken at its word."

It was, however, not just their fanatical anti-Semitism, dispensing with every threshold of inhibition, that drove countless National Socialist climbers toward the permanent intensification of measures directed against the Jews; rather, material interests played a weighty role. Many of the overt executors like Adolf Eichmann or Theodor Dannecker first became ruthless and fanatical anti-Semites in the course of their SS careers, which allowed them to forget about their unfavorable professional situation in civilian life, and they were by no means acting out of ideological motives alone. One searches in vain for differentiated analysis of this kind in Goldhagen.

Goldhagen repeatedly emphasizes that the persecutors imposed fewer inhibitions on themselves vis-à-vis Jews than in relation to other racial opponents of the regime; this was (to the extent that it was even applicable) a result of the fact that Jews were the least protected under the law. It is correct that Jews were assessed as the lowest stratum of the eastern European peoples. But it cannot be denied that the National Socialist extermination machinery, had it not been prematurely broken by military defeats, would have exterminated other populations, likewise asocial or politically disfavored Germans, with the same mercilessness inflicted on the Jews, burdened as they undoubtedly were with the stigma of Occidental anti-Semitism. Independently of that—this goes back to remarks by Götz Aly—a sort of compensatory effect came into play to the extent that the prominent executors, who in the first instance were overwhelmingly concerned with the settlement and resettlement of ethnic Germans, turned toward the Final Solution to the Jewish question to the extent that their "positive" projects (that is, the realization of the gigantic eastern settlement program) shattered at the very outset upon the uncooperative reality of war.

In the differentiated viewpoint of recent Holocaust research, anti-Semitism is seen as a necessary but by no means sufficient condition for the implementation of the Final Solution. The structure of the regime, aligned around permanent competition among self-dissolving institutions, together with processes that discouraged the safeguarding of political interests, fueled a process of cumulative radicalization whose inevitable endpoint was the liquidation of the Jews. Therefore at least as much significance must be attributed to the bureaucratic-administrative factor as to the compensatory hatred of the Jews mounting among the Nationalist Socialist elite.

Given this background, the question of anti-Semitism's relation to the Holocaust must be posed anew. It was not the radical anti-Semitic agitators like Julius Streicher or Joseph Goebbels but, rather, the anti-Semitic men of action who took the steps toward the method of systematic extermination and who engraved a new, internal systematics on the process of eliminating the Jews. However, this process also required social segregation of the groups meant for persecution, wartime conditions, and general anti-Semitic indoctrination. This view of things also forces successor generations to acknowledge how thin the patina of civilization is and how ineffective traditional moral concepts are under constellations of extreme lawlessness and political disorientation. This points to the moral vulnerability of our culture and constitutes an epochal challenge that occasioned Dan Diner to speak openly of a *Zivilisationsbruch* [rupture in civilization].

Goldhagen's book lags behind the entire research discussion sketched here. He mirrors the refusal to recognize that the causes of the Holocaust— of the greatest crime in human history—lie in that mixture of ideological fanaticism, psychopathological aberration, moral indifference, and bureaucratic perfectionism, in the very "banality of evil." Instead he reduces the causes of the Holocaust to a supposedly hypertrophic German anti-Semitism, which early on displayed eliminationist qualities and thereby distinguished itself from the anti-Semitism of other peoples and cultures.

Goldhagen believes that he can demonstrate, in Emile Durkheim's sense, a specific collective consciousness and speaks of "the German cultural cognitive model of the Jew." However, he avoids corroborating this with source material, and he instead refers to a few works on the history of anti-Semitism in Germany whose findings he not infrequently takes out of context and generalizes in a one-sided manner.

Goldhagen charges previous scholarship in general of suppressing the "delight" taken by an entire people in the murder of the Jews. From his perspective, Hitler appears as a necessary consequence of German history, which since the end of the middle ages was shaped by growing anti-Semitism. Accordingly, the German people appear as the very *"Urvolk"* of anti-Semitism. Goldhagen is apparently not aware that he is exposing himself to the suspicion of turning the common anti-Semitic argumentation into its simple opposite and of viewing the Germans' hatred of Jews, as it were, as a historically inherited and innate attribute, even if he disavows this in his answer to his critics and in his supplementary forward to the German edition.

Hitler's immediate exterminationist intent is also not questioned by Goldhagen. He justifies this with Hitler's well-known remark in *Mein Kampf* that one should have held "12,000 of these corrupters of the people under poison gas at the right time" in order to prevent military defeat and the November revolution, and also with a police report summarizing a speech by Hitler from early 1920 in which he on the one hand propagates a "reasoned anti-Semitism" and on the other hand stresses the "thoroughgoing resolve" to "seize the Evil by the roots and to exterminate it root and branch," a remark that remains within the framework of traditional anti-Semitic rhetoric. These are meager proofs for a demonstration that Hitler had the physical extermination of the Jews in mind so concretely from the start. Martin Broszat's shrewd interpretation that the ideology ultimately let itself be "taken at its word" is not taken into consideration any more than is the question of when the systematic intention to exterminate was definitively carried out.

Goldhagen's remarks on anti-Semitism in Germany from the early modern period onward and in the eighteenth and nineteenth centuries rest on a much too narrow, and not always correct, evaluation of secondary literature (his use of sources is, at best, indirect). The derivation of "eliminationist anti-Semitism," as he calls it, from the anti-Semitic rallies of the *Vormärz* [the era leading up to the revolution of 1848—Trans.]—especially the Hepp-Hepp riots of 1819 that were directed against the implementation of Jewish emancipation and that would more properly be credited to the account of a lingering religious-Christian condemnation of Jews than to that of "modern" anti-Semitism—is hardly convincing.

Nobody denies that extreme anti-Semitic views also showed up in Germany; what is questioned is just the imputation that we are dealing with a widespread tendency representative of political culture in Germany. That is emphatically contestable. If Goldhagen's arguments were true, it would be most difficult to explain why there even was a Jewish emancipation in Germany. The author draws with verve from an unpublished Heidelberg dissertation submitted in 1963.[1] Its exaggerated thesis is of an extreme anti-Semitism widespread among the German citizenry. It would take us too far afield to go into every single one of Goldhagen's remarks, which take an anti-Semitic undercurrent making its appearance in the *Kaiserreich* after 1878, raise it to the level of a dominant characteristic of German political culture (in spite of the decline of the anti-Semitic parties after the turn of the century), and simultaneously impute thereunto an "eliminationist" variant, which leads repeatedly to grotesque misjudgments.

The fact that anti-Semitic views were occasionally to be found among Social Democratic supporters does not justify Goldhagen's general assertion that anti-Semitism also became accepted in the working class. Similarly distorted is his analysis of the position of the Catholic segment of the population and the curia on the "Jewish question." Well into the 1930s, clerical "anti-Judaism" undoubtedly did play an important role in that it opened the way, in some respects, for the National Socialist persecution of the Jews. On the other hand, political Catholicism and significant portions of the Catholic clergy were decisive opponents of racial anti-Semitism and cannot, in any event, be added into the postulated camp of "eliminationist anti-Semitism."

It is just as insupportable to denounce nineteenth-century German nationalism generally by making the claims Goldhagen does. Goldhagen's thesis that the National Liberals, and not just their extreme right wing as represented by Heinrich von Treitschke, were carriers of "eliminationist anti-Semitism" is contradicted by the leading role of Jewish liberal politicians in the party. Paradoxically, Goldhagen overlooks *völkisch* anti-Semitism of the kind propagated by those ranging from Richard Wagner through Houston Stewart Chamberlain to Theodor Fritsch, although it is here that one finds the direct precursors of the National Socialist racial ideology. Beyond this, he tends to throw the widespread dissimilating anti-Semitism of conservative provenance, such as found its way into the German Conservatives' Tivoli Program of 1893, into the same basket with *völkisch* anti-Semitism—however little it may be doubted that Germany's upper stratum, especially its military, put up no serious resistance to the National Socialist persecution of the Jews, even when they did not approve of their "methods."

At the same time, Goldhagen argues—in clear contrast to the interpretation of Shulamit Volkov, who characterizes Wilhelmine anti-Semitism as a "cultural code"—that anti-Semitism as a "cultural cognitive model of the Germans" was stamped by an annihilationist intent. The same argumentation is carried through to the period of the Weimar Republic. The early republic was certainly shaped by the massive *völkisch* anti-Semitism that erupted after 1917, finding support in the Supreme Naval Command and increasing greatly in the Munich of the *Räterepublik* [short-lived Soviet-type radical republic—Ed.]. But this no longer applied to the stabilization phase [of the mid-1920s—Trans.], when the anti-Semitic current noticeably flattened out, only to pick up again in the years of the global economic crisis.

Extreme *völkisch* anti-Semitism was represented in the first instance by the Deutsch-völkischer Schutz- und Trutzbund, a front organization for the Alldeutscher Verband, as well as by the Deutsch-völkische Freiheitspartei, the right wing of the DNVP that split off in 1922. The leader of the Alldeutscher Verband, Judicial Councillor Claß, expected that the mobilization of anti-Semitism in 1918 would immunize the working class against the influence of Social Democracy, a strategy that failed down the line (just as had happened to the Christian Social movement mounted after 1878 by the Imperial court preacher Stoecker) because anti-Semitism proved ill-suited as a means of mass mobilization.

At the time of its banning in 1921, the Schutz- und Trutzbund, which embraced nearly the entire potential of organized anti-Semitism in Weimar, had no more than 200,000 members at its disposal. Compared to the mass organizations, from the All German League of Unions (ADGB) trade union confederation to the *Stalhelm*, extremist racial anti-Semitism was therefore quantitatively insignificant, yet it had formative significance for the *Freikorps* movement and for what was (for the time being) its political neighbor, the NSDAP, which recruited a high percentage of its cadres from the Deutsch-völkischer Schutz- und Trutzbund.

Goldhagen's view that anti-Semitism swept Hitler into power—or was successfully used by him for mass mobilization—is therefore incorrect. In the decisive electoral campaigns of 1930 and 1932, which gave the NSDAP its breakthrough as a mass party, anti-Semitic agitation proved, if anything, more of a hindrance, so that the Reich-level campaign leadership consciously played it down. In the decision to vote for the NSDAP, anti-Semitism played a subordinate role, however regrettable it is that many NSDAP sympathizers were hardly disturbed by its extreme anti-Semitism and—in the conservative camp—viewed it as a mere childhood disease that would peter out in time.

It would certainly be misguided to neglect the significance of anti-Semitism as a component of integral nationalism in Germany. The charge that historical scholarship has done this skirts reality. Above all, however, constitutive meaning befits anti-Semitism as a means of intraparty integration. Anti-Semitism was thus capable of patching together heterogeneous ideological elements using the common image of the Jewish enemy.

Goldhagen stands on the extreme wing of the "intentionalist" school and associates himself with the thesis that Hitler constantly had the violent Final Solution in his sights and implemented it as soon as international conditions allowed. He is not bothered, as his critics attest, by contradictory research findings proving conclusively that until 1940 the regime saw no other "solution" than Jewish emigration. He relies overwhelmingly on the interpretation of Richard Breitman[2] without processing it fully. The real question—of why it came to the implementation of systematic genocide, in combination with *Einsatzgruppen* in occupied Soviet territory, the *Aktion Reinhard* in eastern Galicia and in the *Generalgouvernement,* and the *Gauleiter* of the *Altreich* pushing for the deportation of Jews eastward—thereby evades his glance.

Instead Goldhagen concentrates on the mentality of the perpetrators, which he explores on the basis of three case studies. The first one treats the history of the Hamburg Reserve Police Battalion 101 with a look at the role of the police battalions in general. A further case study analyzes two Jewish labor camps, the Lipowa camp and the airport camp in the Lublin district. The third investigation concerns the complex of the death marches. These studies form the core of the book, whose first two parts, although unusually encumbered theoretically, exhaust themselves in a comprehensive exposition for which no archival or otherwise unpublished sources are invoked (and in which secondary literature is cited only in cursory fashion).

Since Reserve Police Battalion 101's intervention in the Final Solution was already thoroughly depicted by Christopher Browning (with detailed and differentiated analyses of the motives of the participants), this case study, even if other police battalions are partly included, contributes no real new research findings (although Goldhagen vehemently states that it does). Although he essentially proceeds from the same material as Browning, Goldhagen arrives at nearly opposite conclusions. Though Browning ascribes a key role to anti-Semitic indoctrination, he delivers—incidentally, against his original expectation—an extremely complex picture of individual motivations for murdering, among which anti-Semitic indoctrination plays no dominant role. That Goldhagen—both in an earlier book review and here again—could portray the experienced and knowledgeable Browning as naive and uncritical is even more problematic in that he follows Browning's treatment of the trial material for broad stretches. In contrast to this, it must be emphasized that Goldhagen's prejudicial approach largely excludes a differentiated analysis that weighs the various activating motives against each other, especially since he refers less to an explanation of individuals' conduct than to proof of their guilty behavior. His wholesale characterization of the interrogations undertaken by the Hamburg judicial authorities as false testimony will also hardly do.

With regard to the Lipowa camp and the airport camp (here, too, he draws largely on the files of the *Zentralstelle der Landesjustizverwaltungen* in Ludwigsburg), Goldhagen endeavors to portray the brutal mistreatment of Jews in as much detail as possible, while a classification of *Aktion Reinhard* and its specific features is not undertaken. Goldhagen is concerned with working out the unspeakable gruesomeness of the German tormentors, which he attributes to specifically anti-Semitic views. He is proud of being one of the first researchers to use photography as a source—contemporary snapshots are to be found in the files of the Hamburg district attorney—but he knows little about the difficulty of determining the documentary relevance, dating, and origins of photographs, which, as a rule, come down to us in isolated fashion. Characteristically, he has not undertaken the certification of origins that a historian is expected to show for photographs reproduced in a book.

The extremely high measure of violence that Goldhagen attests above all for *Aktion Reinhard* is, for him, renewed proof of the Germans' profound anti-Semitic indoctrination. He searches for further confirmation of this in the merciless gruesomeness of the guard personnel accompanying the Jews on the death marches. But even in this commendable portrayal, which clearly goes beyond the previous state of research, amendments must be made. To begin with, Jews were not the only victims of these senseless actions, and it is hardly true that the frequently terrorized population thoroughly approved of the mistreatment and murder taking place before their eyes. These phenomena must, moreover, be placed in the context of the bloody intoxication provoked by the SS and the security organs, such as the leading cadres of the NSDAP, during the last months of the war. Jews were the first but by no means the only victims. The excesses of violence, now also visited upon the Germans, derived from a mixture of habituation to brutality and the use of violence, as well as from a "forward flight" mentality among those who had burned all the bridges behind them.

However, by his emphasis on the violence, sadism, and pleasure taken in murder, Goldhagen diverts attention from the peculiarity of the National Socialist persecution and extermination of the Jews. It was qualitatively different from earlier anti-Semitic outbursts and pogroms, which arose out of a surplus of emotionality but also exhausted themselves therein. Among the Jewish Councils of eastern Europe, the traditional pogrom experience elicited an erroneous appraisal of the persecutors, whom they attempted to bring to reason by passivity and compliance. It was characteristic of National Socialism, by contrast, that the "wild" assaults on the Jews were replaced by planned and bureaucratically perfected segregation, by casting out into pariah status, and ultimately by extermination. That corruption, murderous delight, and sadism would also turn up—although Heinrich Himmler disavowed this and Oswald Pohl as chief of the concentration camp system attempted (in vain) to restrain the use of force in the camps—was hardly surprising under the circumstances and was certainly not a specific feature of the Holocaust.

Moreover, Goldhagen's portrayal of sadistic and gruesome violence releases a certain voyeuristic moment that serious Holocaust research has deliberately avoided in its restrained portrayal of the crimes, particularly since it translates at best into mere *Betroffenheit* [affectation of dismay—Trans.] and contributes little toward real explanation. One may assume that Goldhagen is not sufficiently conscious of this effect, which presumably contributes decisively to the mass marketing of his book. For him, the reference to sadistic terror constitutes decisive proof of the extreme anti-Semitic views of the perpetrators, but this is hardly convincing. Neither Himmler nor Heydrich nor Eichmann and his many subordinates fit into a category of "extreme anti-Semites," and if one is going to speak about the "psyche" of the perpetrators, *Schindler's List* offers an impressive insight into the manifold infirmity of most perpetrators' psychological-ideological constitution.

Goldhagen emphasizes in a somewhat slogan-like fashion that the Holocaust was about the most extreme and thoroughgoing revolution "in the annals of Western civilization." He speaks of a "transformation of consciousness" of the Germans and of the "inculcation of a new ethos" and draws the wordplay-like conclusion that "Himmler's *Kultur*" ultimately became the "*Kultur* of Germany." He sees in the implementation of the Holocaust the expression of "a revolutionary transformation of German society" for which the National Socialist camp system stood as sponsor.

It may be doubted, however, whether it is useful to hypostatize the regime's persecution of the Jews as revolutionary (quite apart from the associated problem of reducing social policy in the Third Reich to the racial question) since this is tantamount to upgrading an exclusively destructive policy of the regime, a policy heading not in the direction of revolutionary change but of human fiasco. Joseph Goebbels's ears would be ringing. Grasped in this manner, the fatefully trivial dimension of what happened and even its psychological repression by major portions of the National Socialist elite disappear completely from view, and what remain are empty formulas like those claiming that there was "a fundamental reshaping of the social and human landscape of Europe."

The corrosive sharpness with which Goldhagen charges the Germans with a will to "demonic anti-Semitism"—and to make them out not as accomplices but as generally pleased perpetrators—is certainly ill suited to quiet resentments, and it is anything but helpful in gaining a sober confrontation with the past in the light of the present.

Originally published in *Die Zeit* on August 31, 1996

NOTES

1. Klemens Felden, "Die Übernahme des antisemitischen Stereotyps als soziale Norm durch die bürgerliche Gesellschaft Deutschlands, 1875–1900" (Ph.D. diss., University of Heidelberg, 1963).

2. Richard Breitman, *Heinrich Himmler and the Final Solution* (Cambridge: Harvard University Press, 1993).

A TRIUMPHAL PROCESSION:
GOLDHAGEN AND THE GERMANS

Volker Ullrich

T
hat a historical work and its author could be awarded such attention is without precedent, declared historian Norbert Frei in the Mozart Hall of Frankfurt's Old Opera. And indeed, the rush to get into all four discussion fora with Daniel Jonah Goldhagen was extraordinary. In Hamburg, Berlin, and Frankfurt, auditoriums had no room to spare; with more than 2,000 visitors Tuesday evening, Munich's Philharmonic Hall was filled to capacity.

Whence the interest? What drew so many people to attend these events? Was it curiosity about the man whose book *Hitler's Willing Executioners* has been arousing such feelings for months? Was it the appeal of being present at the much-anticipated fight exhibiting the fiercely criticized Harvard lecturer in a match against his critics? Or is it the still-open wound of our national history, the penetrating, never-ending questions about why the monstrous crime of the Holocaust was especially possible in Germany?

From the very start, at the Hamburg Kammerspiele last Wednesday, Goldhagen outlined the roles. In his lecture, which he read in German, he presented himself as a reflective scholar who, together with his German colleagues, wanted to find answers to difficult questions of Holocaust research. The panelists on the podium readily took up this offer. Not conflict but the search for common ground and points of contact took center stage initially.

Moving furthest in this direction was Jan Philipp Reemtsma, the head of the Hamburg Institute for Social Research. He spoke about a broad "anti-Semitic consensus" in German society prior to 1945 and called the Holocaust a "collective effort," thus coming quite close to Goldhagen's thesis about a "national project." The Berlin historian and journalist Götz Aly, too, explicitly concurred with Goldhagen that the perpetrators were not "specially selected beasts" but ordinary Germans, a "representative cross-section of society."

So much need for harmony struck the moderator of the evening, Robert Leicht [the editor of *Die Zeit*], as inappropriate. "Let's get the objections on the table!" he asked the participants. The most resolute in doing so was Reinhard Rürup, a historian at the Technical University of Berlin and chair of the foundation for the Topography of Terror museum there. He accused Goldhagen of using source material selectively and in particular criticized his reduction of German anti-Semitism to its "eliminationist" variant. Götz Aly agreed. The introductory chapters of the book stood "on enormously weak feet"; the differentiated picture of state terror and individual patterns of behavior offered by Victor Klemperer's diaries were "ironed flat in a manner unsatisfactory in scholarship" by Goldhagen.

Goldhagen reacted amiably to the criticism, conceding a shortcoming here and making a concession there; but he did not allow any wavering on his basic thesis that the perpetrators were primarily motivated by a lethal anti-Semitism. The public at the Hamburg premiere, visibly moved by the soft-spoken decisiveness of the thirty-seven-year-old American, applauded cordially.

The prospect of Goldhagen's appearance in Berlin the following evening had a special feeling of suspense. Here he was to meet his harshest critic, Hans Mommsen, from Bochum, the doyen of German Holocaust research. He did not let himself be distracted by Goldhagen's conciliatory opening words; supported by Jürgen Kocka of the Free University of Berlin, he immediately attacked him head on. Mommsen exposed the methodological weaknesses of the book and criticized Goldhagen's "circular reasoning." From the Holocaust he draws conclusions about the "eliminationist" nature of German anti-Semitism; from the fact that the members of the police battalions were assembled from all strata of society he draws conclusions about the population as a whole. "As a trained historian I cannot embrace generalizations like that."

Here Goldhagen got into trouble. But then Kocka's Berlin colleague Wolfgang Wippermann, who had previously complained that Nazi racism was narrowed down to anti-Semitism, leaped into the breach. At least Goldhagen's book had stopped the tendency to historicize and relativize Nazi crimes and had forced scholarly research back to the decisive question of why the Holocaust could only happen in Germany and nowhere else. "Goldhagen has done our country's political culture a great service," he shouted into the auditorium of the Jewish Community Center. The audience thanked him for it with thunderous applause.

[At this panel] it became clear that the harder Goldhagen is attacked by German historians, the more forcefully the public takes his side. With his insistence on the perpetrators' individual responsibility, Goldhagen addresses people's feelings better than do Mommsen and Kocka, who ask about complex structures and systemic requirements, and he uses a language that, as it were, focuses on the victims once again. As Kocka remarks that "working" was done differently in the extermination camps than in the police battalion massacres that Goldhagen describes, there is the first stirring of displeasure. It escalates into loud protest when Mommsen claims that many perpetrators were themselves unclear about their motives.

Goldhagen knows how to seize the moment. "Is there anyone here in this auditorium," he asks, "who agrees with Professor Mommsen that the people who were murdering Jews did not know what they were doing?" With his face beet-red and his voice trembling in rage, the Bochum historian protests the misinterpretation of his statement; the confrontation has reached its climax.

Nearly lost in the excitement is Kocka's clever analysis of the success of the Goldhagen book: that its strength lies above all in the way it unflinchingly portrays the everyday reality of the killers and articulates murderous deeds on the border of the indescribable. Here Kocka sees a younger generation of researchers at work whose descriptions of dread approach the aesthetics of the media. Does this perhaps explain why Goldhagen's book resonates especially well with a younger generation of readers?

Friday morning Goldhagen is having a discussion with a group of history students at the Friedrich-Meinecke-Institut in Berlin-Dahlem. Here, too, where Ernst Nolte, the intellectual mentor of New Right historical revisionism, once taught, the Harvard lecturer encounters a wave of sympathy. Might he like to have a discussion with Ernst Nolte? No, Nolte has not even said a word about his book, and what's more, Nolte's position lies beyond the pale of what Goldhagen is ready to discuss.

Might he possibly have too positive a view of conditions in reunified Germany in light of its hostility toward foreigners, not to mention the hysterical defensive reactions to his book? No, says Goldhagen, Germany thoroughly transformed itself after 1945; even if anti-Semitism has not completely disappeared, it has nothing more to do with anti-Semitism before 1945. Is it perhaps Goldhagen's unshakable faith in the Germans' democratic capacity for learning that leads to such an outpouring of sympathy?

Frankfurt, the third stop, was a disappointment. There was no reflective conversation clarifying the different positions, as in Hamburg, no heated dispute, as in Berlin—instead there were just endless monologues. All the panelists gathered on the podium—Heidelberg education scholar Micha Brumlik, Essen political scientist Dan Diner, Munich historian Norbert Frei—know Goldhagen personally, addressed him with the informal "*du*," and spoke past each other in carefully measured statements. During Goldhagen's long-winded reply dealing with all the problems raised, one gets the impression that criticism, which he always receives with gracious thanks, is something he only processes selectively. The public listens patiently to everything and applauds at the end.

This consensual readiness apparently rests on a subterranean feeling that something like a taboo is finally being expressed here: that the distinction between "criminal Nazis" and "normal Germans" is wrong, that the readiness to murder Jews by the millions came out of the very center of German society, that Hitler and Himmler found hundreds of thousands of voluntary executioners, and that the vast majority of the population, though not actively promoting this crime, made it possible in the first place by their moral indifference. That someone is expressing this simple truth apparently has a liberating effect on not a few Germans. The fear that Goldhagen's book might incite anti-Semitic sentiments anew has proven unfounded. On the contrary, it is opening sluice gates and breaking up calcifications as the *Holocaust* series from Hollywood once did.

Goldhagen's impact in Germany—this became apparent days later in the Aschaffenburg roundtable discussion sponsored by the Second German Channel—certainly also lies in his telegenic presence. The way he sits in the circle of somewhat elderly looking German historians (Arnulf Baring, Klaus Hildebrand, Hans Mommsen again) and two witnesses to history (Knight of the Iron Cross Erich Mende on one side, Holocaust survivor Ralph Giordano on the other), wholly attentive and with a winning smile, the way he lightly nods his head, and only occasionally lightly shakes it, to give his discussion partners the feeling that he takes them totally seriously—this has a highly disarming effect. Only Arnulf Baring attempts to stem the tide of sympathy. "You have put your scholarly reputation at peril," he reprimands the Harvard assistant professor with embarrassing arrogance. The public protests, and Baring stoops to a chummy gesture: "You know, I actually like the man, I find him sympathetic."

In Munich, too, the last stop on Goldhagen's trip, on Tuesday evening, the public's sympathies lie with the American, although the historians sitting on the podium—Christian Meier, Manfred Messerschmidt and Moshe Zimmermann—treat him with the utmost respect, offer him virtually loving suggestions for improvement, and voice only restrained criticism. *Frankfurter Allgemeine Zeitung* editor Frank Schirrmacher, who earlier in the year had trashed the book, ended up giving the author a fat compliment: His book marked "a watershed—on a completely different level from the Holocaust movie."

Moderator Guido Knoop spoke in Aschaffenburg of "Daniel in the lion's den." But is this picture accurate? Goldhagen's German tour more closely resembled a triumphal procession. The American political scientist whom Rudolf Augstein had earlier called a "hanging judge" could hardly have reckoned with so much friendly attention, with so much open sympathy, and he was not the only one surprised and impressed. One need not immediately turn this into something negative and see nothing more in it than just another typically German penchant for contrition and devotion to guilt. On the other hand, one should also be on guard about stylizing this event as a graduation test for our democratic society.

The unusual echo shows that even after reunification and the commemoration of the fiftieth anniversary of the war's end, confrontation with the Holocaust has not been removed from the political agenda. Rather, a new sensitivity for the theme is in store. The unexpected success of Victor Klemperer's diaries already point in this direction. Goldhagen's impact in Germany turns the hunch into a certainty.

Originally published in *Die Zeit* on September 13, 1996

TWENTY-THREE

WHY DANIEL JONAH GOLDHAGEN'S BOOK IS MISLEADING

Marion Gräfin Dönhoff

I n a liberal newspaper, there is nobody who tells the others what's what. Problems are talked through, and if agreement cannot be reached on one of the two alternative arguments remaining at the end, then occasionally both of us, Theo Sommer and I, would present our opinions—sometimes even as editorials on page one. The reader gets to decide for himself which argument he finds more persuasive. Sometimes, even Gerd Bucerius, the publisher himself, angrily took up the pen. If he found something wrong with what Sommer or I had said, he wrote the opposite in the next edition.

The case we are dealing with today is called "Goldhagen" and concerns his book *Hitler's Willing Executioners*. I believe that [we at] *Die Zeit* made too big a fuss about the book, which uses questionable methods to advance what looks to me like a theory he cannot prove.

Between April and August we provided a forum for eight historians [see Chapters 1, 6, 8, 10, 11, 12, 13, 14 in this volume]. Then the author of the book, in an article running more than six pages (more than any author has ever been granted), condemned his critics lock, stock, and barrel in a rather authoritarian fashion [Chapter 16]. Finally, last week, Hans Mommsen responded to these comments with another two whole pages [Chapter 21].

Goldhagen's questionable methods: He proceeds from the Final Solution, from the Holocaust, and rewinds the causal chain so that the Final Solution remains forever present through its entire prehistory. In this manner he proves that "all of German society shared Hitler's virulent eliminationist anti-Semitism from way back."

He claims that the executioners constituted a representative sample of the German population. He does not say if his statistics included Austrians, who made up a third of the extermination units in the SS and commanded four of the most important death camps, as Paul Johnson wrote in the *Washington Post*.

When arguments like this are made, one has to ask what such a passionately anti-Semitic people would have done had Hitler fallen on the Western Front, where he was wounded. Undoubtedly an authoritarian regime would have been established in Germany, as in Spain or Italy, but it would certainly not have been Hitlerian National Socialism.

Goldhagen's questionable thesis: He says that the Holocaust was a German "national project." The Germans were not anti-Semitic in the conventional sense; rather, they paid homage to an exceptional anti-Semitism, "eliminationist anti-Semitism." This "eliminationist anti-Semitism" had as its goal the annihilation of the Jews.

If this kind of racism is rooted in the genes, as Goldhagen apparently believes, then one can only wonder at what may have happened to these genes after 1945, for at that point (as he concedes) the Germans totally transformed themselves.

Of course, in the preface the author cautiously protests against the charge that he has postulated any German collective guilt ("I categorically reject the notion of collective guilt"); but talking about "an entire people" or about "all Germans" cannot designate anything other than a collective. Goldhagen further asserts: "The entire German elite wholeheartedly embraced eliminationist anti-Semitism." Once more a collective entity! Goldhagen cites two cases as proof of the Germans' readiness not just to tolerate but to zealously endorse the brutal massacres.

Goldhagen's first proof is that the people cheered Hitler, even after *Kristallnacht* in November 1938. This is a surprise only to someone who has been viewing this entire period monocausally from the perspective of the Holocaust. In fact the people were by no means cheering because of the discrimination against the Jews; many disapproved of *Kristallnacht* in particular. Hitler's great, enduring, and celebrated myth rested much more on a rare combination of success and terror.

Success: Unemployment disappeared, Austria was annexed, the Sudetenland was returned, victory was won over France, which imagined itself secure behind the Maginot Line. Under these circumstances the majority of the people regarded the seizure of power as a commendable national uprising.

Terror: Immediately after the seizure of power, 4,000 Communist functionaries were arrested; in the first year the Nazis had already set up thirty concentration camps for those members of the community who would not toe the line, those who listened to the BBC or expressed skepticism about the regime. Even during the last week of the war, soldiers were executed because they did not believe in ultimate victory; a Catholic clergyman was hanged because he did not tell the Gestapo what he learned from the confession of a member of the resistance.

In light of measures like this, the second proof offered for the supposedly high level of approval all Germans gave to Hitler's Jewish policy is also less convincing. In an interview with *Der Spiegel* [Chapter 17 in this volume], Augstein asks Goldhagen how he knows that "the majority of those [watching the synagogues burn] were supposedly thinking that it served the Jews right." Goldhagen's answer: "The absence of evidence is evidence itself."

Just what does Goldhagen imagine that life in a dictatorship is like? Every person who was seriously in opposition naturally did everything to erase the traces of resistance. The few lists prepared before the assassination attempt of July 20 about who was going to fill key positions (because it was feared that otherwise a power vacuum might arise, leaving whatever *Gauleiter* was in charge to unleash a civil war) turned out to have a fateful impact. Everyone registered there was hanged.

And this further proves that Goldhagen is wrong to maintain that there was no resistance. After the failed assassination attempt, which had been planned for years, the following were hanged: twenty-one generals, thirty-three colonels, two ambassadors, seven diplomats, one minister, three permanent secretaries, the head of the Reich criminal police, and several regional heads of government and police chiefs. The number of death sentences issued by the military courts doubled after 1940–1941. In 1944–1945 it came to 8,200. The People's Court of Justice alone hung 2,140 that year.

The fate of the Scholls and of countless others who remain anonymous should also not be forgotten, even if they were not immediately offering their lives for the Jews but instead keeping their eyes on getting rid of the highest authority: the criminal system. But in many cases it was the barbaric massacres in Poland that strengthened their resolve to join the resistance.

Furthermore, even many Jews did not see themselves in peril. My closest Jewish friends, Professor Ernst Kantorowicz and Richard Meyer, head of the Foreign Office's eastern section, were not ready to emigrate too early; they remained in Germany until well into the 1930s.

Nevertheless, Goldhagen's book is important because unlike any other book it has the capacity to render unimaginable acts of cruelty horribly clear.

It is important, furthermore, because it places in the foreground the question of how ordinary people, from a nation of poets and thinkers, could be capable of deeds like this.

It is regrettable that his theses overstate and exaggerate so much that they elicit protest and a reaction likely to prove negative. Instead of opening to new insights, it is to be feared that people will shut themselves off with the argument that "that's not how it was" and no longer think about these outrages. Unfortunately, concern that the Goldhagen book could revive an anti-Semitism that had more or less died down should also not be so lightly dismissed.

Originally published in *Die Zeit* on September 6, 1996

TWENTY-FOUR

A MORAL JUDGMENT

Robert Leicht

n all the major debates about contemporary history, both preceding and following the *Historikerstreit,* none of the individual contributions to research—no matter how meritorious—played the starring role. One may find this deplorable, especially as promoters of scholarship. But in all these controversies, the main point has always been the proper perspective (whether binding or just politically correct) for viewing history.

In 1979 the TV movie *Holocaust* was highly effective in conveying the Nazi era; it was an immediately understandable epic of everyday life within a family saga. The *Historikerstreit* began in 1986 when Ernst Nolte undertook the crazy attempt to portray Hitler's terror regime as a mere consequence of (indeed as a kind of reaction to) Stalin's reign of terror and when Jürgen Habermas identified this as a mere symptom of a much broader tendency to downplay German history. The translation into the trivial, the flagrant attempt at revaluation, the creeping paradigm shift, and the moral defense— these are the points of departure for those quarrels in the "politics of history" that experts in the "scholarship of history" react to with horror.

If the issue were only critical judgment, or indeed the occasionally militant "defensive consensus" of a majority of historians, then nobody would really even give two hoots about the book by Daniel J. Goldhagen, *Hitler's Willing Executioners.* Nonetheless, the author and his work have encountered an extremely lively interest from the public, even though a considerable portion of the criticism must be taken seriously. This paradox cannot simply be explained away with the single catchphrase "media event."

Why the uproar? It was certainly wrong to expect that our uneasy retrospective on the years from 1933 to 1945 would be a case that automatically closed itself after fifty years. Reunification has certainly answered the German Question but not the many questions addressed to the Germans. The concept of a political "mastery of the past" had always been misguided. But the notion that this portion of our history lends itself to scholarly, that is, to objective, "historicization"—to a certain kind of conclusive clarity, indeed, to "transcendence" in the Hegelian sense—would be naive. Last week in *Die Zeit* [Chapter 21 in this volume], Hans Mommsen charged that Goldhagen's book does not contribute to "a sober confrontation with the past." With all due respect to this unconditionally binding ethos of historical scholarship— sober, past—there is a history that does not lend itself to mastery. Not everything that happened is also done and gone.

Reread in the glaring light of methodological criticism, and saying this wholly without stylized glances at the author's personality, this is, in the first instance, not a historical but a moral book—not a report but a judgment. Moral judgments can be one-sided, even unjust—yet they can still be apt, moving, upsetting, wounded, and wounding. Even after discounting all the mistakes, defects, and high-handedness, there remains a forceful impact from which it is only possible to escape with an extremely cool head and a cold heart. Even the rage in some critiques is a variation on this emotional shock.

Goldhagen starts out by taking a severe look at the perpetrators and offering a drastic portrayal of their deeds. One would have to be made of stone to want to use nothing but methodological objections against this rendering of the singular Holocaust (a big, strange, almost unapproachable word!) into countless wholly concrete individual crimes. The police battalions, the "work camps" for Jews, the death marches—these descriptions cannot be dismissed as all too familiar. Goldhagen's thesis that it was not weak-willed and soulless automatons at work, that it was merely people making decisions about actions, cannot be pushed aside, nor can the fact that there were more perpetrators than we have commonly assumed, that they were often "ordinary Germans" (thus the subtitle) and not completely fanatical Nazis "beyond the pale" of all their contemporaries. Even for members of the successor generations, these crimes get closer to us this way than they do in the demonizing and abstracting isolation of some alienated, wholly remote caste of criminals.

How could it come to this? This outlook on an almost indescribable event—the judge's inquiry, not the scholar's—is certainly morally legitimate, but it does lead with historic inevitability into all those problems of retrograde, backward-moving historical perspective. All actions have causes. But behind every indisputable action that the actors did not shirk, does there always stand an unavoidable logic leading to it? Here is where the dispute begins. Here, too, is where Goldhagen's book is properly controversial. And from time to time it must also be asked: Where does his penetrating impulse bring our knowledge forward, and where does he lead us astray? Consider just two examples.

The Germans: One must agree with Goldhagen that the perpetrators were more like their contemporaries than they (and we) would like. That is the disturbing insight. But Josef Joffe has correctly formulated the problem of retrograde perspective. That the murderers were ordinary Germans cannot mean that (all) ordinary Germans were murderers or that they would have become killers under corresponding circumstances. Goldhagen emphatically rejects any assertion of collective guilt. But it is not just his equivocally alternating use of language ("the Germans," "these Germans"—all in all, his frequent resort to the collective designation "the Germans") that makes it evident that he is imputing a collective disposition. He sees this collective disposition grounded in a general anti-Semitism aiming at the extermination of the Jews, for which the Nazis merely had to open up the sluice gates: Hitler as willing executioner.

Whoever lays Goldhagen's book aside will hardly—if he did not already know better—be able to rest satisfied with some notion of a vague "salon anti-Semitism": widespread, thoughtlessly uttered, but ultimately harmless. The testimony to an animosity toward Jews as it shifted from the religious to the racial is shocking—obscene and immoral even in the absence of concrete practical consequences. Not even clergymen who later joined the resistance had the power to resist it from the start. In 1933 the Protestants could barely bring themselves to put in even a mild word on behalf of baptized Jews, as if this were a question of anyone's particular denomination and not of sheer existence. Even if the potential for evil deeds was not fully charged, the potential for resistance was depleted before it was needed.

But Goldhagen flatly refuses to undertake a comparative analysis of German animosity toward Jews in relation to anti-Semitism everywhere else in Europe. His epistemological circular reasoning is truly peculiar. He is only interested in the German variety, for ultimately the Holocaust emerged only from Germany. But asking about the general along with the particular has nothing to do with relativizing trivialization. Goldhagen's very assertion of a collective disposition can be advanced only if it lends itself to demonstration by comparison.

This brings us back to the heart not only of the historical but also of the moral discussion. If both extremes are wrong—the assertion of a collective guilt (rejected by Goldhagen) as well as the retreat to the personal guilt of a few individuals cut loose from all others (contested by Goldhagen)—the question still remains about the relationship of the socially embedded individual to his political and mental environment. Why should Abel care about Cain, or Cain for Abel? Goldhagen, wounded and wounding, has kicked off this dispute anew—because, and in spite, of his look back in anger.

Originally published in *Die Zeit* on September 6, 1996

TWENTY-FIVE

KILLING FOR DESIRE

Interview with Klaus Theweleit
by Mechtild Blum and Wolfgang Storz

[*Hitler's Willing Executioners* is not the first book on the Holocaust by a long shot, and it is far and away not the best. With this book Daniel Jonah Goldhagen, prize-winning Harvard sociology professor [*sic*], has attracted unusual attention in a way that puts a new focus on the relationship between the concept of democracy and the propensity to violence in Germany. Mechtild Blum and Wolfgang Storz talked about this with Freiburg author Klaus Theweleit.]

BLUM AND STORZ: A widespread discussion on Goldhagen's book, the Holocaust memorial planned for Berlin, a heated debate on the role of the *Wehrmacht*. Fifty years after the fact, has not the National Socialist era been treated only too well?

THEWELEIT: Yes and no. There is a small group of Germans who have been dealing with the topic for years. And there is a majority who are only familiar with the raw data but who have never gotten involved with it all, never asked what this has to do with me and my parents. Therefore, every new book is more good than bad, more useful than useless.

BLUM AND STORZ: In spite of Götz Aly, in spite of Raul Hilberg, why are there such vehement debates around Goldhagen of all people?

THEWELEIT: It can't be just because of the book's content. Goldhagen's thesis—a majority of Germans knew about the Holocaust; many participated in it without compulsion and out of desire—has been said by others. But it's true. This still arouses feelings. What is more, the book is restricted to hammering home a single thesis. These are good prerequisites for a debate. But to me what seems decisive is a forebearance that Goldhagen offers the Germans. He does not describe how "eliminationist anti-Semitism" came about. How did the urge to kill get into bodies? Why did the normal German man become a willing killer? The most delicate question is the one he leaves out.

BLUM AND STORZ: But then why is he the one who is exciting so much attention, and not all the others who have said and described this years ago?

THEWELEIT: Maybe it took reunification and the ascent of a new right-wing radicalism for a broader liberal public to acknowledge that we Germans were not simply seduced and deceived. And they can take this step because Goldhagen is not demanding any more of them. He is not lining up against contemporary Germans. He has given contemporaries a clean bill of health; they are just as democratic as any American.

BLUM AND STORZ: But he has touched a sore spot.

THEWELEIT: Yes, and above all among German historians and some journalists like Augstein who had gotten used to saying repeatedly, "But it was not *all* the Germans"—which, of course, is true. Only it doesn't change the fact that there were a lot of them, and not just SS men.

BLUM AND STORZ: For you it's not the book, to which you attribute a rather limited view, that is decisive so much as the public's reaction?

THEWELEIT: Yes.

BLUM AND STORZ: Were you at all surprised by this understanding and goodwill on the part of the liberal public?

THEWELEIT: This is not something one can anticipate. It requires a clever publisher, and the media have to jump on board. It is difficult to foresee when they will do this. But since there does exist a certain knowledge about the Germans' massive participation in the killing, the topic is bound to find its rhythm.

BLUM AND STORZ: Then the fears that everything will be finally forgotten and suppressed fifty years after the facts are obsolete?

THEWELEIT: Yes and no. Big debates like this can be enlightening, but then they are also staged in order to finish off the topic in stages, as a disposal procedure. A debate that's really meant to have an impact can only begin at a place where there's no stopping at the individual, his stakes, his motives.

BLUM AND STORZ: Haven't we reached this point by now?

THEWELEIT: No, I don't think so. The defensive mantra that started in 1945—no collective guilt and a know-nothing attitude—continues to have an effect, in spite of Goldhagen, in spite of the *Wehrmacht* debate. The phrase "no collective guilt" was held out like a protective shield, above all in front of those who helped kill and then proceeded undisturbed to make careers for themselves in the Federal Republic. The few who attempted to enlighten a bit were denounced as Communists. Before 1970 we hardly noticed what the survivors of the concentration camps wrote. By then the many accomplices had long settled into the framework of the state bureaucracy, into businesses, schools, and associations. It's so crazy. It is what every politically open person knew and said at the end of the 1960s. Writers from R. D. Brinkmann to Heiner Müller, journalists like Erich Kuby wrote it. The liberal public didn't want to hear it.

BLUM AND STORZ: But today this liberal public reacts differently. It accepts it.

THEWELEIT: Some. The vast majority still do not want this kind of argumentation. That remains a taboo. That would get too close to the people. They would have to ask themselves: Who is a perpetrator? Do I know one? My uncle, my relatives? Those who are now in the forty-to-sixty-year-old range would then realize that this has something to do with them, and that a bit of this violence is still inside them, and they wouldn't like this.

BLUM AND STORZ: Fascist, National Socialist violence—is that "heritable"?

THEWELEIT: No. But fascism is not an ideology; rather, it's a way of dealing with reality violently. Everyone is susceptible, in accordance with the violence that has gone into him. For some bodies, violence is a necessity. Let me say this about that: As a rule, perpetrators "heal" themselves with their acts of violence. They begin "to live." Since Goldhagen isn't even interested in what goes on inside the perpetrators, but is only out to condemn them morally, to him the perpetrators are just others, the incomprehensible "Other."

BLUM AND STORZ: Does Goldhagen have a blind spot? What might he not have seen?

THEWELEIT: One need only look back twenty years at the ordinary Americans in Vietnam, or 200 years at the extermination by ordinary Americans of the American Indians, and at the exterminations by ordinary people of the last twenty years in all the corners of the world. There ordinary men exterminate without being anti-Semites, or particularly anti-Indian, or anti-Moslem. The German police battalions that Goldhagen portrays are exactly comparable to these murderers. But the debate doesn't want to go anywhere near that. Historians never wanted to go near it, possibly because they can't do it. They lack psychological awareness, the knowledge of the poets. Perception of everyday violence doesn't count among their "serious sources." Violence between men and women, violence against children, that drops out of the picture, and it's comfortable this way. Goldhagen, that Sonny Boy, provides assistance with all this. He's not the dark, evil Hagen approaching with his spear to stab the clean German Siegfried in the back. He comes from the front, open, sympathetic, a bit of Kennedy plus Günter Jauch, a good Hagen, in other words: a Goldhagen.

BLUM AND STORZ: Goldhagen doesn't have to do everything "for us."

THEWELEIT: Exactly. His work is something we should do. Young Jewish researchers in the United States struggle with the history of the Holocaust because they need that for their identity: They wouldn't even be there if things had proceeded according to "us."

BLUM AND STORZ: Is the democratic Federal Republic by and large just whitewash and not democratic deep down inside?

THEWELEIT: I wouldn't now want to say that it's just whitewash and that violence is lurking underneath. I can say something else. When I was in Yugoslavia at the beginning of the 1980s, in Zagreb, Belgrade, and Split, I saw very civilized people. Had somebody said this slaughter would begin in eight years, I would have said: "Nonsense, here is one of the most civilized regions in the world." Surface appearances can be deceptive.

BLUM AND STORZ: To be a convinced democrat and a racist at the same time, is that a contradiction?

THEWELEIT: No. Democracy isn't the idea that all people have an equal right to life. Democracy only expresses something about institutions of state. In some of them a majority decides. In this sense, we have nothing but good democrats. This doesn't touch upon how far we are prepared to demand equal liberty for all or to let others really live. This is revealed only in crisis situations.

BLUM AND STORZ: How strong is this force in Germany today?

THEWELEIT: If you take the year 1989, the increase in right-wing violence, which was initially tolerated; the dismantling of civil rights, from social welfare aid to kindergartens; the public backlash against feminism—this is all anything but reassuring, not to mention the *Bundeswehr*'s new eagerness for intervention. That speaks not for ample democratic reserves but, much more, for hierarchical thinking and feeling.

BLUM AND STORZ: How was it possible that Germany, in spite of the middle layer of Nazis who were represented in all the institutions even after the Hitler regime, could become as democratic as it is today?

THEWELEIT: Because of countervailing powers outside the institutions, beginning with the extraparliamentary opposition, followed by the ecological groups and the feminist groups. The "long march through the institutions" was a slogan formulated to express the fear that many felt of getting swallowed up by all the institutions of state that were felt to be Nazified at their core. Everywhere in the bureaucracy one encountered this old Nazi middle layer. These gentlemen knew only too well what kind of power they held in their hands, they knew exactly whom they didn't want to allow inside. This created a strong democratic potential among the younger people. And the many people who then went into the institutions after all—as teachers, doctors, psychologists, social workers, lawyers, or in the parties—also had an impact on their inner core. Those born between 1940 and 1960 are the least warlike generation of the last 200 years.

BLUM AND STORZ: Has this generation succeeded in taking what is least warlike and (if anything) comparatively democratic about them and transmitting it to their children, or has this already been broken off again?

THEWELEIT: One seldom passes something on directly to one's children. If that were the case, my generation with its many fascist parents would also have become genuinely fascist. It's also always possible for children to grow up in reaction against parental sympathies. Children in our generation were more likely to have gotten concealed messages, from relatively tolerant parents, in families where politics is discussed incidentally at most, where the main concerns are enjoyment and avoiding stress at work. I don't believe that a special impulse was present in our generation to teach children democracy. We thought they'd learn it all right.

BLUM AND STORZ: In closing, an impatient question: Are the Germans finally making progress in the effort toward a gradually ever more deeply rooted republican tradition?

THEWELEIT: Republican traditions could develop in France or England from their bourgeois revolutions. For us—no longer. Society is too unclear for that. It is disintegrating into enclaves in which individual decisions are made without anybody having something like the nation in view. In any event, nationalism just produces obedient thinking among camp followers. Consciousness about democratic traditions is something we have to take from somewhere else, that we must develop more in small-scale settings. It works, above all, in relationships between man and woman, in other pairs, between parents and children, in schools, at the workplace. Are fairness and equal rights demonstrated or not? Democratic behavior renounces violence in principle, and nonviolence can only be learned by living together at close quarters, or else not at all. So how are things going at school, in the family, in the firm? Are death threats made, or aren't they? When the message is: If you don't watch out, you'll get pushed under, you'll be laid off, you'll be punished. Institutions threaten their members when they don't follow the rules. They have the power to punish. Whoever's inside notices this. And whoever notices this and doesn't want to be killed will conform and will become more ready to pass on an even higher level of the violence to which he himself is subject. That is one of the mechanisms that can lead to a Holocaust.

BLUM AND STORZ: Since this mechanism is everyday and universal, could the Holocaust be repeated at any time and everywhere?

THEWELEIT: Not at any time and everywhere, but always somewhere. Acts of violence are subject to recall. When political power gets in a jam, when a power struggle begins, this usually leads to groups being excluded, to their being declared "subversive," like the Jews in Germany, until a majority seeks their redemption in the destruction of the others. The culpability is taken on by the institutions, whereas the perpetrators feel themselves not only relieved of responsibility but also empowered. The majority of those who go along with those in power take on the assignment and implement it, as can be seen in every single portrayal of all the acts of violence throughout the world, not under compulsion but out of desire. The laughter, born out of fear of one's own ruin, is the feeling accompanying all "willing executioners." Goldhagen's book offers more horrible material underpinning this perception.

Originally published in *Badische Zeitung* on October 15, 1996

"THE KILLERS WERE ORDINARY GERMANS, ERGO THE ORDINARY GERMANS WERE KILLERS": THE LOGIC, THE LANGUAGE, AND THE MEANING OF A BOOK THAT CONQUERED GERMANY

Josef Joffe

W hen the translation of Daniel Goldhagen's *Hitler's Willing Executioners* hit the German market in late August, it was the publishing equivalent of *Independence Day*. Within days, the first batch had sold out; within the next few weeks, more than 130,000 copies of *Hitlers willige Vollstrecker* would be shipped to the bookstores. When the author appeared in Germany in September, the promotion tour turned into a "triumphal procession," as the weekly *Die Zeit* called it. And so it was: from Hamburg to Berlin, from there to Frankfurt, and then to Munich—with a small army of reporters and cameramen clinging to Goldhagen, begging for yet another interview, coaxing him into yet another talk show.

For ten days it was virtually impossible to open a newspaper or switch on a TV set without confronting a flattering image of the youngish Harvard political scientist ("he looks like Tom Hanks"). Essentially, he had told the Germans in 600 pages (700 in translation): The Shoah could only have happened in Germany because you—in your Third Reich incarnation—were the way you were. You did it because you alone among the nations were driven by an "eliminationist anti-Semitism" that turned annihilationist when the time was ripe.

One might have thought that the cruel message would have been enough to turn the heirs of Hitler off and drive them into a boycott, either sullen or aggressive, or at least that their eyes would glaze over because of sheer overexposure as the procession wound its way through Germany. One would have been wrong on both counts. The first public panel discussion in Hamburg attracted 600 onlookers; the last one, in Munich, forced the organizers to switch from a medium-sized theater to a symphony hall with 2,500 seats because tickets ($10 apiece) had been sold out within a couple of days.

Nor does the puzzle end here. When the book was first published in the United States in the spring of 1996, the reaction of professional historians and pundits was so hostile that it was almost bizarre. On this contrast between the experts' militant call to arms in the spring and the public's enthusiastic response in the fall hangs an extraordinary tale entitled "Goldhagen and the Germans."

Hitler's Willing Executioners is an original, indeed brilliant, contribution to the mountain of literature on the Holocaust produced over the last fifty years. Its key merit is a shift of focus. Whereas much of the previous writing concentrated on the victims or on the machinery of destruction, Goldhagen cast his searchlight on the perpetrators; not on the "desk perpetrators" like Eichmann and Himmler but on the "ordinary Germans" of the subtitle. These were not elite SS men but simple, lower-middle-class folks—the members of the *Ordnungspolizei* who moved in behind the *Wehrmacht,* rounding up and slaughtering Jews with perverted gusto. These were the guards of the death marches who went on murdering their prisoners even though the war was already lost, even though Himmler, hoping to mollify the Allies, had ordered a stop to the slaughter.

These case studies chill the blood. Why would ordinary people kill with glee, especially, as Goldhagen argues persuasively, when they did not have to? Why did they *continue* to kill even after Himmler told them to stop in early 1945? The case studies deepen the mystery. Our standard view of the Holocaust is that of a literally dehumanized murder machine—much like a modern car-assembly plant—where a handful of inspectors and troubleshooters supervised an army of robots that precision-slaughtered full-time, twenty-four hours a day. We think of an industry of death, ordered by Hitler, designed by Himmler, and executed by Eichmann with the help of a conspiratorial band of SS fanatics—and far away from their own people, in occupied eastern Europe.

It was not so, counters Goldhagen. Up to half a million Germans may have been involved—in the main, apparently normal people like you and me. How could they turn into willing executioners? How could they torture and humiliate their Jewish victims although refusal would have cost them little or nothing? This is the mystery Goldhagen sets out to solve. His answer, in so many words: Because they were *Germans,* because German culture was shot through with a peculiar "eliminationist" variant of anti-Semitism that imbued "ordinary Germans" with the conviction that mass murder was right and just. Without that almost universal connivance, the Holocaust could not have happened.

We have to reach back to Claude Lanzmann's nine-hour opus *Shoah* for a similar verdict. There, too, we are confronted with "ordinary Germans"— petty officials, train engineers, policemen—who manned and maintained the machinery of death. But the evidence is visual and cinematographic, whereas Goldhagen's is systematic and rigorous, complete with almost 200 pages of notes. As such, *Hitler's Willing Executioners* has already changed the terms of our understanding. And as the furious debate around the world shows, future research will hardly be able to ignore Goldhagen's findings and conclusions.

The German critics did not wait for the German edition. Hardly had the book come out in the United States when almost the entire pack had pounced on *Hitler's Willing Executioners* as if swept up in a feeding frenzy. First of all, the assailants did not argue ad rem, that is, against the theory and the facts. Instead the attack was relentlessly ad hominem, charging the author with malign intentions or insinuating that his biography (as a son of a survivor) had led him to indict German culture as a whole. Another line was to pan the book as unoriginal, sensationalist, and worthless. A third was to depict it, though most obliquely, as an American-Jewish plot against present-day Germany, as an attempt to recycle past guilt in order to stigmatize the Germans forever.

Take the youngish German historian Norbert Frei. Born in 1955, he launched his attack with a slick put down: "Whoever wants to find an audience in the tough, competitive media market of the 1990s needs a thesis with a bang." As we read on, we learn that the "historical-empirical yield" of the book is meager, that a big chunk of it is based on "secondary literature," that it holds "little new" for those in the know. The message to the public is simple: Worthless, sensationalist dribble by a young Harvard punk out to make a name for himself. In short: *Don't read!*

Or take his elder, Eberhard Jäckel, born in 1929. A doyen of Holocaust research in Germany, Jäckel went ballistic. This dissertation was "bad" and a "failure"; it did not measure up "even to mediocre standards"; it was "riddled with errors"; it was "simply bad"; it represented a "relapse to the most primitive of all stereotypes." Though frequently invited, Jäckel refused to take part in any of the public panel discussions. The book was "*unter Niveau*" [not up to standards], he declared during the conference of the Association of German Historians in Munich in September 1996, and hence not worthy of debate. (The conference, at which the German historical profession assembles, did not put the Goldhagen book on its official program, but in response to carping in the press a special panel was hastily arranged.)

Jäckel's colleague Hans Mommsen panned the book as falling short of "the current state of research" in Holocaust studies. Johannes Heil, an associate of the Berlin Center for Research on Anti-Semitism, thought that Goldhagen's theories were "naive" and "not worth debating." The politico and columnist Peter Glotz inveighed against "artificial debates." Rudolf Augstein, the publisher of *Der Spiegel*, huffed: "pure nonsense."

Perhaps this response was sheer resentment on the part of those who have labored hard in the field of Third Reich research for decades without producing a worldwide best-seller. But one may surmise that deeper forces than professional vanity were at work. "Don't read" was the basic point, and this set a key pattern; preemptive censorship worthy of a Vatican cardinal in charge of the Index. Secular historians, of course, do not stamp each other's books with a big, fat *"verboten."* They just call them "unoriginal" or "banal." Reviewing the reviews, the German historian Hans-Ulrich Wehler noted: "With dismaying rapidity, and with a spectacular self-confidence that has frequently masked an ignorance of the facts, a counterconsensus [*Abwehrkonsens*] has emerged."

To be sure, the book is vulnerable on a number of fronts.[1] How does one indict an entire culture? How does one prove that "eliminationist anti-Semitism" is the master variable that explains most of the variance, as social scientists put it? What about a legion of other variables—the unique role of Hitler, the overwhelming impact of Nazi totalitarianism, and so on—that others have used to construct multicausal models?

Goldhagen has argued beyond the bounds of simple logic. Reaching back to Martin Luther and his murderous tirades against the Jews, Goldhagen then moves forward again, laying out a profoundly anti-Semitic German culture and royal road to the explanation of the Holocaust. As he travels across the centuries, he reduces a myriad of germane explanations to One Big One that falls flat even when examined by an intelligent layman. If German culture was indeed the all-powerful, all-pervasive force that turned perfectly "ordinary Germans" into monsters, where is it today? One might think that so potent and enduring a factor would not just vanish from the face of the German earth, yet disappear it did after 1945, and for an elementary reason.

The *political system* had changed. Imposed under the loaded guns of the victors, liberal democracy sank miraculously strong roots in West Germany. Today Germany is a most ordinary member in the community of nations, with only a tiny right-wing party and with probably less racism than France. If culture can be so molded by changing conditions, anti-Semitism could not possibly serve as the massive, overweening explanation for the Holocaust that Goldhagen would like it to be. If Truman and Jefferson could prevail in Germany after 1945, there must be more to German history than Luther's poisonous seed, and certainly less: neither eternal destiny nor damnation.

How can something ("culture") be a master cause if it is so quickly over-whelmed by other factors? If variables *A, B,* and *C* trump *X,* then *X* is either a weak variable that explains little or itself a dependent variable that calls for explanation. Goldhagen's premise crumbles even more when a bit of com-parative history is applied. Polish and Russian anti-Semitism, let alone its Austrian variant, were as "eliminationist" as the German. Britain, a hotbed of murderous pogroms in the Middle Ages, was *judenrein* for 400 years, and so was Spain following the expulsion of the Jews decreed in 1492. Yet the Holocaust was strictly "Made in Germany," and hence other, weightier fac-tors must have been at work.

Goldhagen has also fallen into the oldest social science trap of them all: the confusion of different levels of analysis. Exhibit A is the story of the *Ordnungspolizei,* which moved in behind the *Wehrmacht* as it swept east-ward. These were not SS beasts but a faithful microcosm of German society as a whole (which Goldhagen buttresses with impressive statistics). And yet they killed with sadistic abandon, overfilling their "quotas," even bringing in their vacationing wives to watch the butchery.

But what do these harrowing accounts prove? The Talmud had already, many centuries ago, warned that "for example is not evidence," and the level of the analysis problem cautions that we cannot conclude from one level (the individual) to another (the group), and from neither to the third (the culture)—or vice versa. Expressed formally: Behaviorally, the properties of a set are not identical with the properties of its members. You cannot conclude from "the killers were ordinary Germans" that "ordinary Germans were killers."

Driven by prosecutorial passion, Goldhagen ignores the fact that one cannot reason backward from the behavior of a sample to the culture as a whole, even if the sample's social traits match those of the rest. The oldest saw of sociology since Gustave Le Bon is that groups obey their own rules. Groups in extreme conditions act in extreme manners. Soldiers kill willingly, but that does not prove that their class or their nation is inherently murder-ous. As to the *Ordnungspolizei,* what about the Nazi system in which these "willing executioners" operated? What about the system of indoctrination and training, the Satanic setting, bereft of all civilizing restraints and counteracting values? Or take Bonnie and Clyde. They were killers. Does this mean that their families, closely related by genetics and socialization, were born killers too?

The theoretical part of the argument not only confuses levels of analysis, but it also rests on a grand, circular argument. In his historical analysis of German culture, Goldhagen argues forward from national disposition to group behavior. In so many words, he claims that only because of their anti-Semitism did ordinary Germans turn into mass murderers. Culture, to paraphrase Freud, was destiny. But then he reasons backward again, arguing that the behavior of the *Ordnungspolizei* proves that the culture as a whole was beholden to "eliminationist anti-Semitism." Culture and group thus function as both independent and dependent variables—which is precisely the definition of a circular argument.

If German reviewers had attacked the faulty logic, the overblown conclusions, and the haughty tone of the book, the German story would have been no different from the U.S., British, or Israeli one. Yet the main battle cries were "shoddy," "second-rate," "hype," "old-hat"—in other words: "Don't read!" This led the American political scientist Andrei Markovits to conclude: "When there is something that one does not want to hear, one can always block it out by disputing its value and originality."

What is it that the pundits and professionals did not want to hear? That requires a circuitous answer. In general, postwar (West) Germans have dealt admirably with what they call *Vergangenheitsbewältigung* [coming to terms with the past]—certainly in contrast to Austrians, Japanese, or citizens of the defunct German Democratic Republic. The Japanese have not even begun to search their collective soul; apologies to East Asian neighbors usually refer to the "unfortunate incidents" of World War II. The Austrians took the easiest way out by labeling themselves the "first victims of fascism," conveniently forgetting that they had greeted the *Anschluß* with jubilant applause. The East Germans used a Communist variant of the Austrian strategy: Hitler and his gang were the "bad Germans" who had somehow captured the nation like so many hijackers from outer space. Yet the "Worker and Peasant State" was clean by definition, having vanquished bourgeois capitalism, the source of all evil, and having dedicated itself to ever-vigilant "antifascism."

None of this could be said about the West Germans. Generally, Nazi criminals were hunted down and put on trial. Guilt was accepted, and billions were paid in restitution to survivors and heirs. Anti-Semitism and neo-

Nazi parties were diligently combated. Whereas the GDR slavishly followed Moscow's "anti-Zionist" line, the Federal Republic helped Israel with arms, money, and diplomatic support.

Nevertheless, there is a "but." Subtly, indeed subconsciously, the "Barabas syndrome" of Marlowe's *Jew of Malta* took hold of the official vocabulary: "But that was in another country." And so the crimes had been committed not by Germans but "in the German name," by *them,* by "Hitler and his henchmen." The psychological mechanism was not one of transparent repression or projection, as in the Austrian or German case. The function of these shibboleths was to *sterilize* the festering past, to put a reassuring distance between the murderers and the masses, between Germany then and Germany now.

Enter Goldhagen. The basic message of his case studies is simple, powerful, and frightening. They exploded the careful distinction between "bad Nazis" and "ordinary Germans" by proclaiming in graphic, gripping language: It wasn't so! The executioners were only too "willing," the book roars at today's Germans. And they were not only rigorously selected SS monsters but also your fathers and grandfathers.

This verdict thrust a twisting knife into the wound that was not supposed to ooze any more. Carefully circumscribed for decades, culpability was all of a sudden spread lavishly all over yesterday's Germany again. Little wonder that Frank Schirrmacher, coeditor of the respected conservative daily *Frankfurter Allgemeine Zeitung,* detected a rehash of the old "collective guilt thesis [at] the core of this book." The purpose of the project was to stigmatize Germany here and now, to "again [pin] the Germans," as he delicately puts it, "to a *Sonderweg* for the next century."[2] To top it all off, there was Rudolf Augstein, the Henry Luce of West Germany, who had founded *Der Spiegel* in his early twenties and then parlayed it into the most influential German magazine of the first postwar decades. Denouncing Goldhagen as "hangman in the garb of a sociologist," he declared the "results" of the book "close to zero," and complained bitterly that the "debate about the singularity of Auschwitz . . . cannot be rolled out anew every year" because that "has been settled." Goldhagen's indictment was driven "at best by ignorance, at worst by evil madness."

That was in April. Yet four months later Germany witnessed a "triumphal procession," as Goldhagen's book tour traveled from Hamburg to Berlin, from Frankfurt to Munich. Whatever barriers the self-appointed censors had tried to erect fell before the throngs who fought for tickets so they could hear for themselves. And lo, at least some of the contempt-mongers of the spring reappeared strangely transmogrified in the fall—as respectful, even deferential discussants, no doubt because they had to go up against audiences thoroughly sympathetic to Goldhagen. Take Norbert Frei, one of the most savage early critics. By September, as he faced Goldhagen on the third leg of the tour in Frankfurt, he was ready to extend a benign pat on the back. "The more removed the events in time the more urgent the questions [the author had posed] become." And Frank Schirrmacher, a member of the Munich panel, praised the book as a "watershed."

"Why does this book do this?" asked the moderator of the Berlin panel, "why are 600 people sitting here?" Did Goldhagen win them over with his cuddly looks ("I want to adopt him," enthused one Munich matron)? Was it his courteous demeanor on the podium ("I am happy to be here with such eminent scholars"), which contrasted so starkly with the strident tone of the book? Or his supple defense strategy that recalled Muhammad Ali's injunction to "float like a butterfly"? "Daniel-in-the-lion's-den," as the press liked to call him, would repeatedly yield on this or that point. But then he would come back jabbing, avowing that he had conceded nothing. The problem remained with his critics, who had simply misunderstood his message.

The simplest explanation of the Goldhagen phenomenon might be sheer curiosity, kept alive by relentless media attention. "Who is this young American Jew, and why is he saying this about our forebears?" was written all over the faces of the crowds. Jürgen Kocka of the Free University of Berlin offered another explanation: "Most historians have used more cautious language." That was the understatement of the entire spring-to-fall debate. In the modern literature on the Holocaust, authors have scrupulously stopped pointing at "the Germans." But here was Daniel Goldhagen, slicing through such comforting shibboleths as "Hitler and his henchmen," fingering "the Germans" again.

This new verdict, actually the old one of the late 1940s, was guaranteed to startle, prick, and provoke. Nor was Goldhagen's just yesterday's argument between two new covers. As Dan Diner, a German-Jewish scholar, wrote in the fall issue of the *Frankfurter Jüdische Nachrichten:* "He describes the cruelties of the perpetrators in all of their opulence." Michael Bodeman, a sociologist at the University of Toronto, went one worse in the Berlin *tageszeitung.* "This is pornography," he wrote, because the book, written from the perpetrator's perspective, drives home the "pleasure derived from murder and torture" in a "voyeuristic narration."

The Holocaust à la Goldhagen as Peeping Tom's paradise? The obscenity of this comparison would be hard to surpass. But there is no denying the perverse allure of the book and its author as the caravan wound its way through Germany. Was it the discussions themselves that kept interest at a high pitch? Hardly. The critics were polite, and so was Goldhagen. The debates quickly turned into a stylized routine, much like a minuet where the dancers move up, bow, and turn—and there was a preponderance of historians on the panels. The audiences soon became lost in the fog of academic disputation: "But on page 271, you said . . ." "Yes, but I also wrote . . ." or "This is simply a mistranslation . . ."

Let us try another solution to the puzzle of Germany's "willing listeners." *Hitler's Willing Executioners* dramatized an old insight that first emerged during the German airing of the *Holocaust* TV series in 1978. Put names and faces on the victims, bring the abstract horror of millionfold annihilation down to the flesh-and-blood level of the Weiss family, an emotional impact, a momentary catharsis even is unleashed, that libraries full of learned treatises have not triggered and cannot generate. So it was with the "willing executioners." They, too, had names and faces. These were "ordinary" monsters, who had blotted out images of their own kids back home as they led Jewish children off to the killing pits. People like you and me, perhaps?

And then there is the moralizing voice of the treatise, a literary device that does not normally grace political science dissertations. Listen to Goldhagen as he interrupts his blood-curdling account with questions such as this one: "How could any person have looked upon these pitiable, sick Jewish women without feeling sympathy for them, without feeling horror at the abject physical condition into which they had been plunged?"

This approach, though buttressed by 200 pages of notes, was light-years removed from those thousands of scholarly disquisitions safely ensconced on hundreds of library shelves. Goldhagen's was a stark and enthralling narrative, much like the morality tales about heinous queens, wolves, and witches so beloved by children. Why? Because in the end, trembling and terror are but stepping stones to a morally comprehensible universe. This is the evil that was done, this is who did it; here is why they did it and how they felt. Christopher Browning covered pretty much the same ground with his *Ordinary Men*, a pathbreaking analysis of the police battalions.[3] But his is an academic treatise—minus the moral voice, or more precisely, with the implicit message that "*anybody* could have done it" that leaves the moral puzzle uncracked and the reader as helpless as before.

Only the element of redemption was missing from Goldhagen's story: the punishment of the guilty and the deliverance of the innocents. Or was there redemption after all?

Perhaps there is a three-generational model at work. The grandparents came back from the war and hid behind self-imposed silence. The parents, teenagers at the end of the war, made an unconscious reckoning for themselves along these lines, perhaps: "We were too young to be culpable, but we certainly paid the bill in the coinage of destruction and stigmatization; the accounts are squared and closed." Or they subsumed the crimes of their nation under the sterilizing rubric "in the German name."

Finally there are those younger than forty. They did not hear the story from their parents and grandparents. If they asked, they were not told. Enter Goldhagen. Now they could at least discover for themselves the evil their elders inflicted on the world. With book in hand, they could unearth the repressed knowledge that is the first step toward liberation and even redemption. And this is why they eagerly listened to the harrowing narrative that is Goldhagen's most original and powerful answer to the enduring mystery of the Holocaust, which Elie Wiesel calls "unexplained" and "inexplicable."

But the best explanation of the "Goldhagen phenomenon," one must surmise, is the factor of moral and emotional distance that separates today's Germans from the darkest of all pasts. In the year 51 A.H. (After Hitler), the stigma no longer oozes blood; the unbearable horror was perpetrated almost two generations ago. The clouds of history have settled over Auschwitz and the killing fields of Ponar, and so latter-day Germans need not fear what awaits them if the fog is pierced. It was not they who did it. It was not they who herded the Jews of Białystok into the synagogue, as Goldhagen recounts in unsparing detail—who poured the gasoline and then hurled the incendiary grenades inside.

The ordinary monsters that younger Germans may find in Goldhagen's mirror did their killing "in another country." As Barabas tells Friar Barnadine, "and beside, the wench is dead." Two generations are not enough to deaden the soul, but they are enough to numb the pain and the guilt. Also, in response to his critics, Goldhagen reiterated over and over again that his indictment of German culture did not extend to the postwar period, when a model democracy rose on tainted soil. And so it was safe to relive the dread and the terror, and that is why the Germans of 1996 yielded willingly to curiosity and fascination.

Is the anti-Semitic monster truly dead? One of the critics who was not cowed by the sympathetic reaction of the lay audience was eighty-seven-year-old Marion Countess Dönhoff, the copublisher of *Die Zeit* [see Chapter 23 in this volume]. Like the critics of the spring, she once more accused Goldhagen of having used "questionable methods to advance . . . a theory he cannot prove." And then came the clincher. Would this not "revive an anti-Semitism that had more or less died down"?

That question can be read either way: as a projection of resentment ("anti-Semitism is caused by Jews") that would make Uncle Sigmund's day, or as an honest diagnosis. Why blame the messenger, why worry about lying dogs unless they are alive and ready to bare their fangs at the drop of a book? Reassuringly, the response of the audience has proven the countess wrong. Goldhagen has come and gone, and the dogs have hardly opened an eye.

Originally published in *The New York Review of Books* on November 28, 1996

NOTES

1. The three best critical reviews in the United States are by Clive James, "Blaming the Germans," *The New Yorker,* April 22, 1996; Omar Bartov, "Ordinary Monsters," *The New Republic,* April 29, 1996; and Robert Wistrich, "Helping Hitler," *Commentary,* July 1996.

2. Many historians have used the *Sonderweg* ("separate path of development") to denote a pathological German exceptionalism that led from the refusal of liberal democracy in the late nineteenth century into the totalitarian disaster of the twentieth.

3. Christopher R. Browning, *Ordinary Men: Reserve Police Battalion 101 and the Final Solution in Poland* (New York: HarperCollins, 1992).

TWENTY-SEVEN

THE JEWISH HANGING JUDGE? GOLDHAGEN AND THE "SELF-CONFIDENT NATION"

Wolfgang Wippermann

T he killing itself was a gruesome affair. After the walk through the woods, each of the Germans had to raise his gun to the back of the head, now face down on the ground, that had bobbed along beside him, pull the trigger, and watch the person, sometimes a little girl, twitch and then move no more. The Germans had to remain hardened to the crying of the victims, to the crying of women, to the whimpering of children. At such close range, the Germans often became spattered with human gore. In the words of one man, "the supplementary shot struck the skull with such force that the entire back of the skull was torn off and blood, bone splinters, and brain matter soiled the marksmen." Sergeant Anton Bentheim indicates that this was not an isolated episode, but rather the general condition: "The executioners were gruesomely soiled with blood, brain matter, and bone splinters. It stuck to their clothes."[1]

Absolutely clear: No German historian speaks and writes as graphically as Goldhagen! One can evaluate this positively or negatively. In either case, the problem is that when Goldhagen delivers his thick and empathetic account of the horrible acts of murder, he does not recoil from describing fictitious scenes in addition to real ones in order to arouse the desired emotional effect in the reader.[2] The graphic writing style as well as the mixture of fact and fiction could and perhaps should have been criticized, although this has hardly occurred.[3]

However, Goldhagen's critics have concentrated entirely on his central thesis. It can be quite concisely reproduced as follows: The members of the police battalions, with whom Goldhagen is primarily concerned, were "willing executioners" of Hitlerian anti-Semitism who murdered Jews with almost fanatical zeal. Thereby Goldhagen contradicts Christopher Browning, who took the position in his case study on Reserve Police Battalion 101 that these policemen were "ordinary men" who shot Jews reluctantly and more under pressure from their superior officers than of their own accord.[4] For Goldhagen, however, these policemen were "ordinary Germans" whose anti-Semitic outlook did not distinguish them from other Germans because the members of the police battalions came from all strata of the population and thereby constituted a representative sample.

This methodological procedure is something that Goldhagen has taken from public opinion and electoral survey research, where representative cross-sections (samples) of the population are asked for their opinion on all manner of things—from Helmut Kohl to certain chocolate bars. The fundamental question is whether one can proceed in just the same way when it comes to the Holocaust.[5] Add to this some problems in the critical use of sources. Goldhagen has relied, above all, on the interrogations of these policemen, which German judges and prosecuting attorneys conducted long after 1945 in order to prove criminal charges against them.[6] May one draw conclusions from these interviews concerning the policemen's views about Jews at the time, something that incidentally was of less interest to the lawyers?

As if this were not enough, after attempting to back up his central thesis empirically based on two additional—weaker—case studies in chapters on labor camps (exclusively for Jews) and the so-called death marches at the end of the war, Goldhagen went a step further and maintained that the Germans were anti-Semitically disposed not just during the Nazi period but well beforehand. Within German history and culture, there was a deeply rooted "eliminationist anti-Semitism."

Goldhagen attained this insight not through his own study and research but with the aid of an evaluation compiled from the available secondary literature. This is neither new nor unusual. Historians like Alex Bein, Hermann Greive, Jacob Katz, Herbert A. Strauss, and many others have likewise maintained, long before Goldhagen, that anti-Semitism in Germany stretches in an unbroken continuity, which is why a rather straight line led "from prejudice to destruction" (Jacob Katz).[7]

However, what Goldhagen does not mention is that this interpretation of anti-Semitism has been energetically contested by Werner Jochmann, Reinhard Rürup, Shulamit Volkov, and others because there have also been

phases of German history in which anti-Semitism did not become radical-
ized but weakened instead.[8] This applies to the *Vormärz,* when the proponents of Jewish emancipation were in the majority, and this also applies to
the final years of the *Kaiserreich,* when anti-Semitism certainly became a
"cultural code" (Shulamit Volkov) of bourgeois society but was hardly radi-
calized, as indicated by the dwindling influence of the anti-Semitic parties.
Goldhagen, however, hardly enters into this discussion,[9] something his critics also charged him with, although their professional criticism was insepara-
bly bound up with national indignation. More will be said about this later.

More interesting and more important, it seems to me, is another aspect
of the Goldhagen controversy that has previously been given very low priority. I have in mind the question of whether one can really concentrate on
anti-Semitism alone, the way Goldhagen does (but as other anti-Semitism
scholars also do). Concrete analysis, after all, shows that the German anti-
Semites were by no means merely anti-Semites; rather, they were also preju-
diced against Slavs, Sinti, Roma, and other non-European "races" at the
same time.[10] For Goldhagen, however, anti-Semitism appears to be something wholly special, having almost nothing to do with racism in general.[11]

In general this may be legitimate, but when it comes to the Third Reich
a one-sided concentration on anti-Semitism forces one into a corner. For
this regime was a "racial state" that aimed at "cleansing the body of the *Volk*"
of all "racially alien" and "inferior elements" inside and at establishing a hier-
archically ordered "racial empire" outside, where after murdering European
Jews the "elimination" of an additional 20 to 30 million members of Slavic
peoples was planned.[12] Goldhagen has almost completely filtered out the
racist plans and aspects of National Socialist racial policy and, above and beyond this, has relativized and even partly negated the fact that other groups
of victims besides the Jews were also murdered on equally racist grounds.[13] A
few concrete examples should serve to back up this grave accusation.

Although the researches of Ernst Klee, Hans-Walter Schmuhl, Henry
Friedlander, Michael Burleigh, and others prove unambiguously that the so-
called euthanasia action was the immediate predecessor and necessary precondition for the Holocaust,[14] Goldhagen dealt with this mass murder only
peripherally, and then it is only for the purpose of portraying the murder of
the infirm as less cruel than the Holocaust. This endeavor leads him to the
following truly misplaced remark: "Why did ordinary Germans not act as
modern hangmen do, who are required to administer death in a prescribed
quasi-clinical manner, swiftly, without torment, and with minimum pain—
indeed, in the manner in which the ordinary Germans who killed the mentally ill and others in the so-called Euthanasia Program made efforts to kill?"[15]

No, the murder of helpless persons in mobile gas chambers, which took up to thirty minutes, was just as little painless as was the practice (applied after the presumed halting of euthanasia) of starving infirm patients, including among them many small children, slowly and agonizingly.

The genocide against the Sinti and Roma, too, to which an estimated 500,000 fell victim, is something Goldhagen goes into at only two places in his book. And both of his remarks on the subject are wrong. This applies, in the first instance, to his incorrect assertion that Sinti and Roma, in contrast to the Jews, were not forced to work.[16] Furthermore, Goldhagen is on shaky ground in his supposition that, in contrast to the Holocaust, there was no "comprehensive plan" for the "systematic murder" of Sinti and Roma.[17] Heinrich Himmler, after all, had already publicly announced on December 8, 1938 (as it was worded) the "definitive solution of the Gypsy question . . . from the essence of this race."[18]

In light of the situation of Polish forced laborers in the Reich, who incidentally had already been required to wear a discriminating badge for one year before the Jews were—and in view of the policy toward Poles practiced by the *Generalgouvernement*—one can only see the following sentence of Goldhagen's as cynical: "Germans treated other peoples whom the Nazis and most Germans deemed to be inferior, even 'subhuman,' such as Poles, far differently and better than Jews."[19]

If Goldhagen had looked more closely into the sources and research on the *Generalplan Ost,* which he unfortunately did not do,[20] then he would also not have written the following: "The Slavs, seen as racially inferior, were considered fit to be beasts of burden. The threat that they posed to Germany was understood to be a social Darwinian competition for land and resources. The treatment that the Germans would accord to the Slavs was utilitarian."[21]

Goldhagen will not be spared the charge of having played down the fate of the so-called other victims of National Socialist racism because he wrongly proceeds from the assumption that National Socialists—or, if you will, "the Germans"—only pursued an anti-Semitic and not a racist policy. "The Germans" were "willing executioners" by no means just of Hitlerian anti-Semitism but of a global racist program. Seen this way, Goldhagen is not radical enough.

But as mentioned, this criticism was not at the heart of the Goldhagen controversy. Instead the overwhelming charge was that Goldhagen had offered a monocausal explanation for the multifaceted and complex phenomenon of the Holocaust by focusing completely on the ideology of the regime and the motives of the perpetrators.[22] However, this is a misunderstanding. Obviously Goldhagen is aware that the Holocaust would have been inconceivable without Hitler, the Nazi state, and World War II. He has also obviously taken note of the "historical context" and the "society" from which the perpetrators came. Nevertheless he insists that the "perpetrators" were responsible for their own deeds. In the foreword to the German edition he already writes: "This book shifts the focus of the investigation of the Holocaust away from impersonal institutions and abstract structures back to the actors, back to the human beings who committed the crimes and the populace from which these men and women came."[23]

This is his attack on a group of Holocaust researchers who have acquired a dominant influence in Germany, though things are different in countries like the United States and, especially, Israel. The best known of these "structuralists" (as they are usually known) is Hans Mommsen, who has certainly been the most prominent of Goldhagen's severe critics.[24] For Mommsen the Holocaust was more improvised than intended. It was not based on a "long-developed program" of Hitler or other leading National Socialists. Instead it was a matter of an "accomplished improvisation that in each case emerged from, and escalated, earlier planning stages."[25] Owing to the "administrative turf wars" typical of the "polycratic" Third Reich, it came to a "cumulative radicalization" in which each process that was "set in motion" developed "its very own dynamic." Mommsen accuses Goldhagen of overlooking the fact that "not only ideological motivations but also invented material and psychological predicaments were decisive."[26] For this reason, Goldhagen "plainly lags behind the current state of research." This is not a very convincing argument. After all, Mommsen's thesis (as previously indicated) remains controversial and is not identical with the "current state of research" as such. There are other historians besides Goldhagen who are of the opinion that the decisive "precondition for the Holocaust" was not any kind of anonymous "structure," but, rather, Hitler's anti-Semitism.[27] These historians are usually characterized as "intentionalists." And Goldhagen is in broad agreement with them when he makes the pointed statement "The genocide was the outgrowth not of Hitler's moods, not of local initiative, not of the impersonal hand of structural obstacles, but of Hitler's ideal to eliminate all Jewish power."[28]

But Goldhagen does not stop there. Hitler's anti-Semitic "ideal" was, namely, "widespread in Germany." It was out of the question that there was just a "minority of fanatical racist anti-Semites."[29] Not just the members of the "upper stratum,"[30] but also major sections of the middle class and even the working class were anti-Semitically inclined. For this reason alone the Holocaust was a German "national project," since most Germans were at least latent anti-Semites, which is why they could turn into "Hitler's willing executioners."

This is disputed both by structuralists and intentionalists. Specialized scholarship is also by no means unanimous on how high the percentage of convinced anti-Semites really was.[31] But this is not the defining issue for structuralists like Mommsen. What is decisive for him are the "political-bureaucratic mechanisms that allowed the idea of mass extermination to become reality." This would be "imaginable under other societal conditions as well."[32] Hence, the fact of the Holocaust shows how "thin" the "patina of civilization" can be.[33] The question of whether the Holocaust is a product of modernity or a specifically German project was also at the center of a panel discussion among Goldhagen, Mommsen, Jürgen Kocka, and myself on September 5, 1996, at the Berlin Jewish Community Center.[34] When Mommsen, here as earlier, repeated his oft-repeated remark that the perpetrators "mainly went about their business . . . without thinking about it,"[35] Goldhagen posed the rhetorical question "Is there anyone here . . . who agrees with Professor Mommsen that the people who were murdering Jews did not know what they were doing" and why they did it? The public indicated by its thunderous applause that on this question they were taking sides with Goldhagen and against Mommsen.

Here, too, I agree with Goldhagen. Structures do not kill people. It was undoubtedly Germans who murdered Jews out of anti-Semitic conviction. Hence the Holocaust was indeed a German project and not a product of modernity as such.

This makes it perfectly clear that the Goldhagen controversy is not simply a new installment of the *Historikerstreit*. After all, all the participants are miles away from the positions of Nolte and his followers, who incidentally have not yet spoken up. How does this fit together? Why is it, of all people, the social-liberal historians like Mommsen—who ten years ago was energetically resisting the "disposal of the German past" (Hans-Ulrich Wehler) emanating from the right—who are attacked so fiercely by Goldhagen? One explanation is that Goldhagen has attacked not just the "structuralists" among Holocaust researchers but "structural history" in general. This applies to his remark (cited above) that he is not concerned with "structures" but with individual perpetrators and the motivations behind their actions.[36] At another place in his book he brings this to a head with the pointed claim that he "reverses the Marxian dictum" and assumes "that consciousness determines being."[37] The German anti-Semites and murderers had (to recast another very well-known Marxian quote) made "their own history . . . as they please."[38]

With these words Goldhagen (whether deliberately or not remains an open question here) has turned against the basic maxims of "structural history," which has been described by one of its chief representatives, Hans-Ulrich Wehler, as follows:

> [Only] modern theories of economic growth, of social change, and of the social psychology of collective behavior have made it possible to analyze more precisely the developments in structural history that have prevailed over and above the heads of individuals but that are not perceived as structural processes in their horizon of experience and that consequently are not directly reflected in the sources. Only structural history in this sense makes it possible to concretize Marx's insight that while "men" certainly make "their own history," they "do not make it as they please, not under conditions they choose for themselves, but under conditions immediately found, given, and transmitted."[39]

It is therefore no accident that Wehler, too, has written a more than angry review of Goldhagen's book.[40] Here he takes the side of the critique made by the structuralists (mentioned earlier), according to which Goldhagen has not paid sufficient attention to the "complexity of historical situations" in general and to "cumulative radicalization" in particular. He therefore characterizes Goldhagen's attempt at explanation as "monocausal" because he has ignored another methodological element of modern structural history, namely, "comparison," which Goldhagen avoids "like the plague." That is why Goldhagen's book, like hardly any other, is at a great distance "from the virtues of the comparative method in history and the social sciences." As was already mentioned above, this is a very serious charge, for in place of historicism's *ban* on comparison structural history has postulated an *injunction* to compare.[41] In order to prove the thesis of German anti-Semitism's special radicalism, Goldhagen would have to have undertaken "comparative studies . . . across Europe."[42] In response to this charge, too, leveled by (among others) the Israeli historian and anti-Semitism expert Moshe Zimmermann,[43] Goldhagen has defiantly answered that he is only interested in the Holocaust, which came out of Germany and was carried out by Germans: "No Germans, no Holocaust."[44] Whether the other European nations were less or more anti-Semitically disposed is a completely different question contributing nothing toward an explanation of the Holocaust.[45] Both arguments are subject to dispute. But in my opinion, it is a different matter with Wehler's admonition that the Holocaust must also be viewed from a comparative perspective. With whom or what should we compare so singular a phenomenon as the Holocaust? Wehler mentions the "Turkish massacres of millions of Armenians," the "even more appalling decades of millionfold murder under the dictatorships of Lenin and Stalin" and the "near-extermination of the North American Indians."[46] Goldhagen has certainly gone into these and other comparisons, which (as everyone knows) were at the core of the *Historikerstreit* ten years ago, but he has rejected all of them uncompromisingly.[47] The "Germans' exterminationist drive against the Jews has no parallel, certainly not in the twentieth century."[48] This applies equally to the "geographic scope" and "unprecedented cruelty" as well as to the motivation and the perpetrators' goal of "total extermination."[49] All other "large-scale mass slaughters occurred in the context of some preexisting realistic conflict (territorial, class, ethnic, or religious),"[50] a description that did not fit the Holocaust.

I need not emphasize here yet once more that I regard this singularity thesis as correct—just as I do Goldhagen's uncompromising rejection of the totalitarianism model, which he regards as "wrong in the most fundamental of ways"[51] since it assumes the comparability of the Holocaust. Yet previously I had always seen myself as agreeing with Wehler and other critics of Nolte on this point.[52] Why is this not—or no longer—so?

The answer is baffling. After all, Wehler has turned vehemently against Goldhagen's (supposed!) condemnation of German "national character"[53] and accused him of advocating the "doctrine of collective guilt," which according to Wehler is nothing more than "racism in reverse": "For the 'chosen people,' who were to be obliterated, read 'the Germans' qua degenerate incarnation of evil."[54] With all due respect: Wehler must really know that the collective guilt thesis was at most advocated by journalists, never by serious-minded foreign scholars.[55] It actually exists only in the imagination of conservative German historians like Gerhard Ritter, who (following the pattern "Stop the thief!") wanted to divert attention from their own guilt and responsibility.[56]

The so-called Stuttgart Confession of Guilt of October 1945, always mentioned in this context by others (though not by Wehler), was no simple confession of the Germans' collective guilt—if only because it was issued by representatives of the Lutheran church for the behavior of Lutheran Christians in the Third Reich, who in the very next breath were said to have "struggled over many years in the name of Jesus Christ against the spirit that found its terrible expression in the brutal National Socialist regime."[57] Even the reflections that Karl Jaspers presented as early as 1946 in his "classic" book on the "question of guilt" hardly proceeded from the assumption of a "collective guilt" for all Germans.[58]

The collective guilt thesis is simply a phantom. Nobody, not even Goldhagen, defends it.[59] Goldhagen's book hardly assumes the existence of an unchanged and immutable aggressive German "national character." Instead he has merely asserted that the Holocaust should be viewed as a "national project" of the Germans since it was executed just once, in Germany by Germans who knew they could count on the approval (or at least the silence) of the overwhelming majority of the people, in whom an "eliminationist anti-Semitism" had become deeply rooted and widespread.

Even if all this were to prove wrong, which in my opinion it is not, would this really be so bad? Was it really necessary to break out into nationalistic cries of horror, as almost all German reviewers did initially?[60] One could almost get the impression that the Daniel Goldhagen whom Rudolf Augstein had promoted to "hanging judge" wanted to hack off every finger of each and every one of the reviewers.[61]

This made the defensive strategies turn all the more hectic and ill-considered. So, for example, reference was made repeatedly and vigorously to the "German-Jewish symbiosis,"[62] whose existence, however, is more than dubious.[63] But even if such a harmonious coexistence of Germans and Jews (or of Jewish Germans and Christian Germans) ever existed, does this make the Holocaust more comprehensible or even bearable?

Just as counterproductive were the repeated references to the German resistance.[64] After all, the German resistance *against* Hitler was, at best, only *indirectly* a resistance *for* the Jews. Moreover some participants in the working class and (especially) in the bourgeois-military resistance, as well in the *Kirchenkampf,* had shown a certain (time-bound, though nonetheless hardly acceptable) sympathy for certain anti-Semitic measures of the National Socialist regime, to which Goldhagen has mercilessly drawn attention.[65] But even if the behavior of the German resistance regarding the so-called Jewish Question manufactured by the National Socialists had been different, this would still not constitute an "alibi for Auschwitz."[66]

Totally problematic were those attempts to juxtapose National Socialist crimes against (West) German achievements in "mastering the past."[67] As though one could use mastery of the past to bring the Jews who were murdered back to life! Jost Nolte's lamentations—about the poor Germans in front of whom "a certain type of past keeps looming," which is why they will apparently never "be released from Sisyphus's fate" and are constantly pushed "back into damnation" by the "pamphleteer" Goldhagen—not only have an unintended comic effect but are downright dishonest. This German self-pity is, after all, coupled with sharp attacks on Goldhagen's "speculations about the murderous German soul." Furthermore, Goldhagen's thesis about German collective guilt—indeed, its "original sin"—is "racist." He himself is filled with a "rage of Old Testament breath."[68]

Jost Nolte, whom we have to thank for these wonderful howlers, hit upon a tone that was also struck in many other reviews and public state-ments. We were constantly reminded that this anti-German "interpreter of German guilt" was, after all, a Jew himself.[69] Thus Peter Glotz began his—"naturally" negative—review with the sentence "The author . . . son of a Jewish historian from Rumania. . . ."[70] And at the outset of the review in *die tageszeitung,* incidentally written by a film critic, it says: "The father of the author, Erich Goldhagen, survived the Jewish ghetto in the Rumanian city of Czernowitz and lost most of his family in the Holocaust."[71]

Following this seemingly neutral observation, it was often alleged that Goldhagen (to the applause of "Jewish columnists"[72]) had wanted to quench his "need for Old Testament vengeance" against the Germans because they had persecuted his father.[73] No less nonsensical was the suspicion of *die tageszeitung* film critic mentioned earlier, Mariam Niroumand, that the "Jew Goldhagen's" allusion to the Holocaust serves American Jews "as a useful protective shield against black activist Louis Farrakhan's anti-Semitic rhetoric of insinuation."[74]

In this context Jörg von Uthmann went a step further by engaging in the following almost fantastic speculation about why "Jewish organizations," especially in the United States, must always recall "the gas chambers and concentration camps" over and over again:

> They [the Jewish organizations in the United States—W. W.] thereby pursue a dual goal: On the one hand, the ritual commemoration is supposed to make the government in Washington aware that Israel would be threatened by a second Holocaust if the United States should withdraw its protective hand. On the other hand, it is supposed to commit American Jews, a majority of whom are marrying Christian partners and are on their merry way to assimilating into the main-stream, to a common reference point—if not in the present, then at least in the past.[75]

However, it was not speculation about the emotional state of American Jews that occupied center stage but, rather, the constant references to the collective guilt thesis that Goldhagen was said to be warming up again in order to force the Germans into "self-incriminating rhetoric that has de-cayed into a gesture of self-flagellation."[76] The "hanging judge" Goldhagen, as Rudolf Augstein believed he must be called,[77] was instantly included in the ranks of the "evil Jews" stretching from Ahasver the "eternal Jew"[78] through the notoriously avaricious and usurious "Jud Süß"[79] to the "Jewish avenging angel" Henry Morgenthau.[80] Although Goldhagen was not actu-ally compared to Morgenthau, *Der Spiegel* editor Fritjof Meyer did make a comparison with the otherwise completely unknown and totally uninfluential Jewish journalist Theodore Kaufmann,[81] who supposedly published a book in 1941 with the catchy title *Germany Must Perish,*[82] which Nazis from that time and later revisionists always cite as "proof" of their thesis that it was ultimately the "vengeance-thirsty" Jews who wanted to destroy the Germans and who had even "declared war" on Germany.[83] In this chain of argumentation the ancient anti-Semitic stereotype of the "vengeance-thirsty" Jew, who with "Old Testament severity" seeks retaliation, "an eye for an eye and a tooth for a tooth," gets mixed up with the new anti-Semitism—operating on the slogan "That business about the Holocaust, we'll hold it against the Jews"—that emerged following 1945 not in spite of but precisely because of the Holocaust.[84]

This mind-set received its unsurpassed expression by Jacob Heilbrunn in *Der Tagesspiegel* when he accused Goldhagen of playing "the prosecutor, the avenger of the past," who "puts on the Nuremberg trials a second time in order to punish the Germans finally for their deeds."[85] Andrei S. Markovits is right when he comments on these attacks against Goldhagen, motivated as much by nationalism as by anti-Semitism, as follows: "*Intellectual postmodernism meets old-fashioned anti-Semitism.*"[86]

These and other nationalistic—and (as is so frequent in Germany) also anti-Semitic—reactions to Goldhagen's book seem to indicate that the Germans have in fact become what some nationalistic ideologues want them to be: a "self-confident nation" that indignantly repudiates being "a nation of murderers."[87] To offer just a few examples: The far-right American historian Alfred de Zayas calmed the infuriated Germans in the *Frankfurter Allgemeine Zeitung* (FAZ) with the—demonstrably untrue—assertion that "the Germans" did not know all this because the Holocaust was ultimately kept secret.[88] Furthermore, the Germans could not have been anti-Semites for the simple reason that there were "many German Jews in Bismarck's circle," because there were "many mixed marriages," and finally because "many emigrants came back to Germany after the Second World War in spite of the Holocaust." The good man has really understood nothing and hardly read anything, and that alone makes it a scandal for him to accuse Goldhagen of "ignorance."

Not that much better are the German-national cries of horror into which FAZ editor Frank Schirrmacher erupted when he read Goldhagen's book.[89] Here, too (naturally), an accusatory reference is made to the collective guilt thesis that Goldhagen is said to present in ignorance of the "scholarly literature" (which one?) in a spirit of "chutzpah."[90] With Schirrmacher, to be sure, the "Jews in Bismarck's circle" do not make an appearance, so instead he chides Goldhagen for not mentioning "Mendelssohn and Heine" (as if Heine were the favorite poet of the *FAZ!*). Goldhagen's book is one big "countermanifesto against the civilizing efforts to which the Germans have subjected themselves since 1945." (Obviously, the editorials of the *FAZ* are what he has in mind.) It only leads "back into the Faustian depths of German consciousness" (what this entails I really cannot imagine) and amounts to a "remythologizing of the Holocaust" (what this is supposed to mean I also do not know). Schirrmacher is right on one point: Goldhagen's book— and, even more so, the reaction to it—does indeed raise provocative questions "about the intellectual condition of a society," though not because it "regards such theses as intellectual progress" but because it reacts so hysterically to these theses.

It was certainly no sign of "intellectual progress" (however conceived) in this country when Rudolf Augstein adopted the attitude of a nationalistic mastermind to finish off Goldhagen, while simultaneously emphasizing that these "lowly police battalions [were] not the elite of the nation" but, rather, the "dregs of people with families who could still be trapped into these battalions."[91]

Similarly piqued was the reaction of Peter Glotz (who is otherwise always presenting himself as the brains of the Social Democratic Party, SPD) to Goldhagen's supposed (!) assertion that the Germans were a "nation of killers."[92] He, too, initially obliges with the legend that so many knew so little, only to go on to voice his vehement objection against the thesis of the "German *Sonderweg*," which does not even concern Goldhagen (who is mistakenly awarded "David" as his first name). Genocide is not to be seen as a "German disease," and Goldhagen (who did not even assert this) is seen as someone instigating "trivialization using national psychology."

Almost as frequent as references to the supposedly positive epochs and traditions of German history were the denunciations of the faults and crimes "of the others." For example, Alfred de Zayas did not shy away from referring in this context to the internment of "Americans of Japanese origin" during World War II,[93] whereby he takes up an "argument" frequently employed in U.S. revisionist literature in order to relativize the singularity and brutality of the Holocaust.[94]

But as problematic as all of this was, the height of embarrassment was reached once more by our foreign minister Klaus Kinkel when he believed he also had to say something on the topic. He did this on (of all dates) May 8 and (at all places) before the American Jewish Committee in Washington. He concisely explained to his American and Jewish audience that there could be no such thing as German collective guilt because "guilt . . . is not collective and not inheritable."⁹⁵ There is nothing to object to here, and yet this dressing down of Goldhagen was completely unnecessary and incomprehensible.

By contrast, a very interesting discussion about the lamentations of the right concerning the collective guilt of the German "*Kulturnation*" (Friedrich Meinecke) was conducted in the left-wing paper *Junge Welt.* It began with an article by Uwe Soukop, who said that the FAZ certainly was in the right to criticize Goldhagen for not making "any kind of distinctions among the social, economic, and intellectual milieus within German society."⁹⁶ It would simply not be possible "to explain the emergence of National Socialism without considering the different class interests." For this reason, too, one could not and should not speak about "the Germans." When Soukop was severely attacked by other authors in *Junge Welt* for these remarks,⁹⁷ he defended himself and the Germans with a reference to the revolution of 1918, for if it had succeeded, none of what followed would have happened.⁹⁸ Who would want to contradict this kind of truistic argument—which, however, cannot explain the fact of the Holocaust?

In his review of Goldhagen's book, the Marburg political scientist Reinhard Kühnl simultaneously celebrated the entire "humanistic, democratic, socialist, and antifascist forces and traditions" of Germany because "struggles from Thomas Münzer, across the German Jacobins, through Luxemburg and Liebknecht, and all the way to the struggles of Buchenwald" are "our struggles" and "part of our political identity."⁹⁹ "We Germans" would "make ourselves spiritually defenseless" if "we" (who is we?) allowed ourselves to take all this. Who is up to something so wicked? "Naturally," Daniel Goldhagen, who takes the position of "*völkisch* nationalism" when he is said to make "the Germans" responsible for the Holocaust.

If not "the Germans," then who (one asks in astonishment) was supposed to be responsible? Kühnl's answer is baffling. It was "capitalism as the social system that produced fascism," which is why it was the "annihilation of the political opponents on the left" that stood in the "foreground" of the politics of fascism, which simply cannot "be reduced to an enterprise for the purpose of murdering Jews." For this "*Judenmord*," furthermore, different "social, political, institutional preconditions and interests" (Interests? Who had an interest in Auschwitz?) were decisive. Goldhagen, by contrast, was trying to explain the Holocaust "monocausally from anti-Semitism" and has thereby made himself guilty of a capital crime, namely to believe in the "power of ideas."

Kühnl, too, received a lot of criticism for these remarks in *Junge Welt.* Jürgen Elsässer put it in a nutshell by writing in his commentary: "The reference to the nation as the clincher of the annihilation program makes

Goldhagen more Marxist than Kühnl & Co.—and, in light of this nation's reascent, highly relevant."[100]

Elsässer is right. Just as did the *Historikerstreit,* the Goldhagen controversy has much more to do with the present than with the past. Only when the past is fully "mastered" can the Germans see themselves as a "self-confident nation" again. But for the moment it looked as though "the Germans"—who once again did not want to have been so—did not want to be prevented by this Jewish troublemaker and "hanging judge" from celebrating themselves "again" as a "self-confident nation." The neo-right ideologue and coeditor of the New Right cult book on the "self-confident nation," Heimo Schwilk, could assert with satisfaction on May 10, 1996, in *Junge Freiheit:* "This book promoted by *Die Zeit* is an attempt at ritually reminding the Germans of their failings at ever-shorter intervals. In this case it has not worked because the author has exaggerated. I do not know of a single article that has supported Goldhagen's racist thesis."[101]

However, Schwilk and the other New Right ideologues, who initially regarded it as beneath their dignity to take part in the Goldhagen controversy,[102] celebrated too soon. Although his book was almost unanimously damned, lock, stock, and barrel, Goldhagen encountered a lot of sympathy and approval during his lecture and discussion tour in September 1996. This may certainly be attributed in part to his very winning personal appearance and his skillful style of presentation, incidentally using English exclusively. But that cannot be all there was to it. I believe my spontaneous assessment on September 5, 1996, was correct, when I praised Goldhagen during a discussion in the Berlin Jewish Community Center because we had him to thank now that "the 'goat songs' [war hymns—Ed.] of the 'self-confident nation' were, at least temporarily, dying down."[103] I stand by this positive assessment and believe that Goldhagen's book should be praised, in spite of all the technical defects mentioned above, for the following reasons.

First of all, it sharply rejects all trivializing comparisons between the Third Reich and other regimes, especially the GDR (which is not even mentioned). This is one "controversy about contemporary history" where "Joachim Gauck was not asked for his opinion,"[104] just because the subject was the Third Reich and the Holocaust, which simply cannot be compared, set off against, or even (as happens more frequently in the Stasi [East German Secret Police—Ed.] debate) simply kept hushed up.

Second, Goldhagen should be praised because he has not gotten caught up in the now fashionable discourse on Germany's "tragic middle position," which has apparently baffled different conservative historians and journalists so much that they have not even bothered to speak up. .

Third, Goldhagen has not permitted any doubt that Germany alone was responsible for the outbreak of World War II, which escalated into an unprecedented "war of racial annihilation." He does not acknowledge with a single word the discussion on war guilt newly erupted among us.

Finally, Goldhagen has absolutely no time for the attempts of the New Right ideologues around Rainer Zitelmann as well as among some of the rather naive social historians to relativize the horrors of the Third Reich by reference to the supposedly "good aspects" of this regime, which is said to have promoted a "progressive social policy," or even have become a kind of "welfare state" in which "only minorities and marginal groups" were persecuted. Goldhagen truly does not want to "modernize" the Third Reich.[105]

On the whole, the Goldhagen controversy—which began exactly ten years after the outbreak of the *Historikerstreit* and quite obviously has by no means reached an end—shows that the struggle for cultural hegemony in the present by mastery of the past continues, even if at the beginning of 1996 it still appeared as though the equalizers, relativizers, and deniers had already won.[106] Goldhagen has written an important book at the right time.

Originally published as a chapter in the author's book *Wessen Schuld* (1997)

NOTES

1. Daniel Jonah Goldhagen, *Hitler's Willing Executioners: Ordinary Germans and the Holocaust* (New York, 1996), 218.

2. See for example, ibid., 216, where Goldhagen "describes" the murder of patients in a hospital, for which neither reports nor hearings are available, as follows: "In all probability, a killer either shot a baby in its mother's arms, and perhaps the mother for good measure, or, as was sometimes the habit during these years, held it at arm's length by the leg, shooting it with a pistol. Perhaps the mother looked on in horror."

3. Among the few exceptions: Gertrud Koch, "Eine Welt aus Wille und Vorstellung," *Frankfurter Rundschau,* April 30, 1996.

4. Christopher R. Browning, *Ordinary Men: Reserve Police Battalion 101 and the Final Solution in Poland* (New York, 1992). Goldhagen constantly polemicizes against Browning in a manner that is as tireless as it is off-putting.

5. For more about this method, see Ingrid Gilcher-Holtey, "The Mentality of the Perpetrators" [Chapter 12 in this volume]. Gilcher-Holtey speaks of a "habituation to modes of perception" through "historical analysis of socialization."

6. On the problems with critical use of sources arising from evaluating these interrogations, see Wolfgang Scheffler, "Wider historische Schwarzweißmalerei," *Die Mahnung,* October 1, 1996, pp. 3ff. I cannot go into this any further here.

7. Alex Bein, *Die Judenfrage: Biographie eines Weltproblems,* vols. 1, 2 (Stuttgart, 1980); Hermann Greive, *Geschichte des modernen Antisemitismus in Deutschland* (Darmstadt, 1983); Jacob Katz, *Vom Vorurteil zur Vernichtung: Der Antisemitismus 1700–1933* (Munich, 1989); Herbert A. Strauss and Norbert Kampe, eds., *Antisemitismus: Von der Judenfeindschaft zum Holocaust* (Bonn, 1984).

8. Werner Jochmann, *Gesellschaftskrise und Judenfeindschaft in Deutschland, 1870–1945* (Hamburg, 1988); Reinhard Rürup, *Emanzipation und Antisemitismus: Studien zur "Judenfrage" in der bürgerlichen Gesellschaft* (Göttingen, 1975); Shulamit Volkov, *Jüdisches Leben und Antisemitismus im 19. und 20. Jahrhundert* (Munich, 1991).

9. More on this in Wolfgang Wippermann, *Geschichte der deutschen Juden: Darstellung und Dokumente* (Berlin, 1994), 2ff.

10. More on this in Wolfgang Wippermann, *"Wie die Zigeuner": Antisemitismus und Antiziganismus im Vergleich* (Berlin, 1997).

11. For additional references, see Wolfgang Wippermann, "Was ist Rassismus? Ideologien, Theorien, Forschung," in *Historische Rassismusforschung: Ideologen— Täter—Opfer,* ed. Barbara Danckwortt, Thorsten Quert, and Claudia Schöningh, with an introduction by Wolfgang Wippermann (Hamburg, 1995).

12. For a comprehensive treatment, see Michael Burleigh and Wolfgang Wippermann, *The Racial State: Germany 1933–1945,* 2nd ed. (Cambridge, 1992).

13. This is criticized in the same way by Hans-Ulrich Wehler, "Like a Thorn in the Flesh" [Chapter 11 in this volume], and by Walter Manoschek, "Der Judenmord als Gemeinschaftsunternehmen," in *Ein Volk von Mördern? Die Dokumentation zur Goldhagen-Kontroverse um die Rolle der Deutschen im Holocaust,* ed. Julius Schoeps (Hamburg, 1996), 155–60.

14. Ernst Klee, *"Euthanasia" im NS-Staat: Die "Vernichtung lebensunwerten Lebens"* (Frankfurt am Main, 1983); Hans-Walter Schmuhl, *Rassenhygiene, Nationalsozialismus, Euthanasia: Von der Verhütung zur Vernichtung "lebensunwerten Lebens," 1980–1945* (Göttingen, 1987); Henry Friedlander, *The Origins of Nazi*

Genocide: From Euthanasia to the Final Solution (Chapel Hill, N.C., 1995); Michael Burleigh, *Death and Deliverance: Euthanasia in Germany 1900–1945* (Cambridge, 1994).

15. Thus from the essay in *Die Zeit*, August 2, 1996 [Chapter 16 in this volume]. The point is diluted in the book itself, where it says: "Those whom the Nazis marked for slaughter in the 'Euthanasia' program . . . , if conceived of as being 'life unworthy of living,' were nevertheless thought to be far less of a threat to Germany than were the Jews" (143). In another place: "Coldly uninvolved were the Germans who killed the mentally ill and the severely handicapped in the so-called Euthanasia program. Most of them were physicians and nurses who dispatched their victims in the dispassionate manner of surgeons, who excise from the body some hideous and hindering excrescence" (398).

16. Goldhagen, *Hitler's Willing Executioners*, 313. For a refutation of this insupportable statement, see Romani Rose and Walter Weiss, *Sinti und Roma im "Dritten Reich": Das Program der Vernichtung durch Arbeit* (Göttingen, 1991).

17. Goldhagen, *Hitler's Willing Executioners:* "In some countries, the Germans did treat Gypsies similarly to Jews, exterminating over 200,000 of them systematically. Despite general similarities, the Germans' policies towards the two peoples differed in important ways. To be sure, hundreds of thousands of Gypsies were victims of the Holocaust, but there was not, as for the Jews, a comprehensive plan for their systematic murder" (565).

18. Wolfgang Wippermann, "Ruderlaß des Reichführers SS und Chefs der Deutschen Polizei im Reichsministerium des Innern, Heinrich Himmler, vom 8.12.1939 über die 'Bekämpfung der Zigeunerplage,'" in his *Geschichte der Sinti und Roma in Deutschland: Darstellungen und Dokumente* (Berlin, 1993), 8off.

19. Goldhagen, *Hitler's Willing Executioners*, 116.

20. Mechtild Rössler and Sabine Schleiermacher, eds., *Der "Generalplan Ost": Hauptlinien der nationalsozialistischen Planungs- und Vernichtungspolitik* (Berlin, 1993). The *Generalplan Ost* is not even mentioned by Goldhagen.

21. Goldhagen, *Hitler's Willing Executioners*, 410.

22. This has been the criticism of nearly all professional historians, among others: Norbert Frei, "A People of 'Final Solutionists'" [Chapter 2 in this volume]; Eberhard Jäckel, "Simply a Bad Book" [Chapter 10 in this volume]; Jürgen Matthäus, *Zeitschrift für Geschichtswissenschaft* 44 (1996): 366–68; Manfred Weißbecker, "Goldhagens Suche und die Reaktion," *Antifa*, October 1996,

pp. 25ff.; as well as in the articles, comprehensively discussed below, by Mommsen and Wehler.

23. Goldhagen, "Foreword to the German Edition" of *Hitler's Willing Executioners,* as reprinted in Appendix 3 of the Vintage paperback edition (New York, 1997), 477.

24. On the controversy between "structuralists" and "intentionalists," see Wolfgang Wippermann, "Forschungsgeschichte und Forschungsprobleme," in *Kontroversen um Hitler,* ed. Wolfgang Wippermann (Frankfurt am Main, 1986), 13–118, esp. 8off.; Burleigh and Wippermann, *The Racial State,* 16ff.; Ian Kershaw, *Der NS-Staat: Geschichtsinterpretationen und Kontroversen im Überblick* (Reinbek, 1988), esp. 165ff.

25. Hans Mommsen, "Die Realisierung des Utopischen: Die Endlösung der Judenfrage," in *Kontroversen um Hitler,* ed. Wippermann, 277ff.

26. Hans Mommsen, "The Thin Patina of Civilization" [Chapter 21 in this volume].

27. Even sharper: "That the Holocaust could become reality cannot be adequately explained by ideological factors—like the effect of anti-Semitic propaganda or the authoritarian hue of traditional German political culture" (Mommsen, "Die Realisierung des Utopischen," 28off.).

28. Goldhagen, *Hitler's Willing Executioners,* 162.

29. Mommsen, "The Thin Patina of Civilization."

30. Ibid. In his other publications on this theme, too, Mommsen repeatedly holds the view that the German working class, in contrast to the "upper stratum," was not anti-Semitically inclined.

31. On this point, see Marlies Steinert, *Hitlers Krieg und die Deutschen: Stimmen und Haltung der deutschen Bevölkerung im Zweiten Weltkrieg* (Düsseldorf, 1970). Further: Ian Kershaw, *Popular Opinion and Political Dissent in the Third Reich: Bavaria 1933–1945* (Oxford, 1983); Otto Dov Kulka and Aron Rodrigue, "The German Population and the Jews in the Third Reich: Recent Populations and Trends in Research on Germany and the 'Jewish Question,'" *Yad Vashem Studies* 16 (1984): 421–35; Hans Mommsen, "Was haben die Deutschen vom Völkermord gewußt?" in *Der Judenpogrom: Von der "Reichskristallnacht" zum Völkermord,* ed. Walther H. Pehle (Frankfurt am Main, 1988), 176–200. For a summary of the state of research, see Ursula Büttner, *Die deutsche Gesellschaft und die Judenverfolgung im Dritten Reich* (Hamburg,

1992), 8–29. David Bankier, *Die öffentliche Meinung im Hitler-Staat: Die "Endlösung" und die Deutschen. Eine Berichtigung* (Berlin, 1995). Goldhagen relies exclusively on Bankier's work.

32. Mommsen, "Die Realisierung des Utopischen," 280ff.

33. Mommsen, "The Thin Patina of Civilization." Here Mommsen resorts to theses like those of Peukert and Baumann on the relationship between the Holocaust and "modernity." On this point, see *Wessen Schuld* (Berlin, 1997), 82.

34. See the accounts by Volker Ullrich, "A Triumphal Processional" [Chapter 22 in this volume], and Evelyn Roll, "Eine These und drei gebrochene Tabus," *Süddeutsche Zeitung,* September 9, 1996.

35. I am quoting from Mommsen, "The Thin Patina of Civilization." In the Berlin discussion, Mommsen expressed himself even more misleadingly.

36. Goldhagen, "Foreword to the German Edition," 477.

37. Goldhagen, *Hitler's Willing Executioners,* 454.

38. Karl Marx and Friedrich Engels, *Werke* (Berlin, 1983), vol. 8, 115.

39. Hans-Ulrich Wehler, *Geschichte als Historische Sozialwissenschaft* (Frankfurt am Main, 1975), 27. This is not the place to explore more fully additional details and the broader shape of "structural" or "social history." For an introduction, see the first-rate overview by Georg G. Iggers, *Geschichtswissencharft im 20. Jahrhundert: Ein kritischer Überblick im internationalen Zusammenhang* (Göttingen, 1993).

40. Hans-Ulrich Wehler, "Wie ein Stachel im Fleisch," which first appearing in *Die Zeit,* May 14, 1996; An expanded version appeared in *Ein Volk von Mördern?* ed. Schoeps, 193–209. In what follows I shall quote from this—longer—version, "Like A Thorn in the Flesh" [Chapter 11 in this volume].

41. See esp. Wehler, *Geschichte als Historische Sozialwissenschaft,* 21ff.

42. Wehler, "Like a Thorn in the Flesh."

43. Moshe Zimmermann, "Die Fußnote als Alibi," *Neue Zürcher Zeitung,* April 19, 1996, and in *Ein Volk von Mördern?,* ed. Schoeps, 147–54.

44. As cited by Matthias Heyl, "Die Goldhagen-Debatte im Spiegel der englisch- und deutschsprachigen Rezensionen von Februar bis Juli 1996: Ein Überblick," *Der Mittelweg,* no. 4 (August–September 1996): 55.

45. On this point, see Joscha Schmierer, "Ihr im Polizeibataillon, wir beim Einkaufsbummel," *Kommune* 4 (1996): 20–22.

46. Wehler, "Like a Thorn in the Flesh."

47. See the section "The Germans' Slaughter of the Jews in Comparative Perspective," in Goldhagen, *Hitler's Willing Executioners,* 406–15.

48. Ibid., 412.

49. Ibid., 414.

50. Ibid., 412.

51. This appears in a single note on page 479 of *Hitler's Willing Executioners.*

52. Wehler, however, expresses himself in a very contradictory way when he declares at one point: "The Holocaust was, for the reasons stated, mass murder of a unique kind" and then goes on to insist "but is it proper, in a book of this sort, to gloss over so blatantly all questions of comparison?" (Wehler, "Like a Thorn in the Flesh").

53. Ibid.

54. Ibid.

55. On this point, see Wolfgang Benz, "Kollektivschuld," in *Legenden, Lügen, Vorurteile: Ein Lexikon zur Zeitgeschichte,* ed. Wolfgang Benz (Munich, 1990), 113–55.

56. On Ritter and his controversy with Meinecke, see Wolfgang Wippermann, "Friedrich Meineckes 'Die deutsche Katastrophe': Ein Versuch zur deutschen Vergangenheitsbewältigung," in *Friedrich Meinecke heute,* ed. Michael Erbe (Berlin, 1982), 101–21.

57. Quoted in Helmut Ruppel, Ingrid Schmidt, and Wolfgang Wippermann, ". . . stoßet nicht um weltlich Regiment"? *Ein Erzähl- und Arbeitsbuch vom Widerstand im Nationalsozialismus* (Neukirchen, 1986), 34ff.

58. Karl Jaspers, *Die Schuldfrage: Zur politischen Haftung Deutschlands* (reprint Munich, 1987, first edition, 1946). Jaspers's name, so far as I can tell, was not mentioned even once in the entire debate. This, too, is a sign of how superficial the discussion on the collective guilt thesis was.

59. Among the very few reviewers who have set the record straight is Ulrich Herbert, "Die richtige Frage," in *Ein Volk von Mördern?,* ed. Schoeps, 214–24, 214.

60. I was one of the few exceptions; see Wolfgang Wippermann, "(K)ein Volk von Tätern?," *Allgemeine Jüdische Wochenschrift* 9/96 (May 2, 1996).

61. For the foreign reviewers, who will be mentioned only in passing here, see Heyl, "Die Goldhagen-Debatte," 41–56.

62. Thus Werner Birkenmaier, "Ein zorniges, moralisches Buch," *Stuttgarter Zeitung,* August 16, 1996, simultaneously accuses Goldhagen of conducting "a massive attack against Christianity."

63. Hanno Loewy referred to this in "Ein auserwähltes Volk? Anmerkungen zur schnellen Erledigung von Daniel Jonah Goldhagens Buch 'Hitler's Willing Executioners,'" *Fritz Bauer Institut Newsletter,* no. 11 (September 1996): 32–35, 33.

64. Above all by Marion Countess Dönhoff, "Mit fragwürdiger Methode: Warum das Buch in die Irre führt," *Die Zeit,* September 6, 1996 [Chapter 23 in this volume].

65. Goldhagen, *Hitler's Willing Executioners,* 114ff. Goldhagen is relying here almost exclusively on the essay by Christoph Dipper, "Der deutsche Widerstand und die Juden," *Geschichte und Gesellschaft* 9 (1983): 349–80.

66. Wolfgang Wippermann, "Alibi für Auschwitz? Das Bild des Widerstandes in beiden deutschen Staaten," in *Zeichen für die Völker,* ed. Nes Ammin, 1 (1994): 2–11.

67. See the much too positive account by Friso Wielenga, *Schatten deutscher Geschichte: Der Umgang mit dem Nationalsozialismus und der DDR-Vergangenheit in der Bundesrepublik* (Vierow bei Greifswald, 1995). Also very hagiographic is Christa Hoffmann, *Stunde Null? Vergangenheitsbewältigung in Deutschland 1945–1989* (Bonn, 1992). Informative from an international perspective is Rolf Steininger, ed., *Der Umgang mit dem Holocaust: Europa—USA—Israel* (Vienna, 1994). Very interesting, though restricted to the 1950s, is Norbert Frei, *Vergangenheitspolitik: Die Anfänge der Bundesrepublik und die NS-Vergangenheit* (Munich, 1996).

68. Jost Nolte, "Sisyphus Is a German" [Chapter 5 in this volume].

69. This is quite properly criticized by Loewy, "Ein auserwähltes Volk?," 33.

70. Peter Glotz, "Nation der Killer?," *Die Woche,* April 19, 1996, and in *Ein Volk von Mördern?,* ed. Schoeps, 125.

71. Mariam Niroumand, "Little Historians," *die tageszeitung,* April 13–14, 1996.

72. Thus Matthias Arning and Rolf Paasch in their early review, "Die provokanten Thesen des Mister Goldhagen," *Frankfurter Rundschau,* April 12, 1996. Here it says: "Thus far in the U.S. debate, just what and how much is really new [in Goldhagen's book] has hardly been asked, since those doing the discussing here among themselves are mostly Jewish nonhistorians (substitute: journalists and columnists)." These "Jewish columnists" and "nonhistorians" later surface in Augstein's excoriation; see Rudolf Augstein, "The Sociologist as Hanging Judge" [Chapter 4 in this volume].

73. Henryk M. Broder rolls this out into an entire article, in which he constantly speculates on the father-son relationship between Erich and Daniel Goldhagen. This is more than dubious. See Henryk M. Broder, "Ich bin sehr stolz," *Der Spiegel,* May 20, 1996.

74. Niroumand, "Little Historians."

75. Jörg von Uthmann, "Völkerpsychologie," *Der Tagesspiegel,* April 14, 1996. This is, incidentally, one of most spiteful reviews there was. It ends with a sharp attack on the supposed threat to "freedom of opinion in the United States" because a U.S. publishing house decided not to market a book by the well-known British revisionist David Irving. The editors of *Der Tagesspiegel* have not expressed their regret about these invectives; instead they went on to bring out additional negative articles on Goldhagen that simultaneously polemicized heavily against *Die Zeit.* See Malte Lehming, "Bekenntniszwang," *Der Tagesspiegel,* April 15, 1996.

76. Niroumand, "Little Historians"; likewise with Uthmann, "Völkerpsychologie," and Lehming, "Bekenntniszwang," who lets himself get carried away with the following, completely out of place sentence: "The urge to confess is also a master from Germany."

77. Augstein, "The Sociologist as Hanging Judge." Even the headline for this most remarkable of articles by Augstein is wrong. Goldhagen is a political scientist and not a sociologist. The height of embarrassment was a picture of Goldhagen with the caption "Hangman Goldhagen." All in *Der Spiegel,* April 15, 1996.

78. See Avram Andrei Baleanu, "Der 'ewige Jude,'" in *Antisemitismus: Vorurteile und Mythen,* ed. Julius H. Schoeps and Joachim Schlör (Munich, 1995), 96–102.

79. See Freddy Raphael, "'Der Wucherer,'" in *Antisemitismus,* ed. Schoeps and Schlör, 103–20; Alex Bein, *Die Judenfrage: Biographie eines Weltproblems,* 2 vols. (Stuttgart, 1989), vol. 2, 91ff.

80. See the previously mentioned review by Henning Schlüter of Bernd Greiner, *Die Morgenthau-Legende: Zur Geschichte eines umstrittenen Plans* (Hamburg, 1995), *Frankfurter Allgemeine Zeitung*, September 13, 1995.

81. Fritjof Meyer, "Ein Volk von Dämonen?," *Der Spiegel*, May 20, 1996.

82. This legend is unmasked by Wolfgang Benz, "Judenvernichtung und Notwehr? Vom langen Leben einer rechtsradikalen Legende," in *Rechtsradikalismus in der Bundesrepublik: Vorraussetzungen, Zusammenhänge, Wirkungen*, ed. Wolfgang Benz (Frankfurt am Main, 1980), 169–88.

83. The refutation of this legend, which is always being put forward by Nolte and other revisionists, has been undertaken by Hellmuth Auerbach, "'Kriegserklärungen' der Juden an Deutschland," in *Legenden, Lügen, Vorurteile*, ed. Benz, 118–23.

84. See on this point, Christhard Hoffmann, "Das Judentum als Antithese: Zur Tradition eines kulturellen Wertungsmusters," in *Antisemitismus in der politischen Kultur nach 1945*, ed. Werner Bergman and Rainer Erb (Opladen, 1990), 20–38.

85. Jacob Heilbrunn, "Ankläger und Rächer," *Der Tagesspiegel*, March 31, 1996. This was, incidentally, the first German-language review of Goldhagen's book, and it was devastating.

86. Andrei S. Markovits, "Discomposure in History's Final Resting Place" [Chapter 15 in this volume].

87. Seen this way, what is really an absurd title for the reader edited by Schoeps, *Ein Volk von Mördern*, was actually well chosen, although it must be pointed out time and again that Goldhagen did not even venture such generalizations.

88. Alfred de Zayas, "Kein Stoff für Streit: Goldhagens Unfug, Goldhagens Unwissenheit," *Frankfurter Allgemeine Zeitung (FAZ)*, June 12, 1996.

89. Frank Schirrmacher, "Hitler's Code" [Chapter 3 in this volume].

90. When Yiddish words are employed in attacks on Jews, this is most often a sign of (usually concealed) hostility toward Jews.

91. Augstein, "The Sociologist as Hanging Judge."

92. Glotz, "Nation der Killer?"

93. Alfred de Zayas, "Ein Volk von willigen Henkern?," *Criticón* 150 (May–June 1996): 83–86. This article is otherwise identical with de Zayas's review (already

mentioned) in the *FAZ*, which is hardly remarkable since the *FAZ* and *Criticón* are not that far apart from each other anyway.

94. I refer to an article by the revisionist Bradley R. Smith, which he published in November 1991 in various student newspapers in the United States as an advertisement, for example, in *The Chronicle* (the newspaper of Duke University), November 5, 1991.

95. Cited by Stefan Ripplinger, "Der kollektive Kinkel," *Junge Welt,* May 9, 1996.

96. Uwe Soukop, "Das Holocaust-Personal," *Junge Welt,* April 17, 1996.

97. Among others, by Tjark Kunstreich in *Junge Welt,* May 4, 1996, and Stefan Vogt in *Junge Welt,* May 11–12, 1996.

98. Uwe Soukop, "'Hätte die Revolution doch gesiegt!' Kann man den Nationalsozialismus ohne die Klassenkämpfe in der Weimarer Republik erklären?," *Junge Welt,* May 20, 1996.

99. Reinhard Kühnl, "Kampf ums Geschichtsbild," *Junge Welt,* June 24, 1996.

100. Jürgen Elsässer, "Kollektivschuld?," *Junge Welt,* August 6, 1996.

101. *Junge Freiheit,* no. 20/96 (May 10, 1996): 3.

102. An exception was Hans B. von Sothen, who mocked the "staged commotion" surrounding Goldhagen's book in *Junge Freiheit* and quoted with relish the negative, nationalistic reviews in the *Frankfurter Rundschau* and *die tageszeitung* in order to ascertain—prematurely, as it happened—that "the wind [has] changed direction"; see Hans B. von Sothen, "Vermarktete Anklagen," *Junge Freiheit,* April 26, 1996.

103. Ullrich, "A Triumphal Procession"; Evelyn Roll, "Eine These und drei gebrochene Tabus," *Süddeutsche Zeitung,* September 9, 1996. Very sour, by contrast, is Malte Lahming, "Plastische Nähe: Daniel Jonah Goldhagen in Berlin," *Der Tagesspiegel,* September 7, 1996, and Rolf Schneider, "Ein Historiker und das Marketing," *Berliner Morgenpost,* September 7, 1996.

104. Wolfgang Wippermann, "Auch Gegenwart ist unser Problem," *Thüringische Landeszeitung,* September 21, 1996.

105. See his "Epilogue: The Nazi German Revolution," in which Goldhagen asserts the very opposite, namely, that the National Socialists sought a "*revolutionary transformation of society* in a manner that denied basic premises of European civilization" because the "European social landscape" was to be reshaped

according to "racial biological priniciples" (*Hitler's Willing Executioners,* 458). This is precisely the thesis with which I fully concur.

106. This was my assessment in Wolfgang Wippermann, "Die Entsorgung der Vergangenheit: Der 'Historikerstreit' ist in eine neue Phase getreten," *Evangelische Kommentare* 7 (1996): 416–19.

TWENTY-EIGHT

TURNING AWAY FROM DENIAL:
HITLER'S WILLING EXECUTIONERS
AS A COUNTERFORCE TO
"HISTORICAL EXPLANATION"

Jan Philipp Reemtsma

A book and its effect—that is to be the subject addressed here, not the legend about a book, not the presumed imputation of collective guilt or the alleged assertion of some immutable national character—nor, dear Daniel Goldhagen, is the subject to be something we promised one another in New York a few weeks ago: that the discussion might finally turn to issues of true disagreement. My subject is to be the success of a book in Germany, a success that is not only worth remarking, but also curiously remarkable. As foolish as it is, of course, to trace the book's success, as has happened here and there, to the charm of its author (though I would not wish in any way to dispute that charm), at the very least it takes more than mere quality to make a best-seller. A best-seller supplies a commodity that satisfies a preexistent demand—and of what did that demand consist?

When *Schindler's List* proved to be a success, the film's critics wanted to see it as the acceptance of an offer of exculpation. But they were wrong. Those who saw the film were concerned not with the "good German" who had at last been discovered but, rather, with the issue of individual responsibility—or put another way, with individual freedom. When Daniel Goldhagen's book proved to be a success, it was occasionally regarded as connected with or as a successor to that film, and at times that was meant as a reproach. Unfairly so, I would say. One of the consequences of the years 1933–1945 can be seen in the curious conception of freedom that became popular here in Germany, a conception that revealed itself very clearly whenever someone was admonished that he or she apparently did not know what it meant to live under a totalitarian regime. Individual freedom appeared to be something available in given quantities, and anyone who enjoined responsibility appeared to be someone proceeding from an inaccurate empirical assumption of a given quantum of freedom. As freedom vanished so, too, did morality. The disquieting popularity of a rhetorical phrase such as, "I did it because someone else would have done it in any case," not only fails to recognize that morality begins with the question of what I am to do, and that there is most definitely a decisive difference between whether I or someone else does it, but it also makes a muddle of complicity in a deed and the possible inability to prevent it. The notion of a society in which there is only complicity and suicidal resistance, with nothing in between, is therefore not just a false picture of German society between 1933 and 1945 but also a false picture of human beings in—and here I shall be cautious—almost every society.

There is, however, something like an involuntary consensus between a mentality that insists on the disavowal of freedom and morality and historiography. It may be that the Enlightenment's bias against that discipline originally had something to do with this fact. Even if in writing history one is, of course, not duty-bound by method to record why everything had to happen as it happened, the scope that history can allow to the portrayal of an event as a matter of pure chance is as small as the scope it can give to rhetorical formulas such as "it happened because they wanted it that way." It is a question of genre. That kind of perception of reality lies outside historiography's jurisdiction. That means, however, that it has great difficulty with a mode of presentation systematically focused on making manifest the scope of latitude inherent in a given act. But in writing history, if someone suggests that a person could also have acted differently—a routine occurrence in courts of law, for instance, or in political discussion—that can easily appear to be an admission that one has not worked hard enough to discover why someone had to act as he or she did.

It is interesting to observe why, for this very reason, the discussion of Goldhagen's book as a "historians' debate" had to fail. Only a few weeks ago I heard a well-known historian speak publicly about Goldhagen's thesis that German anti-Semitism is genetically conditioned, revealing by that statement how foreign to him was the very idea that had actually been Goldhagen's chief concern: not to present human beings as acting with no will of their own but to insist that human beings are also responsible for what they believe to be right. And so on various podiums, historians accused Goldhagen of not sufficiently explaining his ideas, while Goldhagen demonstrated that the genre of "historical explanation" is not the only way in which to present historical material and, indeed, is perhaps not even especially useful for some purposes.

It is indeed remarkable that Goldhagen always won his audience over with one introductory statement, often simply leaving his fellow panelists in his wake: For every other great historical outrage, for every other mass killing or genocide, we assume that the murderers did what they did out of conviction that their actions were just—only for the Holocaust do we look for explanations that might make it plausible that the Germans perpetrated, allowed, or intentionally overlooked something they fundamentally did not wish.[1] And indeed this notion is found not so much in the grand theories but in the rhetoric, in the details—when, for instance, one reads in the history of a company that its moral scruples against employing Jewish forced labor fell only after certain events had occurred, but without any documentation whatever that might prove the moral scruples of so much as a single person in the company's upper management.

It was not the apparent simplicity of Goldhagen's theses that led to their success over the more complex theories of the historians but his abandonment of any wish for denial[2]—which had entered into the rhetoric even of historians who are above every political suspicion. I know it sounds somewhat old-fashioned of me to speak of a complementary wish for truth that is in fact capable of prevailing over the wish for denial. But from a psychological viewpoint, truth is often the object of distortion by our wishes because truth itself is such a culturally laden value. There are few social sectors in which the differentiation between true and false, between truth and lies, is irrelevant. Where truth is itself morally laden, it is indeed not easy to live with lies. But this merely in passing. What is of greater importance is that the wish for denial and the wish for truth lay too close together. The outrage that mass killings could be committed in a country that considered itself civilized and the desire to understand how that could have been possible could no more be satisfied by historical research that paid little attention to how its perpetrators thought than it could by research that concentrated solely on the society's elites. The fear of a study of the average man and the possibility of recognizing in him one's own grandfather, father, or uncle (or aunt or mother) has finally been replaced by the willingness to take the risk of such a recognition.

This circumstance made three unexpected successes possible. The first is the Klemperer diaries, which are closer than any text before them to what German policies directed at Jews actually meant in normal everyday life and are likewise a permanent reflection on the question of just how deep the consensus between regime and populace actually was in executing those policies. The second success is "War of Extermination: The Crime of the *Wehrmacht,* 1941–1944," an exhibition mounted by the Hamburg Institute for Social Research—and here, too, the focus is the average man, the point of intersection between the regime and the general population, in this instance, the *Wehrmacht.* And the third, then, is Daniel Goldhagen's *Hitler's Willing Executioners,* subtitled *Ordinary Germans and the Holocaust.* The success of these two books and the exhibition shows that there is a collective willingness to ask the question, and to accept the threefold answer, provided with a different accent each time: that the obsession with Europe's Jewish population as a problem that had to be solved was extremely widespread and that both the formulation of this phantasmal problem and its possible solutions resulted in an increasingly murderous vocabulary—and that the circle of those willing to participate actively was far larger than had previously been assumed.

Evidence for an anti-Semitism in Germany and Austria that was both widespread and rightly termed eliminationist was not first found in Daniel Goldhagen's book, in the letters from the field published in conjunction with the exhibition, or in Klemperer's records of his conversations. In Karl Kraus's *Die Letzten Tage der Menschheit* (Last days of mankind), two men buying newspapers converse at the start of act four: "'And once the offensive starts, just watch—boom, and that's that!'—'Then it's the Jews turn—wipe 'em out !'"[3] And in 1920 Kurt Tucholsky says of the graffiti on the toilets at the University of Rostock ("Jews out !" "Beat the Jews to death!" "Time for a pogrom!"): "The writers of these inscriptions are our future judges, civil servants, prosecutors, priests."[4] The question of why such evidence, even if perhaps it has not totally vanished from the consciousness of written history, has nevertheless been neglected with astonishing unanimity as the explanation for "how it could come to this" leads us to another factor shared by all three aforementioned successes from the years 1995–1996. All three take as their theme that portion of the genocide that lies "before" Auschwitz, both temporally and in terms of being prior to the impetus of escalation. Klemperer writes about the resentment and hatred, the system of regulations, and the Gestapo's terror, which was just as systematic but also depended on the personal initiative and sadistic creativity of individuals; the exhibition on the *Wehrmacht* and *Hitler's Willing Executioners* deal with sectors of extermination policy outside the death camps.

One of the most important presuppositions in Goldhagen's book is the notion that fixating on the thing that is "really" hard to understand—that is, the mass killings, especially those that the equally popular and problematic metaphor calls "industrial"—ultimately hinders our understanding. What has taken place here, if I may put it this way, is an exoneration by the extreme. It was not there from the start; it was the result of a specifically German dynamic of denial.

In her biography of Albert Speer, Gitta Sereny writes about the family of Speer's liaison adjutant to the General Staff:

> When I met the Posers I was already aware of what army people who served in Russia necessarily had to have known about the murders there. Not only because of what the Komissar Befehl and the subsequent verbally transmitted orders told them, but because it was impossible not to either see what was being done or, at the very least (as was the case for many officers on the Chiefs of Staff), hear it described.[5]

And Speer's attorney presents her with this remarkable statement:

> "I, too, after all, knew in the 1930s that Jews were being badly treated, that they could no longer be judges or lawyers. And believe me, I often thanked God that I wasn't a Jew. I had Jewish friends and tried to help, and sometimes one could help. One knew it was miserable to be a Jew in Hitler's Germany, but one didn't know it was a catastrophe; one didn't know what happened to them. Until a day in 1943, when a client of mine who was a medic in Russia came back with photographs of executions of Jews, I knew absolutely nothing of this. I told him to burn or bury the photographs and to tell no one what he had seen. And I didn't tell anybody either, not even my wife . . . I don't think it was a secret that people were being executed; what we didn't know was that they were being systematically mass-murdered."

And later, concerning the Nuremberg trials:

> "Strangely . . . although the shadow of extermination of the Jews hovered over the trial from beginning to end, it was not much discussed . . . You see, they had all these witnesses . . . testifying to beatings and starvation in forced-labor and concentration camps. But somehow those horrors were, well, almost expected . . . Did you notice that even Dr. Gilbert in his book barely mentions the gas chambers? As if even he could not bear to pronounce the word."[6]

Such horrors—the photographs from Russia, the reports from the slave-labor and concentration camps—those were simply to be expected, but not systematic mass killing in camps built for that sole purpose or, in the case of Auschwitz, in a city built for that sole purpose. Nowadays gas chambers and systematic mass killings are denied by only a minority, who are viewed as partly pathological, partly criminal, but talk of those horrors—and shortly after 1945, it was expected that they would indeed be spoken of—can still cause a scandal or two.[7]

Speer is moreover a key figure in this reversal. In Nuremberg he accepted responsibility for Auschwitz and later admitted complicity in its crime—at the same time that he denied ever knowing any specific details. He should have known them, he admitted, and that made him an accomplice. And with that Speer had discovered a downright brilliant turn of phrase. It was a confession of shared responsibility—something demanded both of him and of the German people—but it was more than that, it was a confession of guilt, individual guilt in fact, and yet, as everyone concurred, a confession that, especially at such a high level, almost ennobled him. Yes, a downright brilliant turn of phrase, one can say—in light of his intentional and demonstrable lies about the extent of what he not only knew but had also in fact seen—a turn of phrase that was as breathtakingly impudent as it was thoroughly successful.[8]

And if this division of the Holocaust into two tidily detached operations—killing in the death camps by a murderous elite and killing as an ostensibly war-related act, executed by units in various kinds of uniforms—first led people to overlook the historical uniqueness of the death camps and then to keep their eyes fixed only on them, it also resulted in an understanding of the dynamics of violence that remains inadequate even today. For one statement is true of both parts: "Ultimately the Holocaust took place because at the most basic level individual human beings killed other human beings in large numbers over an extended period of time."[9] The systematic underestimation of anti-Semitism cannot be separated from this reality.

When people accuse Daniel Goldhagen of falling into modes of explanation that date back to the 1950s, they are wrongly insinuating that he grasps anti-Semitism in categories of propaganda and indoctrination, that he regards it as the decisive factor in an escalating dynamic. In Goldhagen's book, however, anti-Semitism appears as a communication system, a code with which a majority of Germans very quickly could come to an agreement about what was true and false. It was precisely the wide dissemination and implicit use of this code that often kept anti-Semitism below the threshold of perception. Telford Taylor reports in retrospect that the judges at Nuremberg would not have paid any notice to Dönitz's statement that naturally he was of the opinion that a necessary prerequisite for Germany's military power had been the exclusion of the Jewish element from the German national community, because Dönitz, who of course claimed he had never been an anti-Semite, had himself not noticed that his judges would see anything out of the ordinary in such a statement.[10] The trial of Reserve Police Battalion 101, which is investigated by both Christopher Browning and Daniel Goldhagen, proves that in the 1960s and 1970s the question of an anti-Semitic consensus was no longer posed, which is why the topic no longer appears in the court records or, as a result, in Browning's book.[11] Once the court had excluded the topic, the murderers could provide only fragmentary information about their deed. "A few of the policemen made the attempt to confront the question of choice, but failed to find the words. It was a different time and place, as if they had been on another political planet, and the political values and vocabulary of the 1960s were useless in explaining the situation in which they had found themselves in 1942."[12] As Goldhagen shows, it was only by indirectly speaking of an anti-Semitic fantasm that, prior to their first killing mission, the troops could come to an understanding of its necessity.[13]

The loss of the vocabulary in which to speak about motives and preferences of action brings with it the loss of any notion of free choice, which, as the records prove beyond a doubt, had been present. "Most of the interrogated police denied they had any choice."[14] The words with which they could have described why they acted as they had, why they felt that what they had done was right, were no longer available to them. The court had no interest in these words being uttered again, and the defendants surely knew that their use would have been anything but helpful to them. And here the viewpoint one ought to take of such matters in a court of law can be instructive for historiography: a confession that one has taken part in the killing of Jews because one considered Jews inferior and dangerous should not have led to an acquittal on the grounds of unaccountability due to indoctrination and propaganda but to a conviction based on admitted base motives.

It would be incorrect if I were to advance Daniel Goldhagen's book merely as an indication that things have changed somewhat in our country. A book is not only accepted, but it also serves to make people aware of, and to help them reformulate, their readiness to accept those things with which it deals, for mere diffuse sentiment does not suffice. I believe that with this Democracy Prize, the *Blätter für deutsche und internationale Politik* wanted to express their gratitude that with his book—and this can surely be said even at such close temporal proximity—Goldhagen has made a contribution to the discussion of historical factual material, a contribution that can never be ignored in the future, and that (and I say this in the face of those political sectors who are currently busy loudly protesting that there has not been any progress whatever in this direction) alone is in a position to overcome what Hannah Arendt, on a visit to Germany in 1950, saw as a "general lack of emotion," "an apparent heartlessness, sometimes covered over with cheap sentimentality," that is "only the most conspicuous outward symptom of a deep-rooted, stubborn, and at times vicious refusal to face and come to terms with what really happened."[15]

Translation by John E. Woods
Speech originally published in *Blätter für deutsche und internationale Politik* (April 1997)

NOTES

1. Cf. Daniel Jonah Goldhagen, *Hitler's Willing Executioners: Ordinary Germans and the Holocaust* (New York: Knopf, 1996), 29.

2. To speak of a "wish to repress" is incorrect, even in a psychological sense.

3. Karl Kraus, *Die letzten Tage der Menschheit* (Munich: Piper Verlag, 1974), 428.

4. Kurt Tucholsky, *Gesamtausgabe,* vol. 4 (Reinbek: Rowoult, 1996), 277ff.

5. Gitta Sereny, *Albert Speer: His Battle with Truth* (New York: Knopf, 1995), 458.

6. Ibid., 581ff.

7. Ibid., 333ff.

8. Ibid., 585ff., 563ff.

9. Christopher R. Browning, *Ordinary Men: Reserve Police Battalion 101 and the Final Solution in Poland* (New York: HarperCollins, 1992), xvii.

10. Telford Taylor, *The Anatomy of the Nuremberg Trials* (New York: Knopf, 1992), 406.

11. The investigations ran from 1962–1987.

12. Browning, *Ordinary Men,* 72.

13. See Goldhagen, *Hitler's Willing Executioners,* 212.

14. Browning, *Ordinary Men,* 72 .

15. Hannah Arendt, "The Aftermath of Nazi Rule: Report from Germany," in *Essays in Understanding, 1930–1954* (New York: Harcourt, Brace, 1994), 249.

TWENTY-NINE

GOLDHAGEN AND THE PUBLIC USE OF HISTORY: WHY A DEMOCRACY PRIZE FOR DANIEL GOLDHAGEN?

Jürgen Habermas

T he Democracy Prize, last awarded in 1990 to Bärbel Bohley and Wolf-gang Ullman on behalf of the civil rights activists of the GDR, is given to this year's recipient on the following grounds: through the "urgency, the forcefulness, and the moral strength of his presentation" Daniel Goldhagen has "provided a powerful stimulus to the public conscience of the Federal Republic"; he has sharpened "our sensibility for what constitutes the background and the limit of a German 'normalization.'" This reference to the rhetorical effect of the book, and to the controversial issue of normalization (which poses itself anew in the transition to a Berlin Republic) makes clear what the Board of Trustees of the *Blätter für deutsche und internationale Politik* has in mind in awarding this prize—and what it does not. It cannot and will not enter into a controversy among professional historians. In Germany as well as the United States, a number of prominent historians have contributed greatly to the research on the Nazi period and to the political enlightenment of German citizens concerning the complex prehistory of the Holocaust, often with the devotion of an entire professional career. Here I will name only Martin Broszat, Hans Mommsen, and Eberhart Jäckel and younger historians such as Ulrich Herbert, Dietrich Pohl, and Thomas Sandkühler as representative. The question is not who among contemporary historians deserves the attention of a wider public but, rather, how we are to understand the unusual degree of public attention that Daniel

Goldhagen's book has in fact received. Awarding this prize expresses the conviction that the public response that both book and author have received in the Federal Republic is as deserved as it is welcome.

This view has been the subject of vehement dispute. The book's detractors claim that it offers a global and one-dimensional presentation of a highly complex event, thus satisfying the mass public's demand for oversimplified explanations. Some object that the book employs an aesthetics of the gruesome as a stylistic tool, generating emotional effects that dim the capacity for sober judgment. Other criticisms refer less to the text itself and far more to the motives of those who buy and read it. Here we encounter the familiar stereotypes: "do-goodism," "negative nationalism," "flight from history." With a retrospective identification with the victims, so it is said, the descendants of the perpetrators have gotten themselves a free and self-justifying kind of satisfaction, or have again seized the opportunity to reject their own tradition and to flee into the chimerical dream of a postnational nation. I must confess that I do not entirely understand these agitated reactions. They are trying to explain a phenomenon that stands in no need of explanation.

Clearly a broad public response to a book such as this cannot come as a great surprise. One need only see how Goldhagen's analytical case histories of the annihilation of the Jews mesh with the expectations of a reading public as it searches for an understanding of this criminal chapter of its history. Goldhagen's investigations are tailored to address precisely those questions that have polarized our public and private discussions for the past half century. From the very beginnings of the Federal Republic there has been a fundamental disagreement between those on the one side who would rather interpret the breakdown of civilization as a natural event and those on the other side who insist on seeing it as the consequence of the actions of responsible persons—and not just of Hitler and his inner circle. Today both sides square off with mutual suspicions of each other's respective motives. The diagnosis of denial thus stands opposed to the accusation of self-righteous moralizing. This hopeless battle only serves to conceal the truly fundamental question at issue: What does it mean to assign the responsibility for historical crimes retrospectively—if it is just this reckoning that we are now undertaking with the goal of generating an ethical-political process of public self-understanding? Goldhagen provides a new stimulus to a reflection about the proper public use of history. In public discourses of self-understanding, which can be touched off by films, television series, or exhibitions just as much as by historical works or "affairs," we argue not so much over short-terms goals and policies as over the forms of a desired political existence and over the values that shall predominate in it. Moreover, such discourses concern how we as citizens of the Federal Republic can have mutual respect for one another and how we wish to be acknowledged by others. National history constitutes an important background for this. National traditions and mentalities reach back far behind the origins of this republic, forming a part of our personal identities. This connection between political self-understanding and historical awareness also determines the point of view from which Goldhagen's book is relevant for us. This singular crime— a crime that first generated the notion of a "crime against humanity"—has issued from the very midst of our collective life. For this reason, all those members of later generations who struggle to come to terms with their political existence in this country confront the same question: Can the responsibility for mass political criminality ever be laid as a burden on individual persons or groups of persons? If so, who were the responsible actors, and what were their reasons for acting as they did? And insofar as normative justifications were of decisive importance for the actors, were these rooted in the culture and in particular ways of thinking?

Goldhagen ascribes to a representative group of somehow convinced perpetrators a subjective justification for their acts that formed an integral part of the basic cultural convictions that were dominant at the time. "The rupture in the German cultural fabric that the Jews represented to Germans . . . was such that cultural taboos failed to hold sway when the Germans discussed the Jews."[1] This cannot fail to have a powerful impact on our own self-understanding. Present and past generations are bound up with one another, in their forms of thinking and feeling, their gestures and expressions, and in their ways of seeing, in a tapestry composed of countless cultural threads. To the extent to which it is legitimate, an assertion such as this must shake any naive trust in our own traditions. This critical attitude toward what is most our own is precisely what Goldhagen's study demands—and what calls forth the concern of some conservatives.

These conservative circles believe that only unquestioned traditions and strong values make a people "able for the future." Hence each and every skeptically probing backward look at tradition falls under the suspicion of being another instance of unbridled moralizing. Since 1989 a new sort of patriotic spirit has strengthened in the unified Germany, a spirit that regards the learning processes of the last forty years as already having gone "too far." On June 19, 1948, Carl Schmitt noted that a "repentance preacher" like Karl Jaspers was beneath attention. The wretched vocabulary of repression audible in this indescribable "glossary," which registers every word of self-criticism as a "false eagerness to repent," was later reconstructed in Weikersheim; today it continues to exert its influence far beyond the circle of the incorrigible, in the wake of successful diversionary tactics against "political correctness." Even those who think differently than these hard-core conservatives seem to worry that Goldhagen's study will provoke a dubious moral judgment of the "unknowing" contemporaries of the Holocaust. And yet it is just this study that can serve as an illustration of how historical problems of subjective accountability bear an entirely distinct status once they enter the contemporary context of an ethical-political process of self-understanding. I will first recall the general sense in which a public use of history can be legitimate and then go on to explain why Goldhagen's case histories are well suited for an ethical-political process of self-understanding free from moralistic misunderstandings.

Modern historiography addresses itself to two different audiences: the guild of professional historians and the general reading public. A good work of contemporary history should simultaneously satisfy both the critical standards of the profession and the expectations of an interested public. Of course the view of the historian must not be directed by the interests of general readers, who come to the historical text in search of explanations of their own historical position. The moment that the analytic perspective of the observer blurs with the perspective assumed by participants in a discourse of collective self-understanding, historiographical science degenerates into the politics of history. The union of historicism and nationalism once arose from just this confusion; a similar confusion is reflected today in tendencies that attempt to continue the Cold War with historiographic means. It goes without saying that only historians of integrity, who insist upon the difference between observer and participant perspectives, are capable of being reliable experts.

Political criminal justice, for example, depends on historical experts. In cases of mass political criminality, both jurisprudence and contemporary historiography deal with the same questions of accountability. Both take an interest in who participated in crimes, whether the responsibility for the consequences of criminal actions should be borne by individuals or ascribed to circumstances, whether those involved could have acted differently, whether in a given case they acted on the basis of normative convictions or out of self-interest, whether another choice of behavior could reasonably have been expected of them, and so forth. But the criminal judge can only benefit from historical documentation—just as, conversely, the historian can only benefit from the official proceedings of the office of the public prosecutor—as long as both, judge and historian, view the same phenomenon from different perspectives. The one side is interested in the question of culpability for an act; the other in the explanation of its cause. From the historian's perspective, accountability for actions is not resolved in terms of guilt or innocence but in terms of what kind of explanatory grounds exist. However that explanation will look—whether the causes lie predominantly in persons or in circumstances—a causal explanation can neither condemn nor excuse the actors. Only from the perspective of participants, who now encounter one another whether in a court of law or on the street, and call each other to account for themselves, do questions of accountability transform themselves into legal—or moral—questions.

The moral point of view also concerns the judgment of justice or injustice, although of course without the strict rules of procedure of a criminal proceeding. Historical knowledge can be put to use for moral controversies that take place in the context of the everyday just as much as for the ends of jurisprudence—as for example in the proverbial conflict between "fathers and sons." In both cases, historical knowledge becomes relevant in the same regard for those affected. However, this view of justice differs sharply from the point of view from which members of a current generation seek to secure for themselves a historical heritage that, as citizens and members of a collective political life they must inherit in one way or another. It is this difference that concerns me. From the point of view of the ethical-political processes of self-understanding of citizens, the explanatory accounts of the historian have a different function than they would have in moral or legal discourses.

Here, in an ethical-political discourse, the question is not primarily the guilt or innocence of the forefathers but, rather, the critical self-assurance of their descendants. The public interest of those born later, who cannot know how they themselves would have acted, directs itself toward a different goal than the zealous moral judgments of the contemporaries of the Nazi years, who find themselves in the same context of interaction and demand a moral reckoning from each other. Painful revelations of the conduct of one's own parents and grandparents can only be an occasion for sorrow; they remain a private affair between those intimately involved. On the other hand, the later generations, as citizens, take a public interest in the darkest chapter of their national history regarding themselves—and in relation to the victims and their own descendants. They are not pointing a finger of blame at anyone else. They are trying to bring about some clarity about the cultural matrix of a burdened inheritance, to recognize what they themselves are collectively liable for, and to decide what is to be continued, and what revised, from those traditions that had earlier formed such a disastrous motivational background. An awareness of collective liability emerges from widespread individually guilty conduct in the past. This has nothing to do with the ascription of collective guilt, a notion that is simply incoherent on conceptual grounds alone.[2]

Goldhagen's case histories, particularly his studies of police battalions and death marches, are intended to lead to conclusions, within a particular theoretical frame, that refer observed modes of behavior to orienting interpretive patterns and mentalities. The studies read like retrospectively conducted experiments, and in this sense they conform to the standards of autonomous research. At the same time, however, in the land of the perpetrators the analytical perspectives encompassing the responsible perpetrators, the motivational grounds for their extraordinary actions, and the fundamental cognitive patterns that generated them meet our public interest in a forthright, nonmoralizing self-understanding. A clear strategy for analysis does not, of course, guarantee the correctness of its results. But in the meantime, a number of professional controversies over the details of Goldhagen's work have been helpful in de-dramatizing its reception. Specialists familiar with the historical material have raised a host of objections concerning specific details, while taking Goldhagen's approach seriously.[3]

I myself am won over by the clear argumentative strategy. Goldhagen defines the circle of perpetrators that he is investigating as constituted by membership in the institutions of murder and direct participation in the operations of killing of Jews. These perpetrators may be said to stand at the end of a complex chain of events. Defining the perpetrators in this way solves by implication questions of objective accountability, which are far from easy to decide with regard to the highly anonymous, differentiated, and administrative execution of organized mass murder. At the same time, other questions—which norms were violated, and whether the perpetrators had knowledge of them—are settled by simple reference to the form of the crime itself. The analysis proper then starts with the questions of whether the perpetrators acted in a subjectively accountable manner, whether they were aware of, and desired, the foreseeable and avoidable consequences of their actions. From the logic of everyday situations both within and outside of the murderous "service" itself, Goldhagen infers that the perpetrators must have had enough latitude for a reflective relation to their own action and involvement. "The perpetrators lived in a world in which reflection, discussion, and disagreement were possible."[4]

This leads Goldhagen to probe the question of what ought reasonably to have been expected of the perpetrators. Given the circumstances, did they have no choice but to act in the way that they did? Here Goldhagen points to killing operations that were manned by volunteers or that perpetrators undertook on their own initiative, refusals of chances to voluntarily excuse themselves from participation in massacres, and opportunities on the scene to refrain from taking part in killing operations without the threat of punishment. Supposedly the men also understood that they could, if nothing else, request to be transferred to another position and that they could even refuse to follow orders without placing their own lives in danger. "Superfluous" violence, or the excessively gruesome nature of the killing operations (which Goldhagen describes for analytical reasons) also speaks against the assumption that the perpetrators found themselves trapped in a state of coercion. Goldhagen believes that he can rule out other possible grounds for excusing the perpetrators, such as the social-psychological effects of group pressure, a habituation to state-sanctioned mass criminality, or an unconscious attachment to state authority. There is a natural suspicion that this type of perpetrator may have been unusually fixated on the authority of his superior officers; Goldhagen refutes this, too, by pointing out instances of opposition and open subordination in other situations having nothing to do with the murder of Jews. Nor does self-interest seem to have been a decisive motivation. In any case, the proposition that corruption, ambition, or interest in professional advancement played no decisive motivational role is important for Goldhagen's argument; one confirmation for this assumption is the truly bizarre behavior of the teams of guards on the death marches during the final days of the war. If these people acted willfully, without any drastic outward coercion or obvious inner compulsion, if they did not even act on utilitarian grounds, then we are forced to confront a picture of perpetrators who lacked the awareness that they were committing an injustice.

Philosophically Goldhagen's study is inspired by the idea that evil is not to be understood as sheer aggression as such but, rather, as the kind of aggression that the perpetrators believe themselves to be justified in committing. Evil is distorted good. With a wealth of details, from the absence of concern for secrecy to obscene sessions of posing for photographic mementos, Goldhagen argues that many of the perpetrators must have regarded their murderous action as legitimate. But anyone who can appeal to his convictions in order to participate in an act that would count as criminal by any normal standard—indeed, in an act that must count as the monstrous itself—must have some powerful normative basis to justify such a dramatic exception. Here Goldhagen naturally refers back to the conception of "the Jew." Since he is obliged to reconstruct the bases for the morally selective perception of the perpetrators from their manifest acts, he collects evidence for the sharply differential treatment of designated victims. The anti-Semitic syndrome expresses itself in the fact that in comparable situations Jews consistently met a worse fate than did Poles, Russians, political prisoners, and others. The perpetrators behaved more cruelly toward Jews than toward their other victims. As the current discussion on the Berlin Holocaust memorial continues, anyone inclined to mock the wish of survivors for a memorial that differentiates between different victims should pause to remember who it was who first set up this "hierarchy of victim groups." Following this course, Goldhagen reaches his central contention: In the end, anti-Semitic conceptions explain the murderous actions of these perpetrators.

The concluding step of the argument is supported by a fact already suggested in the title of the exemplary study by Christopher Browning. The perpetrators were in fact "quite ordinary men."[5] Goldhagen sharpens this thesis to "ordinary Germans." With the help of the usual statistical criteria he documents that the composition of Reserve Police Battalion 101 was roughly representative of the male population of Germany at the time. Naturally, retrospectively determined data of this sort cannot simply be equated with data derived from public opinion research. This is why serious qualifications are needed before one treats this police battalion as a representative sample and draws the conclusion that "the antisemitism [that] moved [them] would have [similarly] moved millions more had they found themselves in the same situation."[6] In the present context, it should be emphasized that such a conclusion ought not to mislead us into making the stigmatizing reproach that the Germans were a "nation of murderers,"[7] or even only "potential murderers." Such counterfactual moral accusations are meaningless. Face to face, moral reproach can relate only to concrete, factual actions or omissions. But Goldhagen's counterfactual reflection is quite a different matter, which in a historical context very sensibly refers to the undisputed and widespread anti-Semitic dispositions in the German population during this historical period.

The question of the rootedness of anti-Semitism in German culture during this period transcends the boundaries of any case study. Goldhagen is obliged to expand the scope of his analysis from the already considerable number of perpetrators to the vast number of those who were indirectly involved. From 1933 onward the Jewish population was systematically excluded from every sphere of German society, a process that was carried out in full public view. This would not have been possible without the silent complicity of broader strata of the German population. Referring to social elites, Goldhagen justly asks:

> How many German churchmen in the 1930s did not believe that the
> Jews were pernicious? . . . How many generals . . . did not want to

cleanse Germany of the Jews? . . . How many jurists, how many in the medical community, how many in other professions held the ubiquitous, public anti-Semitism, with its hallucinatory elements, to be sheer nonsense? . . . To be sure, not all churchmen, generals, jurists and others wanted to exterminate the Jews. Some wanted to deport them, a few wanted to sterilize them, and some would have been content to deprive the Jews "only" of fundamental rights. Nevertheless, underlying all of these views was an eliminationist ideal.[8]

The only objection that comes to my mind is that Goldhagen forgot the German professors.

On the other hand, these facts are not sufficient to justify speaking of the extermination of the Jews as a German "national project." Goldhagen himself refers to the medium of "society's conversation," in which all of these eliminationst intentions had to be articulated. The intersubjective constitution and the dynamics of public communication require a more differentiated picture. Even under the asymmetrical conditions of dictatorship, beliefs gain credence only in competition with other beliefs; cognitive models only against other cognitive models. But the objections of professional historians focus in the first place on the polemical thesis of a "road to Auschwitz [that was not twisted]."[9] The impression that Goldhagen's intentionalist argument overextends the credit of his empirical work by drawing global explanations from it can be countered by Goldhagen himself, who firmly refuses monocausal explanations and insists on a comparative approach. Goldhagen certainly understands that in finding explanations for the Holocaust one "[cannot] limit one's self to anti-Semitism alone, but [must] deal with countless other factors."[10] As a nonhistorian who has familiarized himself with the range of controversies in the broad field of Nazi research, I got anyway the impression that competing interpretive approaches tend to complement rather than contradict one another.

But it is not for me to offer a professional judgment on these matters. On the present occasion we are evaluating the contributions that an American, a Jewish historian, has made toward Germans' search for the proper way to come to terms with a criminal period of their history. In conclusion I want to consider a proposal that the legal theorist Klaus Günther has made for the problem of how to cope in public with the history of political crimes. How we decide questions of accountability for crimes depends not only on the facts but also on how we view the facts. How much responsibility we ascribe to individuals and how much to historical circumstances, where we draw the boundaries between individual freedom and constraint, guilt and innocence— these decisions depend on the particular preunderstanding with which we approach the events. The hermeneutic ability to recognize the true scope of responsibility and complicity for crime varies with our understanding of freedom: how we value ourselves as persons and how much we expect from ourselves as political actors. An ethical-political discourse of collective self-understanding raises just this preunderstanding as a topic of discussion. How we see the distribution of guilt and innocence in the past also reflects the present norms according to which we are willing to accord one another mutual respect as citizens of this republic. And historians who participate in this discourse do so no longer as experts but, like us, in the role of intellectuals.

Here is where I see Goldhagen's real contribution. He is not arguing for supposed anthropological universals or regularities to which all persons are equally subject. Such regularities may well serve to explain a portion of the unspeakable, as some comparative research in genocide maintains. Goldhagen's work, however, refers to very specific traditions and mentalities, to ways of thinking and perceiving that belong to a particular cultural context—not something unalterable to which we have been consigned by fate but factors that can be transformed through a change of consciousness and that in the meantime have actually been transformed through political enlightenment. The union of anthropological pessimism and a fatalistic kind of historicism in this country is in fact a part of the very problem whose solution it pretends to offer. Daniel Goldhagen deserves our thanks for strengthening our ability to take another view of the past.

Translation by Max Pensky
Speech originally published in *Blätter für deutsche und internationale Politik* (April 1997)

NOTES

1. Daniel Jonah Goldhagen, *Hitler's Willing Executioners: Ordinary Germans and the Holocaust* (New York: Knopf, 1996), 63.

2. Herbert Jäger, who himself published an early study of criminal violence in the Nazi regime, emphasizes that Goldhagen does not argue for a collective guilt, as he is often accused of doing, but rather that his book "reveals a massive individual guilt"; "Die Widerlegung des funktionalistischen Täterbildes," *Mittelweg 36* (February/March 1997).

3. Dieter Pohl, "Die Holocaust-Forschung und Goldhagens Thesen," *Vierteljahreshefte für Zeitgeschichte*, 1997, 1–48.

4. Goldhagen, *Hitler's Willing Executioners,* 267.

5. Christopher R. Browning, *Ordinary Men: Reserve Police Battalion 101 and the Final Solution in Poland* (New York: HarperCollins, 1992).

6. Goldhagen, *Hitler's Willing Executioners,* 9.

7. Julius H. Schoeps, ed., *Ein Volk von Mördern?* (Hamburg: Hoffmann and Campe, 1996).

8. Goldhagen, *Hitler's Willing Executioners,* 430–31.

9. Daniel Jonah Goldhagen, *Hitler's Willing Executioners: Ordinary Germans and the Holocaust,* paperback edition (New York: Viking Press, 1997), 479.

10. Ibid.

THIRTY

MODELL BUNDESREPUBLIK:
NATIONAL HISTORY, DEMOCRACY, AND INTERNATIONALIZATION IN GERMANY

Daniel Jonah Goldhagen

eorge Santayana's famous aphorism, "Those who cannot remember the past are condemned to repeat it," captures something important about the relationship between learning from the past and political action. Yet it is contestable. What he might have said—though it would have been less lapidary and therefore perhaps none of us would now know it—is "those who study history, may learn from it, and may therefore be less likely to repeat its darkest chapters." If I understand the *Blätter* correctly, then it is this nonaphoristic formulation that informs its members' thinking. I share this view, and I wish to use this occasion to discuss facets of the learning of history and of democracy in the Federal Republic and to suggest that the success of each are related.

How does one learn from history? How does a nation learn from history? Whatever else is necessary, an accurate and properly interpreted history has to be available. This requires that certain proclivities in the writing of history, and here I speak specifically of national history, must be resisted, or more likely, counteracted.

By "national history" I do not mean just the history of a given country or nation. I refer to the dominant framework for understanding that history. This is not confined to or necessarily governed by how academic history is written, though it may include that. It encompasses how a national history is represented more generally in the public sphere—in newspapers and magazines, on television and film, in textbooks and popular works of history, and in public memorials and rituals. These shape a people's images of its past far more than do the scholarly books of academic historians.

Because national histories are principally composed by members of the nation, they bear some obvious relationship to autobiographies. The author and the subject of autobiography are the same. The authors and the subjects of national history share an identity. Autobiographies generally present their subjects in an overly favorable light. National histories generally prettify and glorify their subject, the nation's past. Autobiography tends toward individual narcissistic self-exaltation, namely, self-hagiography. National history tends toward collective narcissistic self-exaltation, namely, nationalist history.

Developing an accurate view of each requires that the subjects be cast in the critical light of outside perspectives. For the portrait of the individual, the outside perspective comes from the biographer. For national history, the external perspective comes from abroad. But because composing national history differs from providing an account of one person's life, merely having available an external perspective is not enough.

The individual's portrait—whatever the success of an autobiography— does not remain in that individual's hands. For national history, it is the opposite. Because whatever the success of external perspectives, national history does not pass into the hands of those outside the nation but continues to be composed by members of the nation, by those who share the identity of their subjects. It continues to be composed in a country's own newspapers, television, textbooks, and history books.

So unlike the rendering of an individual's life, the writing of an accurate national history requires that some outside perspectives be integrally incorporated into the composition of national history itself, which means into the framework of understanding used by the people who must depict subjects with whom they share a fundamental identity. This is rare. Yet as I shall discuss in a moment, it has happened, to some great extent, in the Federal Republic of Germany.

Turning to politics, I need hardly belabor the point that the nation-state tends toward nationalism, the exercise of power, and the pursuit of its own material, positional, and symbolic interests to the detriment of those of other states and other peoples. Democracy serves to counteract these tendencies (though without guaranteed success; witness the history of colonialism). Democracies go to war, particularly against each other, far less frequently than nondemocracies do—indeed, it has almost never happened. Democracies have far more cooperative and mutually beneficial economic relations. The balance between emphasizing the welfare of their own citizens, on the one hand, and pursuing international power or prestige, on the other, is more heavily weighted to domestic well-being among democracies than among nondemocracies.

Yet democratic institutions alone fetter the nationalist tendencies of elites (and of peoples) imperfectly, particularly when a country is far more powerful than its neighbors. This has been recognized as a problem throughout the history of the Federal Republic. Yet these nationalist aspirations have, by and large, been tempered or, certainly, held in check to an extent that few would have imagined possible in 1945 or 1949.

Two parallel, indeed surprising, developments characterize the Federal Republic: the emergence of a relatively nonnationalist and remarkably self-critical national history and a relatively nonnationalist, internationally responsible nation-state.

In my view these developments are not unrelated. A powerful, common mechanism has influenced the development both of historical understanding and of democracy in the Federal Republic: internationalization. Historical understanding and democracy in the Federal Republic are related in another way. The development of an appropriate general framework for understanding the past has been critical in the development of a responsible democratic political system.

I began thinking about these issues when, at an academic conference last fall, the discussant on a panel mentioned that German history had been "internationalized." Unlike the history of other major countries (and probably of most countries), the main contours of modern German history have not been drawn solely by Germans. The commentator observed that more professors of German history teach at U.S. universities than at German universities. No matter how Germans would like to write their own history, a powerful external check exists from abroad.

However some in Germany might have wished or even tried to write a sanitized German history, it has simply not been possible because it would have necessitated altering the dominant framework of understanding, which has not been entirely under national control. Whatever the challenges to it or variations upon it, this framework consists of these only sometimes articulated notions:

1. Nazism was not an accident of German history.
2. The rise of Nazism is owed fundamentally to the failure to develop in Germany a genuine understanding and sufficient acceptance of democratic beliefs and liberal values and therefore to produce sustainable democratic institutions.

3. The Holocaust was not accidental to but an organic outgrowth of Nazism.

4. The Holocaust was therefore made possible by the failure to develop a firm national democratic orientation and political system.

5. Because the unsurpassed catastrophe that was the Holocaust was not an accident, it (even more than Nazism itself) is the central event of modern German history. Because the failure to develop a democratic orientation and a sustainable political system made the Holocaust possible, this failure is its central feature.

Had a defeated Germany in 1945 been left to rebuild itself in accordance with its own purely domestic political impulses, then perhaps this framework of understanding would still have developed and become dominant within Germany. I doubt it. But it did develop and it did so in part because the understanding of German national history both in the Federal Republic's popular media and also in the academy was subject to international influence. The consequences of this internationalization of German historical composition are significant.

In the Federal Republic people have been exposed to a more accurate account of their own history than they otherwise would have been and than the peoples of other countries typically are. I know of no other country that has dealt so openly and consistently with the inglorious and horrific portions of its own past as has the Federal Republic. This does not mean that the record in Germany has been perfect; far from it. But in comparative terms, the public discourse about German history looks extraordinarily honest.

External pressure has, to some extent, induced Germans to do this. Because so much attention outside of the Federal Republic has been paid to German history, specifically to the Holocaust, and to how Germans discuss, commemorate, and deal with their past, Germans' treatment of their own history has been an international political issue and has been seen at times, rightly or wrongly, as an indicator of Germans' political rectitude, specifically, that they have rejected and abandoned all that was Nazism.

Internationalization has taken a second form: the direct involvement by non-Germans in the composition of German national history; on television, for example, with the *Holocaust* series; in film by, among many other examples, *Schindler's List;* and in the academy by an array of non-German authors who have written books considered to be standard works. But the dominant framework for understanding German national history did not develop as it has merely because it was imposed from outside or because non-Germans have had access to the institutions of the German public sphere.

A third aspect of the internationalization of national history writing has been the enormous influence of these outside perspectives upon the perspectives of those in Germany who have shaped the understanding of national history and who continue the ongoing process of framing and interpreting the past. This influence dovetailed with these Germans' own democratic beliefs and values, which, even if at first haltingly, gradually became dominant in the Federal Republic. The democratic aspirations of the first postwar generation of Germans, the "68ers," produced independent demands for a more accurate reckoning with the past.

These three aspects of the internationalization of German national history writing—pressure from the outside, direct participation by outsiders, and the intellectual influence of external perspectives—have, at their core, a common feature: the incorporation of the critical perspectives of outsiders into national history in what might be called a pluralized national history (or at least a more pluralized national history). It is not a coincidence that the country that has succeeded best at dealing honestly with the least savory part of its past, Germany, is the country that has had the least control over the construction of its national history. There is a more positive way to frame this. Germans have succeeded best at constructing an accurate national history because, drawing on both domestic and international sources, they have succeeded best at counteracting the prettifying, mythologizing, and self-deluding tendencies of national history writing.

Similar features can be observed in German democracy. The development of a democratic orientation among the vast majority of Germans and of stable democratic institutions in the Federal Republic is the great cultural and political success story of the postwar period. The transformation from Nazi Germany to a genuinely democratic Federal Republic did not, of course, occur overnight. It, too, had much to do with the internationalization of German political life, which continues to this day.

This internationalization has had three dimensions analogous to the three that have influenced national history writing. The western part of Germany was initially given no choice but to adopt democratic institutions. (Many Germans adopted them gladly not only because they believed in democracy's desirability but also because the threat from the Communist east during the 1950s made the western camp the only feasible choice.) Second, German sovereignty has also been penetrated, and therefore circumscribed, first by the absence of full sovereignty until 1955, then by the continuing presence of mainly U.S. troops as part of NATO, and also by the growth of the European Union. Finally, the development of the Federal Republic's political self-understanding has emerged at least partly through the internalization of the values of their conquerors, who then became their allies. In these and other ways the conduct of the Federal Republic has, over the years, been greatly influenced by the views of others.

This internationalization of the Federal Republic can be seen in two characteristics of its elites. No other major country has an elite that is so internationalized and comfortable in a second language, not the United States, France, Italy, Britain, Russia, China, or Japan. (This linguistic facility is undoubtedly also true of the German people compared to their counterparts in other major countries.) The political elites of no other major country seem to have cared as much about how they are viewed abroad as have those of the Federal Republic. Aside from matters that directly and tangibly affect their interests, the U.S., British, and French political elites care little for how their actions are viewed abroad. In Germany, this "other-directedness" has led to the incorporation of outside perspectives into the decision making of German politics more than it has in other countries.

Looking at oneself through the eyes of others is a self-correcting mechanism. In the case of Germany, such a gaze revealed its neighbors' frequent suspicion and apprehension at what a rebuilt, then resurgent, then united, and powerful or even dominant Germany might do. This, among other things, has contributed to turning Germany—with all the disheartening exceptions—into a responsible actor in international affairs, especially in the evolution of the European Union, though also beyond.

Without minimizing the powerful domestic sources for the enormous accomplishments of German democracy, democracy's success at home and the Federal Republic's comparatively good record as a member of the community of nations is significantly owing to its internationalization.

German national history and German democracy are connected by more than their common internationalization. Knowledge of history has itself been critical for the success of the Federal Republic.

I mentioned earlier that for people to learn from their history they must have an accurate account of it. The internationalization of German history has helped to that end. Still, what sorts of learning take place and how has the Federal Republic, in particular, benefited from such learning? Two kinds strike me as particularly relevant.

The first is the learning from the past that is self-consciously and explicitly undertaken in order to provide a how-to guide to constructing a different future. A classic, successful example can be seen in the construction of the Federal Republic's political system. Its framers crafted many of its crucial features in order to make the reemergence of Nazism less likely, which included avoiding the institutional weaknesses of the Weimar political system.

A second kind of learning is not so self-conscious and goal-directed. It is people's reassessment of their beliefs and values in light of experience and in light of competing beliefs and values. This takes place every day, is carried on by every person. Sometimes the vast majority of the people of a given society learn from common experience in the same way. This happens typically after a national trauma or when fundamental institutions of society are transformed. Examples besides Germans include the Japanese, who after World War II transformed their deeply militaristic culture into one that now has a strong pacifist component, and the whites of the U.S. South, who with the overthrow of legal segregation have substantially altered their understanding of the place of blacks in society.

This learning process is not automatic, nor does it occur overnight. It is gradual. In the case of the Federal Republic the important learning occurred principally during the first two postwar decades, and here I refer to democratization and also, though more slowly and less completely, to its citizens' views of Jews. (I am surprised that, during the last year, so many people have objected to the notion that learning has taken place in the Federal Republic regarding Jews, especially since the evidence, including survey data, overwhelmingly indicates that it has.)

A proper understanding of German national history does not provide an unambiguous blueprint for the future. The past can never do that. But it can open future possibilities. It does so by clarifying the dangers that inhere in certain beliefs, practices, and institutions and by providing powerful negative models that people conclude must not be repeated.

This is what a proper understanding, the internationalized understanding, of German national history furnished for the builders of the Federal Republic, who included certain prominent individuals, groups of elites, and, let us not forget, that portion of the German people who found themselves in the west. The more or less inescapable conclusion that followed from the dominant framework—that held the Holocaust to be the central event of modern German history and its cause to be the failure of democratic values and democratic institutions in Germany—was rightly understood to be that the only future for Germany is one firmly anchored in democratic values and institutions and therefore bound to the Western community of nations that, however imperfectly, lives by them.

Germans learned well from their history. Because so many drew the right conclusions, it has made it easier for this dual process of internationalization to go forward in Germany. After all, it was not just other countries that wanted to bind Germany in the Western institutions of the European Union and NATO. Many Germans have seen these institutions as a means of preventing any recurrence of the past by creating a set of institutional constraints and incentives for maintaining the political orientation of the Federal Republic.

Some might think that it is a shame, perhaps even Germany's shame, that the Federal Republic has lived and continues to live looking over its shoulder in a way that no other people has and that, in their view, is unbefitting a country of its power and stature. They are wrong. It is precisely the opposite. The Federal Republic's political practice should be a source of satisfaction. Its mode of political activity, which has been a constituent feature of German democracy, has been an undeniable strength of the Federal Republic that should be understood, applauded, encouraged, and furthered by Germans and non-Germans alike.

The Federal Republic of Germany—and other countries—ought to be judged not according to some nationalist, that is to say, egoistic, benchmark but according to a universal standpoint and standard. It ought to be assessed realistically compared to other countries. Comparatively, the Federal Republic, as I have already said, looks good. Its honesty regarding its past, the development of its democracy, and its conduct internationally have, whatever the flaws, been better than most and in some ways exemplary.

To the extent that internationalization has facilitated this, it should be a source not of discontent but of satisfaction in the Federal Republic. But satisfaction should not lead to complacency. As fine as the Federal Republic's record has been, the task of constructing an accurate national history and a responsible democracy is not and can never be finished because it is forever ongoing. The Federal Republic should move still further down the path of internationalization on which it has already set out.

It should be recognized, for example, that there are still aspects of the Nazi period that have never been fully discussed and victims who have received insufficient acknowledgment and no recompense. This includes many Jews and also members of other victim groups, such as homosexuals, the Sinti and Roma peoples, and millions of other Europeans whom Germans over fifty years ago killed or enslaved. Acknowledging the past does not shame today's Germany but emphasizes to the whole world that the Federal Republic is different and that it abhors such deeds and the beliefs that led to them.

I say this in part to underscore that no one should understand my appreciation for the genuine, enormous achievements of the Federal Republic to imply that a *Schlußstrich* (an endpoint) can now be drawn. The self-

defeating strategy of a *Schlußstrich* calls to mind an observation by de Toc-
queville: "As the past has ceased to throw its light upon the future, the mind
of man wanders in obscurity." Putting this past behind—in the only important sense in which it can be kept at arm's length, in the sense of making sure
that it does not become the basis for creating a future in its own image—can
be done only by keeping it alive in people's minds. When one wanders in
obscurity, there is no telling where one might end up.

Still, the Federal Republic's achievements are great, and with respect to
this mode of cultural and political practice the Federal Republic should be a
model for other countries. All countries would benefit from greater internationalization in the two ways that I have discussed. The external perspectives of others correct, at least somewhat, for two of the nation-state's greatest failings: its tendency to glorify itself, for which national history is a
critical component, and its drive to pursue its own self-understood interests
even to the enormous detriment of others. All national histories should be
internationalized. All democracies, all democratic elites in particular, should
be induced to care more about how other nations view their actions.

It would be too much to expect, and perhaps not even desirable, that all
states and peoples adopt a cosmopolitan perspective, namely, a perspective
that is not rooted in anything particular to that country. Yet it is possible for
states and peoples to adopt more of an international pluralized perspective, namely, a perspective that admits and grapples with the viewpoints of
others. Outside perspectives, in this case, are almost inevitably critical perspectives that if taken seriously compel a people to reassess and then justify
or alter their own views and practices.

My book focuses exclusively on the past. My task, as I understood it,
was to illuminate why and how the Holocaust occurred and unfolded as it
did. My task was therefore not to render moral judgment but to explain why
things happened. It seemed to me that for this to be possible a shift in perspective was necessary. The longstanding focus on abstract institutions and
structures—like the Nazi Party, the SS, and the terror apparatus—had to be
replaced by one that put at the center of our inquiry and interpretation the
human beings who contributed, however they did, to bringing the Holocaust about, which includes the actors' understanding of their deeds.

Since its publication I have come to realize that my book is not just
about the past. The enormous discussion that it has triggered, especially here
in Germany, has led me to understand ever more that the book is relevant to
the future. Much of what I have said this evening attempts to explain why
this is so. By helping to produce a discussion that both reinforces and aug-
ments the basic framework of understanding for German national history,

my work seems to have reminded people that there is no usable German political model prior to the Federal Republic that is to be recaptured, that can serve as a model for the future. The democratic principles, the Western anchor, the internationalizing orientation of the Federal Republic are and must remain its strengths.

By understanding what happened in Germany during the Nazi period, a period that entailed a thoroughgoing rejection of the Enlightenment image of humanity and of the democratic political values and institutions that have governed the Federal Republic; by understanding what this rejection produced in Germany and Europe, a catastrophe unmatched in modern European history, for Jews, for Sintis and Romas, for Communists and Socialists, for the mentally ill, for homosexuals, for Poles, Ukrainians, Russians, and other Europeans, and ultimately for the German people itself; by understanding why so many ordinary people lent their bodies and souls to producing this catastrophe, it becomes less likely that old forms will appeal to people today.

Versions of a mythical and sanitized past have, at times, found currency in Germany since 1945. Some attempts to "normalize" Germany's past would have produced such an outcome. The *Historikerstreit* was fought over this terrain. Recent protests against the *Wehrmacht* exhibit by the Hamburg Institute for Social Research reveal continuing resistance to facing basic truths. Mythologizing and sanitizing constructions have not been buried for good. Yet I do believe that the discussion in Germany during the last year shows that such constructions have become ever less plausible to ever more people.

This issue is of some moment. German power has grown. The unusual postwar constellation of German and of international politics that produced the Bonn Republic has come to an end. The restraints of the Cold War have dissolved. The nation-state's will to power stands against the tempering effects of the internationalization of Germans' self-image and of German democracy, as well as the continuing domestic and international institutional restraints upon German power.

Which will prevail? Now that German democracy, and therefore Germany, is "mature," is it time for the internationalization of German national history and of German democracy to end?

No. The successful groundwork that has been laid by the Bonn Republic, including its unusual self-understanding and politics, needs to be carried over to the Berlin Republic.

In this respect it is not the Federal Republic but other countries that should change. It is also time for this German model to be internationalized, time for other nations to emulate Germany in constructing their national histories and contemporary national self-understandings.

If I understand the *Blätter* correctly, it is its members' interest in the future—particularly on this issue—and their understanding of the relationship between illuminating, discussing, and learning from the past and creating a democratic future that has brought us here today. Their commitment to the principles that have governed the Federal Republic and also to this view of the relationship between learning from history and constructing a desirable future is one reason, among others, for inviting Jürgen Habermas and Jan Philipp Reemtsma to speak here. No one has been a more articulate and tireless public champion both of the principles of the Federal Republic and of this understanding of national history than Jürgen Habermas. No one has been a more courageous and forceful proponent of presenting an unadorned, unsparing view of the past than has Jan Philipp Reemtsma. So I feel especially grateful not only for their generous words but also that they accepted the *Blätter*'s invitation in the first place.

By awarding me its Democracy Prize, the *Blätter* has done me a great honor and given me a gift: a better understanding of the possibilities of my own work. For the honor and the gift, I thank you with my head and my heart.

That I am being so acknowledged in Germany for writing a book with the unsettling and painful content that mine has is the strongest testimony to everything that I have said this evening, to the character and the democratic promise of contemporary Germany, and to the fact that it is really all the people in Germany, responsible for making the Federal Republic the democratic country that it has become, who deserve this prize.

Originally published in *Süddeutsche Zeitung*

Chapter 1 first appeared in *Die Zeit*, April 12, 1996; reprinted by permission of the author. Chapter 2 first appeared in *Süddeutsche Zeitung*, April 13–14, 1996; reprinted by permission of the author. Chapter 3 first appeared in *Frankfurter Allgemeine Zeitung*, April 15, 1996; reprinted by permission of the author and *Frankfurter Allgemeine Zeitung*. Chapter 4 first appeared in *Der Spiegel*, April 15, 1996; reprinted by permission of the author and *Der Spiegel*. Chapter 5 first appeared in *Die Welt*, April 16, 1996; reprinted by permission of the author. Chapter 6 was presented to the United States Holocaust Museum and Memorial on April 8, 1996, and first appeared in publication in *Die Zeit*, April 19, 1996. An English version also appeared in *History and Memory* (1996). The work is reprinted here by permission of the author. Chapter 7 appeared in *Berliner Morgenpost*, April 24, 1996, and *Rheinischer Merkur*, April 26, 1996; reprinted by permission of the author. Chapter 8 first appeared in *Die Zeit*, April 26, 1996; reprinted by permission of the author. Chapter 9 first appeared in *Profil 18*, April 29, 1996; reprinted by permission of the author. A slightly different version of Chapter 10 first appeared in *Die Zeit*, May 17, 1996; reprinted by permission of the author. An abridged version of Chapter 11 appeared in *Die Zeit*, May 24, 1996. The English translation appeared in *German History* 15, no. 1 (1997). The work is reprinted here by permission of the author. Chapter 12 first appeared in *Die Zeit*, June 7, 1996; reprinted by permission of the author. An abbreviated version of Chapter 13 appeared in *Die Zeit,* June 14, 1996; reprinted by permission of the author. Chapter 14 first appeared in *Die Zeit,* June 14, 1996; reprinted by permission of the author. Chapter 15 first appeared in *Blätter für deutsche und internationale Politik,* June 1996; reprinted by permission of the author. Chapter 16 first appeared in *Die Zeit,* August 2, 1996; reprinted by permission of the author. An altered version, entitled "Motives, Causes, and Alibis: A Reply to My Critics," appeared in *The New Republik* on December 23, 1996. Copyright Daniel Jonah Goldhagen. Chapter 17 first appeared in *Der Spiegel* 33 (August 12, 1996); reprinted by permission of *Der Spiegel* and the author. Chapter 18 first appeared in *Neues Deutschland,* August 17–18, 1996; reprinted by permission of the author. Chapter 19 first appeared in *Süddeutsche Zeitung,* August 28, 1996, and in English in *Yad Vashem Studies* 26 (1997); reprinted by permission of *Yad Vashem Studies* and the author. A much shorter version of Chapter 20 was translated into German for publication in the Berlin daily *Die Tageszeitung,* August 29, 1996; reprinted by permission of the author. Chapter 21 first appeared in *Die Zeit,* August 31, 1996; reprinted by permission of the author. Chapter 22 first appeared in *Die Zeit,* September 13, 1996; reprinted by permission of the author. Chapter 23 first appeared in *Die Zeit,* September 6, 1996; reprinted by permission of the author. Chapter 24 first appeared in *Die Zeit,* September 16, 1996; reprinted by permission of the author. Chapter 25 first appeared in *Badische Zeitung,* October 15, 1996; reprinted by permission of *Badische Zeitung.* Chapter 26 is adapted by Josef Joffe from his article in *The New York Review of Books,* November 28, 1996; published with permission from *The New York Review of Books,* copyright 1996 Nyrev, Inc. Chapter 27 first appeared as a chapter in the author's book *Wessen Schuld* (Berlin: Elefanten Press, 1997) and is reprinted here by permission of the publisher. Nachdem dieser Artikel seine Erstveröffentlichung im dem Werk des gleichnamigen Autoren mit dem Titel *Wessen Schuld* erfuhr (Berlin: Elefanten Press), wird er nun hier mit freundlicher Genehmigung des Verlags neu abgedruckt. The German version of Chapter 28 appeared in *Blätter für deutsche und internationale Politik* (April 1997) as well as in the German- and English-language paperback *Aus der Geschichte lernen (How to Learn from History),* 2d ed. (Bonn: Blätter für deutsche und internationale Politik, 1997). Copyright Blätter für deutsche und internationale Politik (Bonn); reprinted by permission. The German version of Chapter 29 appeared in *Blätter für deutsche und internationale Politik* (April 1997) as well as in the German- and English-language paperback *Aus der Geschichte lernen (How to Learn from History),* 2d ed. (Bonn:

Index

ROBERT R. SHANDLEY is assistant professor of German at Texas A&M University. He has published articles on German film, literary fairy tales, intellectual history, and the Holocaust. He is currently completing a book on immediate postwar Germany.

JEREMIAH RIEMER received a Ph.D. in government from Cornell University. He has taught comparative European and American politics at several universities, most recently at the Johns Hopkins School of Advanced International Studies and the Freie Universität Berlin.